Oracle Streams
High Speed Replication and Data Sharing

Oracle In-Focus Series

This book is dedicated to the Information Technologists who day and night involves themselves in the task of data management

Oracle Streams
High Speed Replication and Data Sharing

By Madhu Tumma

Copyright © 2005 by Rampant TechPress. All rights reserved.

Printed in the United States of America.

Published in Kittrell, North Carolina, USA.

Oracle In-focus Series: Book 20

Series Editor: Don Burleson

Editors: Robin Haden

Production Editor: Teri Wade

Cover Design: Janet Burleson

Printing History: February, 2005 for First Edition

January, 2007 for Second Printing

ISBN: 0-9745993-5-2
ISBN-13: 978-0974599359
Library of Congress Control Number: 2004096471

Table of Contents

Using the Online Code Depot

Purchase of this book provides complete access to the online code depot that contains the sample code scripts.

All of the code depot scripts in this book are available for download in zip format, ready to load and use and are located at the following URL:

rampant.cc/streams.htm

If technical assistance is needed with downloading or accessing the scripts, please contact Rampant TechPress at info@rampant.cc.

Are you WISE?

Get the premier Oracle tuning tool. The Workload Interface Statistical Engine for Oracle provides unparalleled capability for time-series Oracle tuning, that is not available anywhere else.

WISE supplements Oracle Enterprise Manager and it can quickly plot and spot performance signatures to allow you to see hidden trends, fast.

WISE interfaces with STATSPACK or AWR to provide unprecedented proactive tuning insights. Best of all, it is only $349.95 for the Enterprise Edition. Get the WISE. Download now!

www.wise-oracle.com

Get the Oracle Script Collection

This is the complete Oracle script collection from Mike Ault and Donald Burleson, the world's best Oracle DBA's.

Packed with over 500 ready-to-use Oracle scripts, this is the definitive collection for every Oracle professional DBA. It would take many years to develop these scripts from scratch, making this download the best value in the Oracle industry.

It's only $49.95 (less than 7 cents per script!). For purchase and download go to:

www.oracle-script.com

Conventions Used in this Book

It is critical for any technical publication to follow rigorous standards and employ consistent punctuation conventions to make the text easy to read.

However, this is not an easy task. Within Oracle there are many types of notation that can confuse a reader. Some Oracle utilities such as STATSPACK and TKPROF are always spelled in CAPITAL letters, while Oracle parameters and procedures have varying naming conventions in the Oracle documentation. It is also important to remember that many Oracle commands are case sensitive, and are always left in their original executable form, and never altered with italics or capitalization.

Hence, all Rampant TechPress books follow these conventions:

Parameters - All Oracle parameters will be *lowercase italics*. Exceptions to this rule are parameter arguments that are commonly capitalized (KEEP pool, TKPROF), these will be left in ALL CAPS.

Variables – All PL/SQL program variables and arguments will also remain in lowercase italics (*dbms_job, dbms_utility*).

Tables & dictionary objects – All data dictionary objects are referenced in *lowercase italics (dba_indexes, v$sql)*. This includes all *v$* and *x$* views (*x$kcbcbh, v$parameter*) and dictionary views (*dba_tables, user_indexes*).

SQL – All SQL is formatted for easy use in the code depot, and all SQL is displayed in lowercase. The main SQL terms (select, from, where, group by, order by, having) will always appear on a separate line.

Programs & Products – All products and programs that are known to the author are capitalized according to the vendor specifications (IBM, DBXray, etc). All names known by Rampant TechPress to be trademark names appear in this text as initial caps. References to UNIX are always made in uppercase.

Acknowledgements

It was the encouragement and guidance of Don Burleson that steered this book into print. I want to sincerely thank Don.

I was fortunate to get tremendous help from Robin Haden. She was an excellent reviewer and painstakingly improved the content and offered suggestions. Much of the content was revised and made into a nice and readable form. Thank you very much, Robin.

I wish to thank the production team at Rampant Publishing, especially Linda Web, Janet Burleson and John Lavender.

I also want to thank my coworkers at Credit Suisse First Boston with whom I am privileged to work. Directly and indirectly many of them have helped me in this book venture.

Madhu Tumma
Princeton, New Jersey
Dec 15, 2004

Feedback

In this book, I have broken down and simplified the Oracle Streams concept. The narration and the examples shown in the book are largely tested and verified. However, if you find any mistakes let me know.

I will be very much interested in knowing what you think of this book. Please write to me with your comments. I can be contacted at info@rampant.cc

Thank you,

Madhu Tumma
Princeton, NJ
December 15th 2004

Preface

Data

We live in a world of data, data accumulation, data consolidation, data movement, and data sharing. Data is a key component in the business and corporate world. Data management is an essential component and key requirement for businesses in this modern information age. The Oracle data management products are a preferred choice in many organizations.

In my 18 year IT career, I have always been fascinated by data analysis, data modeling, data handling, data usage, and data management. Whether it is the mainframe-based data systems, the database systems of the open system era, or the clustered scalable data base systems of today, the management of data in these systems has been a challenging part of providing data services to end users. Regardless of the system, data always has to be moved, transported and shared.

I have been using data replication and architecting data solutions for years using different RDBMS systems. Oracle Database System, with the introduction of the Streams methodology has opened up a new vista in the data sharing and data replication arena. For a long time, the Oracle user community has felt the need for an effective, flexible, easy to use, non-intrusive and asynchronous data replication method. Here it is …!! Oracle Streams based Replication.

There is no doubt that the basic replication and advanced replication methods that we have been implementing are still here for us to use. However, advanced replication was not without its complexities and challenging issues. It was a never a simple setup, simple to manage situation.

Now, Oracle Streams based replication provides us with a simple, yet flexible, methodology for data sharing. For the last year, I was involved in learning and implementing this new methodology. This book arose out of my desire to share my experiences along the road to understanding Streams replication methodology.

What is Streams Replication Anyway?

Oracle Streams is a new method of replication for many of us. But, it is much bigger than that. It is a paradigm shift on the part of Oracle in the implementation of data sharing techniques. For example, even advanced queuing is now Streams based.

Oracle Streams extracts changes from the transaction (redo) logs to propagate them to the destination database. Does this remind anyone of the popular Sybase Replication? Sybase Replication has been a strong player in the Wall Street IT industry, where I currently work. Sybase database system has been particularly effective in providing a non-intrusive, flexible asynchronous replication methodology.

By reading the transaction logs with the help of a separate Sybase RepServer, Sybase Database organizes the data flow to single or multiple data destinations. The financial services industry, which relies heavily on data replication to send and receive data across the pond, is very much interested in a product like Oracle Streams because it provides log based replication. Besides the financial services industry, big enterprise such as the pharmaceutical industry and other industries which have multi site operations will benefit from this new flexible method of data replication.

How does Oracle Streams differ from the Oracle Data Guard solution and the Oracle RAC solution? Both Streams replication and Data Guard rely on the same underlying technology. Both of these methodologies read the redo log files for the database changes. The database transactions are recorded in the redo log files, which are extracted by the log transport service in the case of the Data Guard setup and by the Capture process in the case of the Streams methodology.

The Data Guard solution primarily focuses on providing a standby database. It is more of an Oracle Disaster Recovery (DR) solution. The Data Guard database is a peer host system with an independent database which can be put to use immediately in case the primary, or source, database is lost or rendered inoperable. However, it lacks some of the flexibility offered by the Streams solution.

The Real Application Cluster (RAC) database is basically a parallel database with clustered multiple instances that access the same database system. The Oracle RAC database system offers scalability and high availability solutions.

Scalability is achieved in terms of adding multiple instances each with its own host resources meeting the ever increasing user transaction load. High availability is a built-in feature of the RAC database.

Oracle Streams now offers a different solution that is broader in its perspective. Streams based replication can provide an alternative data source. It is a much more flexible solution than the Data Guard solution, and it can very well act as the DR solution. Since it is a pure data solution, data can be maintained as either a complete replica of the source database or as a subset of the data. In the Streams method, data can be transformed as desired and can also be sent to multiple destinations. With the help of apply handlers, a variety of data transformations are possible. Auditing routines can be developed and tracked. PL/SQL routines can be devised to control the data transformations.

As you can see, the RAC, Data Guard, and Streams based replications offer different solutions for data management issues.

This book is about the Streams Replication methodology. There are many methods that can be used to configure the Capture and Apply processes to conduct the replication methodology. There are many choices. There are many issues that must be understood so that an efficient data solution can be configured. This book is an attempt to simplify the subject of Oracle Streams and present it in a coherent manner.

Organization of the book

This book is organized into 10 chapters.

Chapter 1 is an introductory chapter where the significance of data accumulation, data transfers and data flow needs is presented. Data sharing and data synchronization are essential parts of modern database systems. This chapter also introduces the Streams methodology and discusses the enhancements introduced in the Oracle 10g database release. It also provides a brief overview of the other competitive replication products that are out in the market.

Chapter 2 provides a look into the basic architecture of the Streams process. The Streams components are highlighted and examined. Streams data flow involves the use of the producer and consumer model. The producer is the source database system where the database changes are effected by transactional activity on the database objects. The consumer is typically the destination database where database changes or user messages received from the producer are consumed. The basic components include the queues, Capture, Propagation and Apply processes. A detailed account of Supplemental logging at the source database is also covered.

Chapter 3 is an overview of the replication methodology using the Streams technique. Data replication is the main benefit of the Streams processes. The Capture process can be local to the source database, but it can also function on a remote database, which it is termed Down Streams capture. This chapter also presents various replication-related issues such as type of changes, streams tags, and multi-way replication challenges.

Chapter 4 covers the configuration of Capture and Propagation processes. It covers topics ranging from the environment setup, supplemental logging, creating queues, and creating the Capture process to the configuration of Propagation. Examples have been included to illustrate the replication flow. There Capture process can be configured at various levels within the database. These levels are table level, a subset of table level, schema level and database level. Each level is detailed and examples are included.

Chapter 5 explores the configuration of the Apply process. It shows the creation of the Apply process as well as how the apply is managed thereafter. The Apply process can be created by using different procedures. The Apply process can be extended by setting up apply handlers. This chapter provides some examples for illustration.

Chapter 6 covers extensions to the Apply process that are called apply handlers. Apply handlers are a useful feature Streams replication because they provide an elegant method of transformation of data, creating a suitable auditing mechanism, etc.

Chapter 7 covers monitoring and troubleshooting topics. It presents a survey of the relevant static and dynamic dictionary views and constructs useful SQL queries for monitoring the Capture, Apply and Propagation processes. There many useful examples provided to illustrate process flow and latency determination, etc. Various troubleshooting tips are also included.

Chapter 8 is devoted to the topic of Down Streams capture. Down Streams capture helps divert the Capture process load from the source database. This chapter also includes details on Down Streams configuration methodology.

Chapter 9 presents information on the Streams methodology in a RAC environment. A RAC database involving multiple instances has a different method of configuration. With multiple instances in a RAC environment, the ownership of queue table and buffers becomes important. Even though the RAC database has multiple instances, only one instance has the ownership of queues and queue tables. When propagation is directed to the RAC, it has to be directed at the instance-owning buffers or the propagation will fail.

Chapter 10 covers the details of heterogeneous Streams replication to a non-Oracle database and the use of User Application enqueue mechanisms to replicate changes from non-Oracle to Oracle databases.

What Next?
Read the book ...

What is Streams?

"Ms. Jones, we need to share data at high speed and we want to remain competitive. Please find-out what Oracle Streams is all about."

Introduction

In this introductory chapter, an overview of some key concepts of data sharing and data synchronization needs that originate both within and outside of enterprises will be presented. How the Oracle Stream technology fits into the data sharing realm will also be examined.

Oracle Streams provides a queue-based and non-intrusive methodology that can be used to transfer the changed data across databases. It offers a new method of data replication for the Oracle Database environment. It is asynchronous in nature and as a result, it has minimum impact on the source database system. In keeping with market demand, Oracle has developed this revolutionary stream replication method which reads the redo logs with the intent of capturing the database transactions for onwards propagation and consumption. This is a timely departure for the Oracle database environment which hitherto depended on trigger snapshot replication and synchronous advanced replication

Streams replication is the new kid on the block!!

There is a strong and growing need for data sharing among the different internal and external users in an organization. This is becoming more important due to the rapid globalization of business operations. Oracle Streams is well positioned to offer a simple and flexible, yet revolutionary, method to move data between databases at high speeds. Streams based replication involves data exchange between the peer database systems. It readily provides an alternate database, which can serve as the primary whenever the original primary database is lost or inoperable. In a way, it can be designed to be disaster recovery solution. For performance reasons, the destination database which is maintained by the Streams replication process can be used as the access point for many of the applications because the data resides in the near vicinity of the application location. The flexibility and overall utility of the Streams processes are what make it a database revolution.

IT Operations and Databases

Today, enterprises depend on structured data for running business operations. At all levels within the organization, there is heavy dependence on databases for performing business tasks. With e-business applications and the globalization of business, on-line database systems are essential for day-to-day operations. The Internet, with its potential to connect virtually every computer in the world, has made database technology more crucial than ever. With hundreds or thousands of users connecting concurrently to databases to query and update data, high performance database systems are essential.

The need for high quality business data is ever-expanding. In the mid-eighties, databases much larger than a couple of gigabytes were rare and qualified as Very Large Databases (VLDB). Now, normal databases are in the multi-gigabyte range and the VLDB domain does not start until the terabyte range, with petabyte sized databases looming on the horizon. A 10 or 20 Gigabyte database would have been considered large a decade ago.

An ever-increasing amount of information is collected and organized into relational databases. Statutory requirements sometime dictate the accumulation process. Many times, business competition warrants the heavy growth of organized data. Again, the same data is needed for analysis and research.

Information Technology (IT) plays a vital role in the shape and conduct of businesses all over the globe. There has been an explosive growth in the amount computer dependent operations for core activities. In order to keep up with that growth and with the goal of gaining a competitive advantage, the commercial, government, and non-profit organizations have become quite sensitive to the changes occurring in information technology. The economics of its use are also a primary area of focus.

Data Sharing

Data accumulation usually happens where business operations normally occur. As a result, there are often islands of data within the organization. Even though there is usually some effort within organizations to consolidate and reduce the number of data centers and database systems, the existing systems are often resident in varied platforms and operating systems.

The situation involving multiple databases located in different geographical areas necessitates data sharing. While data explosion and data accumulation is occurring at one end of the system, the need for sharing the same data is growing with equal speed on the data access end of the system. With global operations becoming the order of the day, data sharing and data duplication are becoming significant aspects of data management. This is where data replication plays a key role. With the help of methods such as Oracle Streams, data movement is organized and the sharing of up-to-date data is made possible for more users. Streams replication, for instance, is capable of transferring the database transactions in near real time to the destination site.

The maintenance of a data replica site in a remote location or in a distributed environment allows the system to fail over to the replicated site when the need arises. The replicated data also serves a key role in disaster recovery as Streams can be configured to ensure that the risk of losing data is very small.

Growing Need for Data

Data management is a critical function for the IT division in any enterprise. As more and more business functions use and revolve around the IT functions, the dependence on organized database systems is growing. Any business operation needs to retrieve stored information in order to make business decisions or to execute business activities. Business operations are recorded in database systems for later retrieval and further analysis.

Data is everything. Data is power. Data is an asset.

With online shopping sites like Amazon.com or Expedia.com, millions of transactions take place every day. Pricing and product information is retrieved for the shopping activity. Sale transactions are recorded into databases. A look at the financial markets today, whether it is stock trading activity or stock research activity, reveals that database systems provide the real foundation of their business.

It may not be far from the truth to say that database systems touch every aspect of modern life. As a result, database systems that are accumulating business and transactional information are constantly growing in size and complexity.

💻 **Code Depot Username = book, Password = shield**

Global Operations

When the Internet is combined with advancements in networking technology, computer systems are able to communicate very effectively across countries and continents. Globalization of business activity is a primary benefit of the expanded and innovative IT infrastructure. With the help of improved communication facilities and better IT systems, business organizations are able to transact globally.

To meet the goal of globalization of trade and commerce, database systems need to be fully geared up for providing the information and analytical capability. As operations tend to spread across states and countries with offices located in different geographical areas, data availability in the various office locations becomes an important issue. This accentuates the common and essential need for data sharing. Even though the business or corporate data is collected and stored in different locations, all data has to be made available to IT applications running at these many business locations. Data replication, based on methods such as Oracle Streams, provides the necessary infrastructure for effective data movement and data sharing across distances great and small.

For instance, the corporate head office located in Chicago would be interested in monitoring and tracking product distribution through information on daily sales and inventory levels from its country wide offices. The Streams based data replication method would configure data movement to the corporate database system asynchronously.

The country-wide data could be monitored in a near real-time way, thus helping the sales and inventory analysis in timely manner so that adjustments in other business processes could be made to increase income for the corporation. In another instance, traders located in the London and Singapore offices of a financial services organization would like keep track of the trades and price movement executed in New York location for derivative products.

Data replication conducted using the Streams replication process is an ideal choice for achieving the above mentioned objectives. Users in all locations would have the updated information in a time efficient manner. Worldwide decisions could be made effectively because all users would be confident that they had the best data on which to base their business decisions.

Heterogeneous Systems

The next important data sharing challenge is the wide variety of systems and formats with which corporate data is collected and stored. The data may be resident in legacy systems or may be located in open systems. There are many widely used relational database systems such as Oracle, Sybase, MSSQL, and IBM-DB2 where the organized data gets accumulated. With regard to the formats of the data, sometimes the data resides in pure flat files and sometimes it is buried within spreadsheets.

Information integration is a real challenge for data administrators and IT mangers. They must manage diversified data formats and database systems and make the data shareable. There are many interoperability issues. Even though the data sits in a variety of formats and systems, the entire data set needs to be seen transparently from the users' point of view.

Database systems have different access interfaces, data types, and storage attributes. Even the concepts and administration of these relational database systems differ.

Fortunately, there are many tools that can be used to move, migrate and transform data from one heterogeneous system to another. For instance, there are many gateways provided by database vendors to manage the data transfer from one relational database system to another.

There are many independent vendors who provide interfaces and data sharing tools which can access the variety of relational database systems. These tools provide the methodology required to move, transform and migrate information from one relational database system to a different relational database system.

Data Synchronization

As the need for data sharing and data movement to desired locations and application sites is evaluated, one prominent goal of the effort would be data synchronization.

Since it is more and more likely that the data will be pulled from a variety of internal and external locations, there is a need to examine the ways in which each data set is synchronized or refreshed. Assuming that the accumulated data from one location is needed for other locations, the data has to be moved, transformed, and/or replicated. All of these methods of data handling are generally used within any given organization. Each of these methods is applicable in different circumstances.

Streams is well-equipped to perform such data synchronization. For example, Streams has built-in flexibility that allows the design of apply handlers and on-the-fly data transformation methodologies. When multiple sites participate in the data transfers, the goal should be to have the data from other sites as soon as new data available. Streams can move the data and synchronize it at multiple sites.

Data Movement

Data residing in database systems or data being changed in the database systems has to be propagated to database systems situated in other geographic locations. Data Movement includes a variety of ways in which data is transferred to different databases. To refresh or synchronize the data, it can be extracted and transferred to the desired location, overriding previously loaded data.

A simple method may involve extracting the necessary data into text files and moving such files by the FTP process to the desired host machine to load into the relational database. In another method, third party tools such Informatica or other data handling tools, which connect to multiple database systems concurrently, can move data by using the extract-transfer mechanism. Products such as DBArtisan can do transfers from one database to another, on demand, by managing internally using a bulk transfer mechanism.

For instance, production database system data is often moved into a development or QA database system. This may be done on a scheduled basis or can be done on-demand. In another example, data at the end of business hours may be sent to external agencies or to internal data warehousing systems to be used for refreshing the summaries.

Data Movement is often a time and resource consuming activity. However, it is a critical activity that is required to maintain current data.

Data Transformation

Data Transformation is a process in which the data being sent out and applied at remote destinations is modified. The modification could be for the accommodation of the different data types and formats. Sometimes, it is method of data cleanup.

A simple scenario would involve translating certain code values into more detailed values. This might be required in order for the values to make sense at the destination after the updates to the target site have been applied. The goal would be to have properly formatted data that is appropriate for the destination system. Transformation may be used when the data type of a particular column in the source table is different from that of the destination database. Such a column could be a NUMBER column in the source database and a VARCHAR2 column in the destination database.

The Streams based replication methodology comes equipped with transformation handlers. These handlers are simple PL/SQL procedures which act on the destination or apply site to transform the data as desired.

Another example would be to apply a filter to the extracted data so that only data satisfying the filter conditions is moved to the destination system. Some rules may be applied to the data movement and transformation process that controls the data format and refresh process.

Data Replication

Data Replication is the process in which the data is duplicated at the destination database. Data Replication is normally a built-in methodology in all relational database systems. Some relational database products even support replication to heterogeneous database systems.

A typical Data Replication process captures the changes at the source database and applies those changes at the destination database in a continuous or scheduled manner. There are many reasons why data replication is a widely used database option. Some of the main reasons are as follows:

Global Organizations - An organization operating at multiple locations often needs all of the data to be available at every location. Data may be accumulated and maintained at remote sites which are not accessible for the applications. As a result, the local application requires its own data site. In such a situation, the data is sent by using data replication methodology.

Site Autonomy - In many situations, the local sites run their own applications and want to maintain their own data, but they also want to get the remote data on a periodic or continuous basis. The data replication process can help achieve the data independence by obtaining the necessary data from the remote locations.

Enhanced Performance - For performance reasons, the data is often maintained close to the application that is processing it. Remote access to the data may involve additional network traffic delays. Centralizing application access from various locations to a common database may have a huge impact on the performance of the database. By maintaining the independent data locations or database systems, yet synchronized from remote database systems, application performance is generally improved.

Availability and Data Protection - By maintaining the replicated database site, an indirect benefit of data protection is achieved. Since the replication is a peer-to-peer system, the infrastructure facility of the remote database system provides true database system availability. When the remote system is located in a distant place, it can very well act as the disaster recovery database system. When the local database system is unavailable due to an unforeseen catastrophe, the remote database is kept up-to-date by the replication process and can easily provide the database service.

Oracle's Streams based replication was developed to address all of the above mentioned objectives. The Streams process is so comprehensive that it has become Oracle's preferred method and technology for conducting data replication both within and outside the Oracle database environment. Knowing that the worldwide thirst for current data is only going to grow, Oracle is committed to supporting, developing and enhancing its database's features further.

Replicated Systems and Distributed Systems

In a distributed environment, disparate peer systems communicate with each other. Each database system in the distributed environment has its own data. The database system in which users primarily connect is a local database system. Any additional systems accessed by these local database system users are called remote systems. A distributed environment allows applications to access and exchange data from both the local and remote systems. All the data can be simultaneously accessed and modified. There is no active transfer of data between the systems.

In a distributed database environment, the data is partitioned into disjointed fragments which are located at particular sites. There is only one image of the data. Access is usually granted by federating all the database systems or by creating database links from one database system to another.

In the case of replicated data, multiple copies of the data are stored at different sites. These multiple copies are refreshed periodically from one another. Changes at one database system are synchronized by applying the transactions to the replicated databases.

Traditionally, data replication follows two major approaches in terms of transaction execution, Tight Consistency and Loose Consistency.

Synchronous Replication – Tight Consistency

Tight Consistency involves synchronous transaction propagation. In the synchronous replication method, data changes at the source are propagated simultaneously at the replicated site. There is no lag in synchronizing the data.

Transactions are applied completely at the source and destination sites at virtually the same time. If the change cannot be applied at the destination site, the whole transaction is rolled back.

The Two-Phase Commit (2PC) is used to replicate transactions as they occur. Transaction Commit is successfully completed only when a transaction succeeds at the source and at the destination. This method always ensures the synchronization of data between the source and destination sites.

However, there are many issues with this approach. Transactions cannot be executed if the destination system is not available or is interrupted by network failures. Since the whole transaction completion depends on the successful application at the destination site, it can unduly impact performance at the source site. This method involves high overhead in terms of preparing, propagating and applying the changes at the remote site.

Oracle Streams follows a far simpler approach. Streams achieves bi-directional and multi-directional data replication without going through the hassle of 2PC. Data flow in each direction is independent of the flow in the other direction. There are well- defined conflict resolution methodologies for Streams processes. Conflict resolution will be presented later in this book.

Asynchronous Replication – Loose Consistency

Loose Consistency involves the asynchronous propagation of data changes. The transaction executed at the source database gets completed irrespective of the propagation result. In other words, the data change at source is completed even before the change is applied at the destination database.

Under normal conditions, the elapsed time may be as short as a few seconds before the change is actually applied at the destination site and the data is synchronized. This method does not affect the performance levels on the source transactions. This method is very flexible and easy to manage. In fact this is the basis behind the Oracle Streams based Data Replication Mechanism.

What is Oracle Streams?

Oracle Streams is Oracle database's new method of data sharing. Oracle Streams provides a mechanism for the propagation of database changes within the database or to the external database system. Oracle Streams, simply called Streams, keeps track of all the database changes in terms of Data Manipulation Language (DML) commands and Data Definition Language (DDL) commands. It then stages those changes into queues and later moves them to the destination queues where they are applied to the destination database objects.

Streams provides a flow mechanism in which the database changes flow in a streamed manner, hence the name Streams. Besides the database changes, Streams can also capture user defined events, stage them, and apply them at the destination database. To apply changes means that based on the specification or rules defined, the changes can be made at the destination. In fact, they are consummated at the destination site. As shown in Figure 1.1, Streams provides a data flow mechanism which continuously keeps moving and transferring messages. This becomes the basis for many data sharing and messaging functions.

Streams Information Flow

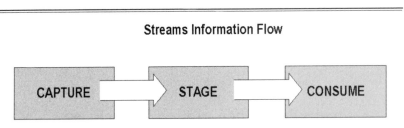

Figure 1.1 - *Simplistic View of Streams Data Flows*

Typically, the capture of database changes involves extracting changes made to the tables, schema, or entire database objects by reading the redo log files. Redo Log Files record all changes made to the database object whether they are rolled back or committed.

All the captured changes are converted into events called Logical Change Records (LCR). The Capture process enqueues them into the appropriate queues. Besides scanning and extracting the changes, there is another facility where user applications can explicitly create events. This can be LCR(s) or user messages. These are known as user-enqueued events.

Streams provides a rich set of methods that allow DBAs to control what kind of data and information is placed into Streams and how the stream flows or is routed from one system to another. There are rules, transformations, and configurations that control the entire flow of capture and apply.

Where to use Streams

The Oracle Streams methodology provides an integrated infrastructure in which a variety of messaging functions and data flow systems are implemented. Streams Methodology supports Oracle functions such as message queuing through advanced queuing, data replication, event management and notification, data warehousing loading, and data protection by way of the standby database.

How do the Streams differ from the Oracle Data Guard solution and the Oracle RAC solution? Both the Streams replication process and Data Guard rely on the same underlying technology. Both of these read the redo log files for the database changes. Database transactions are recorded in the redo log files. In the case of Data Guard, the transactions are extracted by the log transport service. In the Streams process, the changes are extracted by the capture process.

The Data Guard solution focuses primarily on providing a standby database. It is more of an Oracle provided Disaster Recovery (DR) solution. The Data Guard database is a peer host system with an independent database that can be put into use immediately in the event the primary, or source, database is lost or rendered inoperable. The Data Guard standby database is constantly kept in recovery mode and the all the redo log changes received from the primary database are applied regularly. It has one-to-one matching with that of primary database. It is fairly simple to configure and maintain.

A Real Application Cluster (RAC) database is basically a parallel database with clustered multiple instances accessing the same database system. The Oracle RAC database system offers scalability and high availability solutions. Scalability is achieved in that multiple instances can be added, each with its own host resources aimed at meeting the ever-increasing user transaction load. High availability is a built-in feature of the RAC database. Since the database can be accessed and handled through any one of the instances, failure of the host does not cause database failure or database service loss. The Oracle RAC database system uses shared storage to host the database structures.

Streams offers a different solution that is broader in its perspective. Streams based replication can provide an alternative data source. It is a much more flexible solution than the Data Guard solution in that it is designed to do more than simply provide a standby database for failover or disaster recovery;

although, it can very well act as the DR solution. Since Streams is a pure data solution, data can be maintained as either a complete replica of the source database or as a subset of the data. With Streams, data can be transformed as desired and can also be sent to multiple destinations. With the help of apply handlers, a variety of data transformations are possible. In addition, auditing routines can be developed and tracked. PL/SQL routines can be devised to drive the data transformations based on the needs of the users.

RAC, Data Guard and Streams offer different solutions. Each methodology has its strengths, but the Streams methodology has cleverly incorporated some of the strengths of RAC and Data Guard.

Message Queuing

By using the Streams based Advanced Queuing (AQ), user applications can enqueue messages into queues, then propagate them to the subscribing queues. The AQ process sends notifications when messages arrive into queues, allowing the specified action routine to execute. Usually, the action routine involves processing the messages by de-queuing them at the destination.

Oracle AQ has all the standard features of the message queuing systems. It allows the establishment of multi-consumer queues, publish and subscribe methodology, content based routing, transformations, and gateways to other messaging subsystems. Oracle Streams based AQ is fully integrated into the database systems. As a result, the maintenance of persistent queues becomes really robust. AQ stores the messages in the database objects in a transactional order. The messages are available later, even after they are de-queued, for secondary uses like auditing and tracking. This is one of the main reasons for the popularity of AQ.

Event Messaging and Notification

Business organizations need to propagate a variety of messages between different applications running on different systems and supporting a variety of business users. Events are basic units of business communications that convey a certain message, situation, or status, which in turn could trigger a specified action. The alert mechanism or notification mechanism is built upon the simple premise of a cause and effect paradigm.

Streams Methodology event management systems allow the applications to enqueue explicitly. The captured events may be DML or DDL changes. Through the use of multiple queues and queue tables, events are propagated to the desired queue systems. These messages can be explicitly de-queued by writing a suitable application routine. This routine may update certain database objects or trigger some other specific action or series of actions.

Message Systems are important components in the overall business communication process. Based on the appropriate rules, a messaging client or an application can de-queue the messages. This kind of event based system has the added advantage of having the capability of alerting the appropriate monitoring systems or applications groups. They can also develop a suitable auditing mechanism allowing further analysis of the actions that have taken place. User developed application routines can be used to harness the database to perform actions that range from notifying the user that a set criteria has been met or the database can de-queue the messages in a manner determined by the user.

Data Replication

Data Replication is one of the most widely used methodologies for the maintenance of different sets of data within or outside business organizations. It is used to keep those sets of data synchronized, as required. Data Replication is one of most significant benefits of the Stream Methodology.

Oracle Streams keeps track of database changes and captures those changes in the form of events. These database changes can be DML changes or DDL changes. The changes are wrapped and formatted into Logical Change Records (LCR) and are propagated to the destination system where they are applied to synchronize the database systems.

Streams based replication provides a useful asynchronous replication. This allows the maintenance of remote database systems without affecting performance levels at the source database system. Since the extraction or capture of database changes is effected from the redo log files, it does not delay any transaction activity and does not affect the normal Online Transaction Processing (OLTP) or DSS activity of the source database.

Data Warehousing Loading

Data Warehousing Systems are huge accumulations of data from different sources. The accumulation process is dynamic in nature, and periodically, huge amounts of fresh data are loaded and updated. Summarized data is a derivative of base data. When new data arrives into the data warehousing system, most of summarized data needs to be refreshed to reflect the new values. Usually, changes in the base relational data systems, along with changes from many other sources, are propagated to the data warehousing systems.

The Oracle Streams methodology provides an effective process for capturing the database changes and then applying them to the data warehousing systems. By using Streams, the capture of redo log information avoids unnecessary overhead on production systems. By using built-in data transformations and user-defined apply procedures, the system has enough flexibility to reformat data or update warehouse-specific data fields as data is loaded. Besides the usual Streams replication technology, Change Data Capture uses some of the components of Streams to identify data that has changed so that the changed data can be loaded into a data warehouse.

The main benefit of the Streams Methodology is the ability to avoid performance overhead. By creating the database changes from the redo log files, near real time data propagation is made possible. Compared to traditional 'select source and load' methods at scheduled intervals, Streams based data loading provides a more controlled and faster refresh of data warehouses. With the built-in, robust rules engine, a variety of data transformations are possible before the data is applied to warehousing systems. Thus, the Streams methodology can be designed in such a way that it can offer many of the standard Extract, Transform and Load (ETL) features for data movement and data loading.

Data Availability and Protection

Data protection and disaster recovery are among the most important requirements of most business environments. Setting up a logical standby database in a remote location using Streams based methodology provides two distinct solutions.

The first solution is to provide a remote copy, which is a near-real-time image of the database that can be used immediately when the primary database is not available. In this way, Streams methodology offers data protection.

The second solution is to provide a logical standby database, which is opened for read-only or read/write access. The secondary database can have its own attributes in terms of additional indexes or additional objects for query optimization. By diverting queries to the secondary standby database system, overhead on the primary production system is avoided.

Streams Historical Growth

Seasoned Oracle Database users and administrators have been using traditional basic and traditional advanced database replication methods for a long time. Both of these systems worked very well, in their own right, for a number of years.

The basic replication system used the store and forward mechanism to transmit the database changes to the destination system. Snapshot based replication was well-suited for the situations in which delays in data refreshes are tolerated. With advanced replication, multi-master replication was possible. By using the 2 phase-commit, real time data replication was possible.

Both of these methods served effectively in most situations, but they caused performance overhead on the source database systems. When database systems were low in both activity and size, the performance degradation was not noticed as much. However, problems were often encountered with large data changes. Plus, configuring, troubleshooting, and resolving conflicts resulted in an increase in administrative overhead.

Oracle Streams, for data replication, is a major feature enhancement that was introduced in Oracle Database Release 9.2. The use of Streams for data replication altered the way in which database changes could be captured, propagated, and applied at the replicated site. This was a big change in replication technology for the Oracle Database system.

Note: Even though Streams supports data replication, it is still possible to configure data replication using traditional advanced replication.

Streams First Release in 9.2

When Streams was first made available in Oracle Database 9i Release 2 (9.2.0), DBAs were presented with a new method of data replication and data sharing. This Streams based data replication reads the database changes out of the redo log files. The propagation of the database changes are managed by the *dbms_job* scheduler, and the apply process manages the apply functionality at the destination.

Scanning and extracting the database changes from redo log files is called Hot Mining. However, when using Real Application Clusters (RAC), the captured changes are confined to the archived redo log files. This can cause a definite latency or delay in capture, propagation, and apply.

New Streams Features in 10G

With Oracle Database 10g, Streams functionality matured greatly. Oracle has added many new features that made it a viable option for data sharing and data replication. A brief overview of the new features that were introduced in the 10g release will be presented here. Detailed explanations of these features will be presented in later chapters.

The Capture process can run on a database other than the source database. The redo log files from the source database are copied to the other database, called a downstream database, and then the capture process extracts changes in these redo log files to propagate to the destination.

Streams processes such as capture processes, propagations, apply processes, and messaging clients can use two rule sets: a positive rule set and a negative rule set. The negative rule set helps to discard specific changes so that they are not processed by Streams processes. Previous releases allowed only positive rule specification. The positive rule set indicated that any changes which met the rule conditions were selected by the Streams client.

Subset rules can be used for capture processes, propagations, and messaging clients, as well as for apply processes. Subset rules permit the use of a condition similar to a WHERE clause in a SELECT statement.

Specific memory areas within the SGA can be allocated for Streams. This memory area is called the Streams pool. To configure the Streams pool, specify the size of the pool in bytes using the *streams_pool_size* initialization parameter. The Streams pool also contains buffered queues, which are used for internal communications during the capture and apply. Many dynamic performance views have been added to allow the DBA to look into the buffered queues.

Support for Streams in the RAC environment has been considerably extended. In prior releases, whenever there was a failure of a RAC instance, there was a bit of manual work required to restart the capture or apply process. For capturing the events, archive logs were read instead of online redo log files. These two issues have been addressed through enhancements.

- The default tablespace for LogMiner has been changed from the SYSTEM tablespace to the SYSAUX tablespace.

- There is a new parameter called *and_condition* in some of the procedures that create rules in the *dbms_streams_adm* package. This parameter enables the DBA to add custom conditions to system-created rules.

- *set_rule_transform_function* is a procedure that has been added to the *dbms_streams_adm* package. This makes it easy to specify and administer rule-based transformations.

- Streams capture and apply processes now support the additional data types: NCLOB, BINARY_FLOAT, BINARY_DOUBLE, LONG and LONG RAW.

- Streams capture and apply processes now support processing changes to Index Organized Tables (IOT).

- A new procedure, *set_execute,* has been added to the *dbms_apply_adm* package. This procedure enables the DBA to specify that apply processes do not execute events that satisfy a certain rule.

- There is a new type of apply handler called a pre-commit handler. This handler serves to record information about commits processed by an apply process. This helps to develop a suitable audit and tracking mechanism.

- Streams capture and apply processes now support processing changes to tables that use function-based indexes and descending indexes.

- A new parameter, *drop_unused_rule_sets*, has been added to the following procedures:

  - *dbms_capture_adm.drop_capture*

- *dbms_propagation_adm.drop_propagation*

- *dbms_apply_adm.drop_apply*

- A new procedure, *remove_queue,* has been added to the *dbms_streams_adm* package. This procedure enables the DBA to remove a SYS.AnyData queue. This procedure also has a *cascade* parameter. When *cascade* is set to TRUE, any Stream client that uses the queue is also removed.

- The *dbms_streams_tablespace_adm* package provides administrative procedures for copying tablespaces between databases and for moving tablespaces from one database to another. This package uses transportable tablespaces, Data Pump, and the *dbms_file_transfer* package.

- A package called *dbms_streams_auth* was introduced. It provides procedures that make it easy to configure the Streams administrator.

- *remove_streams_configuration* is a procedure added to the *dbms_streams_adm* package. This procedure permits the removal of the entire Streams configuration from a database, when required.

- New options such as the FOREIGN KEY columns and the ALL columns have been added to the database supplemental logging.

- In addition to original export/import, Data Pump export/import, transportable tablespaces, and RMAN can be used to perform Streams instantiations.

- A new recursive parameter in the *set_schema_instantiation_scn* procedure and the *set_global_instantiation_scn* procedure permits the setting of the instantiation *scn* for a schema or database, respectively; and for all of the database objects in the schema or database.

- Two functions have been added to the *dbms_streams* package. They are: *get_streams_name* and *get_streams_type*. These functions return the name and type, respectively, of a Streams client that is processing an LCR.

- The *include_extra_attribute* procedure in the *dbms_capture_adm* package can be used to instruct a capture process to include certain extra attributes in LCRs. These attributes are: ROW_ID, SERIAL#, SESSION#, THREAD#, TX_NAME, and USERNAME.

- A procedure called *get_scn_mapping* has been added to the *dbms_streams_adm* package. This procedure gets information about the *scn* values to use for Streams capture and apply processes in order to recover transactions after a point-in-time recovery is performed on a source database in a multiple source Streams environment.

Streams Based Oracle AQ

In Oracle 10g, the Oracle Advanced Queuing system has been integrated with Oracle Streams. The original Oracle Advanced Queuing system has been renamed as Oracle Streams AQ (AQ). The new Streams AQ provides message queuing functionality which is fully integrated into the database system. It is built on top of Oracle Streams and leverages the functions of the Oracle Database so that messages can be stored persistently, propagated between queues on different computers and databases, and transmitted using Oracle Net Services and HTTP(S).

Since the AQ is fully integrated, it has the benefit of high availability, scalability, and reliability that are applicable to the regular database system. Usual database features like recovery, security, and access control are automatically available to the AQ. It is a significant development from the Oracle's commitment point of view. The integration of AQ into Streams and the use of queuing for replication simplify queuing, and each approach compliments the other. This integration is a good step in the direction of providing a comprehensive data management practice. Oracle's future product development efforts will likely be designed to benefit both the Streams and AQ options.

Other Replication Products

Though data sharing and data replication are now implemented by Oracle Streams through the use of redo log files for capturing transaction changes, the concept of using the transaction log to construct the database changes to propagate to the destination database is not new. Competitive RDBMS products and other third party data sharing products have implemented such methodology in the past. Sybase is well known for a robust replication methodology and has implemented a transaction log based data replication method.

Quest software's SharePlex product implements a redo-log capture based data replication methodology for Oracle databases. GoldenGate software also provides a data replication product. These two products will be introduced, in brief.

GoldenGate Data Synchronization Platform

GoldenGate Software provides an innovative product that can be used to support data replication in the Oracle Database environment. GoldenGate's solution reads the Oracle redo log files and captures the database changes for propagation and application to the destination. However, the extract and apply processes are not part of the database. They are an operating system level process.

The data synchronization solution consists of three modules: Capture; Delivery; and Manager. The Capture also known as the extract process and the Delivery process do the bulk of the data replication and data sharing functions. These two processes are de-coupled and run independently. The Manager module provides an interface to configure and manage the replication process.

The Capture module is configured on the source database system. It retrieves the insert, update and delete transactions and outputs the information to the platform queues. Queued records are stored in GoldenGates's universal data format. Queued records are usually written to binary flat files on the target system.

The Delivery module, an independent operating system level process on the destination system, performs the function of applying changes to the designated tables of the destination database system. As soon as the data is available in queue records or flat files, the Delivery process reads transaction details and posts them to the designated destination database objects. Changes are applied in the same order as they are committed at the source database system to ensure data and referential integrity.

The Manager component is the main interface that is used to manage the whole replication platform. Manager tracks the growth queue records, starts and restarts the processes, and also monitors.

The GoldenGate solution is a non-Oracle and multi-process system and consequently, it is not affected by resource levels within the database. At the same time, since GoldenGate processes are outside the database system, it does not create any overhead in the primary database system. Details on GoldenGate solutions are available at www.goldengate.com.

SharePlex Data Replication

Quest Software has been providing Oracle data replication products for a long time. Quest's replication product is called SharePlex and has been used in many enterprises. SharePlex uses the transaction details stored in the redo log files for data replication.

SharePlex focuses on diverting the replication scheme from the primary database system to the data stored in the redo log files. As a result, the SharePlex replication process does not impact the source database transactions. SharePlex works outside of the database to capture the database changes and transmits them to the destination database. SharePlex does not use the Oracle database engine for the capture and propagation of changes.

SharePlex log-based replication captures every modification to selected objects immediately. As soon as the changes are written to the Oracle Redo log, even before the transaction is committed, they are extracted by the SharePlex module. Therefore, it can update the changes at the destination site very quickly. SharePlex also completely follows the Read Consistency Model so that the target instances are accurate representations of the source database. Thus, it is a logical solution that replicates transactions as they occur without waiting for the commit. Details on Quest's solutions are available at www.quest.com.

Now, the Oracle Streams methodology has been developed to include the best features of the existing RDBMS and third party data sharing products. Many of these features have been built into Oracle10g Database. In addition to the built-in features, Streams allows the implementation of user developed PL/SQL routines and other applications to achieve specific data replication goals. This combination has yielded an extremely powerful and flexible data replication package over which the DBA still retains ultimate control.

Conclusion

In this chapter, increasing data growth patterns in global business operations have been examined. The need for internal and external data sharing and data movement is ever-growing.

Data replication is an important function of database systems. Oracle Streams provides a new method of data replication and data sharing. The Oracle

Streams data sharing methodology is based on the extraction of the database changes from the Oracle Redo Log files. Initially introduced in version 9.2, Oracle Streams is now a fully matured product. The Oracle10g release has brought in many useful features. Some of those new features were highlighted in this chapter as well.

The main points of this chapter include:

- Data accumulation and data synchronization are an important need for many business organizations. It is much more significant for the organizations with multiple sites due to the need to have data exchanged efficiently between sites.

- Data replication conducted by the Oracle Streams replication process helps to achieve data synchronization very effectively by offering time efficient data transfer as well as built-in functionality in the areas of failover and disaster recovery.

- The producer and consumer database model was introduced and was followed by a description of the Oracle Streams methodology.

- Additionally, some third-party products that provide replication and other data sharing capabilities were also examined.

In the next chapter, more details regarding the Oracle Streams process, architecture, and resources will be presented.

Streams Components and Processes

"Ms. Jones, there appear to be too many components in Streams."

Introduction

In this chapter, the basic architecture of Oracle Streams will be presented. The details will include an overview of all the resources, processes, and components that make up the data flow using Oracle Streams. Familiarity with the details of the components and the inter-relations among them yields a quick view of the overall process. The material in this chapter is the basis for Streams configuration details that will be presented in later chapters.

The basic objective of Streams is to capture, propagate, and apply database changes and user input messages. This data flow process revolves around the 'producer and consumer' model.

The Producer and Consumer Model

The producer is the source database system in which database changes are effected by transactional activity on the database objects. Besides the transactional input, user applications can produce the input messages which

---

are ultimately converted into queued events for propagation. Input to the source queues may initiate from the local database system or it may come from another database, as is the case with downstream capture. Downstream capture refers to situations where the database changes are captured in an intermediate database other than the database where the transactions are initially performed.

For instance, in a source database the table 'orders' is updated by application transactions. This action generates redo entries into the redo logs. The changes are produced at the source database and this database becomes the producer. These transactional changes are then routed to a destination database where the Streams client, via the Apply process, consumes them to update the orders table. The destination database becomes the consumer. There could be even multiple consumers especially when the changes are routed to multiple destinations.

Thus, the consumer is typically the destination database in which database changes or user messages that have been system generated by the producer are ultimately consumed. Once changes are generated at a source database, they may be consumed by more than one remote database. In addition, any application can consume messages. This model of "producer and consumer" controls the nature of the data flow origin and ultimate usage.

Streams Clients and Event Flow

In the Streams environment, there are four distinct entities which act as the clients. They are called Streams Clients. These distinct entities are: the Capture process, the Apply process, the Propagation process and the Messaging client which is typically a user application. All operations are conducted by these four entities, and they act as the producers and consumers. Any activity for data flow within Streams is controlled and managed by these four Streams Client processes. They are typically the Oracle processes which perform the data flow.

In Figure 2.1, a complete Streams-based data flow system with components and resources is shown. In the diagram, all of the Streams components and their interrelations are depicted. A typical event flow using the Streams process from a source database to the remote database is represented.

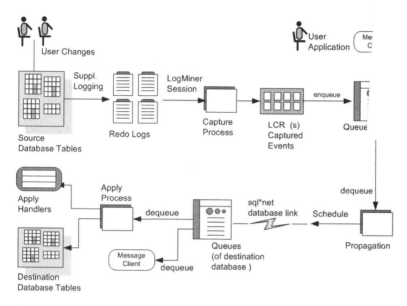

Figure 2.1 - *Event Flow Using Streams*

When database changes are made, they are recorded into the Redo Log files. If supplemental logging is enabled when the Redo Logs record the transactional activity, extra columns of information are also recorded. The Capture process scans the redo entries and converts them into Logical Change Records (LCR) or LCR events, and then it enqueues them into the source database queue. These events are then known as Captured Events. Alternatively, the User Application, a messaging client, may directly enqueue LCR or events into the queue. In this case, the events are called user-enqueued events.

Once the events are queued, another Streams client, the Propagation process sends them to the queue of the destination database. The process of sending the messages or LCRs to the remote database is called the dequeue. It is also possible to dequeue by a user application.

Once the remote database queue gets the LCRs and messages, the Apply process dequeues events and either applies each event directly to a database object or passes the event, as a parameter, to a user-defined procedure called an Apply handler. Apply handlers include Message Handlers, DML handlers, DDL handlers, pre-commit handlers, and error handlers.

The Streams clients are controlled by rules. A rule is a database object that enables a Streams client, such as Capture, Apply, or Propagation, to perform an action when an event occurs and a condition is satisfied.

All about Queues

Queues are an important component in the Streams Infrastructure. Streams processes use queues to stage events in preparation for sending them to the remote database by Propagation or consumption. Propagations send events from one queue to another. These queues can be in the same database or in different databases.

The queue from which the events are propagated is called the source queue, and the queue that receives the events is called the destination queue. Typically, the source queue stays in the source database, and the destination queue will be in the remote database. In terms of sending the messages, there can be a one-to-many, many-to-one, or many-to-many relationship between source and destination queues. It is more like a transfer to another staging area for further use. Events that are staged in a queue can be consumed by an Apply process, a messaging client, or by an application.

Messages are propagated between a source queue and a destination queue. Although Propagation always occurs between two queues, a single queue may participate in multiple Propagations. That is, a single source queue may propagate events to multiple destination queues, and a single destination queue may receive events from multiple source queues. However, only one Propagation is allowed between a particular source queue and a particular destination queue. A single queue may also be a destination queue for some propagations and a source queue for other propagations.

Secure Queues

In the Oracle Database environment, queues can be of type Secure or Non-Secure. When the queues are created, if they are set up with attribute secure set to TRUE, they are known as Secure queues. 'Secure queue' implies that only the owner of the queue can perform queue operations such as dequeue and enqueue; however, database users who are created as secure users can also perform the queue operations on these secure queues.

All the queues typically included in the Streams environment are SYS.AnyData queues which can stage any data type. All SYS.AnyData queues created by using the *set_up_queue* procedure of the *dbms_streams_adm* package are secure by default. Thus, the Streams environment ensures that the queues it uses are only handled by the appropriate secure and explicit users.

Typed Queue and SYS.AnyData Queue

In the Streams environment, the bulk of the time the DBA deals with a Sys.AnyData type queue. The Capture process enqueues events into a SYS.AnyData queue. A SYS.AnyData queue can stage events of different types. Users and messaging clients may enqueue events into a SYS.AnyData queue or into a typed queue. A typed queue can only stage events of one specific type.

Transactional Queue

When dealing with user enqueued events, a user application can group the events and enqueue them as a single unit or single transactions. In such situations, the Apply process, a consumer, performs a COMMIT only after all the events in the groups are successfully applied. Queues that deal with this process are called transactional queues. In the case of non-transactional queues, each event is a transaction by itself. Therefore, the Apply process performs a COMMIT after each user-equeued event is applied.

When a queue is created using the *set_up_queue* procedure of the *dbms_streams_adm* package, it creates a transactional queue by default. With captured events, the distinction of transactional and non-transactional is not particularly relevant because the Apply process preserves the original transaction order.

Enqueue and Dequeue

Enqueue consists of inputting or placing something into a queue. Enqueues can be accomplished in the following ways:

- The first method of enqueue is through a Capture process. In this method, the Capture process enqueues captured changes in the form of events. Those events contain Logical Change Records (LCR). These events are referred to as captured events. This is because the basic origin of the event is a typically a Capture process. The Capture process is not user written program or application. It is an Oracle background process.

- The second method of enqueuing events is through the use of a user written application. A user application typically constructs an event in the form of an LCR record. The user application will then explicitly enqueue the LCR records into a source queue. Events placed into the queue in this way are called user-enqueued events.

The difference between capture events and user-enqueued events is important because various Streams processes can be configured in different ways based on the method used to enqueue the information.

Dequeue consists of consuming or sending messages or events out of a queue. Events can be dequeued by an Apply process or a user application.

- A typical Apply process can dequeue both the captured events and the user-enqueued events. The Apply process handles all events containing LCR(s) automatically. It uses the specified rule conditions to apply directly to the database objects, or it may also use a user specified procedure to do the transaction processing. When there is no LCR in the event and there are only user messages, the Apply process reacts differently. When it can rely only on user messages, the Apply process can call upon a user-specified procedure to process the messages. These procedures are called Message Handlers.

- User written applications can be developed and used to explicitly dequeue the user-enqueued events. These applications may or may not rely upon the Streams messaging client. It is important to remember that captured events can not be dequeued by a user application. Only the Apply process is able to dequeue the captured events. The only technical exception is when an Apply process calls a user procedure such as a message handler that enqueues an event explicitly. This event is considered a user enqueued event and can be dequeued explicitly even though the event may have originally been a captured event.

The different types of queues and the various ways that events can be queued and dequeued are some of the exciting features of the Streams methodology.

Queue Tables

In reality, the information on queues brings to light that there are two distinct parts. The first part included the queue buffers which are part of the SGA, and the second part included the associated physical tables, which are called queue tables. Every queue has its queue table and the queues make use of these queue tables for storing the events or messages when they spill over from the buffers.

Capture Process

The Capture process is an Oracle background process that scans the database redo log files to extract the DML and DDL changes that were done on the database objects. The database in which the database changes occur is called the source database.

A typical database transaction initially creates a redo entry in the log buffer, which is a part of the SGA. The background process log writer (LGWR) subsequently writes those redo entries into the online redo log files. The LGWR also writes the commit records into the redo logs. The Streams Capture process can only read the redo logs or archived redo logs when extracting the transactional information. It does not read the log buffer.

The Capture process usually runs on the source database system where the actual transactional activity takes place. In which case, the Capture process is called the local Capture process. However, the Capture process can also run on a remote database other than source database, in which case the remote database is called a downstream database. When the Capture process runs on a downstream database, it cannot read the redo log files of the source database; rather, it scans and extracts information from the archived log files of the source database copied to the downstream database.

If the Capture process is disabled on the source database for an extended period of time and the redo log file is archived in the meanwhile, the redo log file is no longer available for the Capture process when it resumes the scan. In that case, the Capture process reads the archived redo log files. In this way, the disabled or deleted Capture process does not hold up the database activity and the redo log switching activity. By scanning the archived redo logs in addition to online redo logs, the Capture process is guaranteed to be able to extract all the transactions in a transactional order. As a result, the process acts as a backup plan because it will search for any and all data that might have been missed by the Capture process while it was out of commission.

The Capture process, which extracts the database changes from redo log or archive log files, formats the information into events called LCR events. The term event denotes that something has occurred which could cause some action. A more detailed explanation of the LCR is presented in a later section of this chapter.

After capturing the database changes and converting them into LCR events, they are inputted to a source queue. There may be more than one queue to receive the LCR events. The queues act as staging areas. A Capture process is associated with a single SYS.AnyData queue. There may be more than one queue defined for the database.

The Capture process follows rules that define, dictate, or decide if the Capture process has to extract or discard the database changes into LCR events. The rules can be specified in a positive or negative rule set for the Capture process. If a rule evaluates to TRUE for a change and the rule is in the positive rule set for a Capture process, the change is captured.

If a rule evaluates to TRUE for a change and the rule is in the negative rule set for a Capture process, the change is discarded. If a Capture process has both a positive and a negative rule set, the negative rule set is always evaluated first.

Salient Features

In a typical Streams configuration, for administrative and performance reasons, multiple Capture processes can be created. When the DBA wants to have different sets of data streams going to different destinations with data that may vary in nature, multiple Capture processes should be considered.

The Capture process has to be associated with pre-created queues. It is possible to use one queue associated with the multiple capture processes. Oracle recommends that each Capture process use a separate queue to help keep the LCRs from different capture processes separate.

The *streams_pool_size* initialization parameter controls the size of the Streams Pool within the SGA of the database. This parameter was newly introduced in Oracle10g database. In earlier versions, there was no way that the allocated SGA resources for streams could be increased except by increasing the total SGA size. Oracle10g provides a way to have better control over the memory resources allocated for Streams.

Each Capture process uses one LogMiner session. The LogMiner session is constantly scanning the redo log files for database changes and converting them into LCR events. The LogMiner process and methodology can be used independent of Streams to extract the transactions and know the SQL Statements executed during a particular period. Using the LogMiner session, the Capture process internally reads the same set of redo entries and converts them into the LCR objects needed for the Streams operation.

Buffered Queues

There are buffered queues that are extremely useful for the Capture process. A buffered queue includes the following storage areas:

- SGA memory associated with a SYS.AnyData queue that contains only captured events.

- Part of a queue table for a SYS.AnyData queue that stores captured events that have spilled from memory.

Recall that every queue has a buffer part and the table part. Oracle uses these queue buffers to stage the captured events. The buffers are part of the SGA, and as such they help to optimize and process at very high speeds. Buffering of captured events in a SYS.anyData queue is the default behavior. The buffering of captured events is not just confined to the source database. Buffering also happens at destination databases and at intermediate databases when they are configured as Down Stream databases.

The user-enqueued LCR events and user enqueued non-LCR events are stored in the queue tables associated with the appropriate queue. Queue buffers are not used for storing these events. This may have a slight performance impact if there is a large quantity of user-enqueued events.

Another group of events that use the queue tables includes the apply error transactions. When the Apply process fails to apply transactions, they are immediately moved into the error queue and are stored into the associated queue table. This keeps the buffers free for the current events that are being processed. This makes sense in terms of efficiency as the DBA may chose to attend to the error transactions at later time while keeping the Apply process moving forward.

What is SYS.AnyData?

Events of different data types can be staged into a SYS.AnyData queue. The SYS.AnyData type is defined at the database level. Almost any type of payload can be wrapped in a SYS.AnyData queue. To do this, the *convertdata_type* static functions of the SYS.AnyData type can be used. In this case, data type is the type of object to wrap. These functions take the object as input and return a SYS.AnyData object. Since the database table columns routinely have different data types in their definition, the Streams processes deal the columns a uniform data type during the data flow. At the end of Streams flow, they are converted back to the original data type. The transmission of a single, uniform data type facilitates the smooth, consistent, and efficient exchange of data.

Users and applications may enqueue events into a SYS.AnyData queue or into a typed queue. Remember, a typed queue can stage events of one specific data type only.

Data Types Captured

Table 2.1 shows the data types that can be part of Streams staging and consumption.

VARCHAR2	TIMESTAMP WITH LOCAL TIME ZONE
NVARCHAR2	INTERVAL YEAR TO MONTH
NUMBER	INTERVAL DAY TO SECOND
LONG	RAW
DATE	LONG RAW
BINARY_FLOAT	CHAR
BINARY_DOUBLE	NCHAR
TIMESTAMP	CLOB
TIMESTAMP WITH TIME ZONE	NCLOB
TIMESTAMP WITH LOCAL TIME ZONE	BLOB and UROWID

Table 2.1 - *Data Types that can be captured*

Oracle Background Process

A Capture Process is an optional Oracle background process whose process name is *cnnn*, in which *nnn* is a capture process number. Capture process names include *c001* through *c999*. A Capture process captures changes from the redo log by using the infrastructure of LogMiner.

Streams configures LogMiner automatically. The DBA can create, alter, start, stop, and drop a Capture process. Capture process rules that control which changes a Capture process captures can be defined by the DBA. More details about Capture process maintenance will be presented in later chapters of this book.

Log Based Changes – Hot Mining or Cold Mining

From the information presented earlier, it is clear that the Streams main functionality is based on the information available from the database redo log files. Redo log files record all database changes. Since they have a complete journal of database changes, redo log files become the perfect place to extract the database changes to propagate to the destination database.

How does this method of redo extraction differ from the queue methodology? In fact, the Streams method uses the queue mechanism in its data flow path. Staging into the queue and then subsequent propagation are the main steps. Rather than relying on enqueued events, LogMining of the redo logs and the archived redo logs can be used when there might be a lapse in information in the queued events due to a shutdown of the Capture process.

Many times, the Capture process is temporarily stopped or disabled while the transaction activity continues and log switching occurs as usual. When the Capture process resumes, the LogMiner session will go back to the point where it left off. It is possible that the starting point will be located in an archived log file.

When the transactional activity contents are extracted from the redo log files by the LogMiner Session for the Capture process, the process is called Hot Mining. When LogMining has to be done on the archived redo log files, it is called cold mining. This condition often occurs when the capture process falls back in time and frequent log switching takes place.

Supplemental Logging

Redo log files record all of the information needed for instance recovery. Now that redo log files and archived redo log files are being used for the likes of Oracle Streams and LogMiner, some extra columns of information need to be added to the redo log file. The process of logging extra columns to the redo log files is called Supplemental Logging. Thus is not a default behavior. It has to be enabled either at the database level or at the object level.

Why is this additional logging needed? When a particular column is updated at the source database table for a set of rows, the values in the column or columns are logged by default. When these values are moved to the destination side, to which rows does Oracle apply them, or how does Oracle identify the rows to be updated? Supplemental logging provides the answers to these questions. The additional column values are used by Oracle to identify the rows that are to receive the information.

When Supplemental Logging is enabled, either some selected columns or all columns are specified for extra logging. They are called a supplemental log group and consist of nothing but a set of additional columns that are being logged. There are two types of supplemental log groups that determine when columns in the log group are logged:

- **Unconditional Supplemental Log Groups** - The before-images of specified columns are logged any time a row is updated, regardless of whether the update affected any of the specified columns. This can be referred to as an ALWAYS log group.

- **Conditional Supplemental Log Groups** - The before-images of all specified columns are logged only if at least one of the columns in the log group is updated.

Supplemental Logging can be enabled at database level or at the table level. When it is enabled at database level, there are two types:

- Minimal Logging
- Identification Key Logging

Database Level Logging

With the minimal database level supplemental logging, the database logs the minimal amount of information needed for LogMiner or for the Streams

Capture process to identify, group, and merge the redo operations associated with DML changes.

To enable minimal supplemental logging, the following statement can be executed:

```
SQL> ALTER DATABASE ADD SUPPLEMENTAL LOG DATA;
```

When using the identification key logging method, the database can be instructed to log all the columns in primary key, foreign key, and unique constraints. This would be applicable for the tables in the source database. This method is followed when the intention is to capture changes for the entire database.

The following SQL statement sets up the database level logging using the identification key log method:

```
SQL> ALTER DATABASE ADD SUPPLEMENTAL LOG DATA
     (primary key, unique, foreign key) COLUMNS ;
```

There is also an available option for specifying a particular type of attribute or ALL. These concepts are explained next.

- **ALL** - This option specifies that when a row is updated, all columns of that row, except LOBs, LONGS, and ADTs, are placed in the redo log file. To enable ALL column logging at the database level, execute the following:

  ```
  SQL> ALTER DATABASE ADD SUPPLEMENTAL LOG DATA (ALL) COLUMNS;
  ```

- **PRIMARY KEY** - This option causes the database to place all columns of a row's primary key in the redo log file whenever a row containing a primary key is updated, even if no value in the primary key has changed. To enable PRIMARY KEY logging at the database level, execute the following:

  ```
  SQL> ALTER DATABASE ADD SUPPLEMENTAL LOG DATA (PRIMARY KEY) COLUMNS;
  ```

- **UNIQUE index** - This option causes the database to place all columns of a row's composite unique index key or bitmap index in the redo log file if any column belonging to the composite unique index key or bitmap index is modified. To enable UNIQUE index key and bitmap index logging at the database level, execute:

  ```
  SQL> ALTER DATABASE ADD SUPPLEMENTAL LOG DATA (UNIQUE) COLUMNS;
  ```

- **FOREIGN KEY** - This option causes the database to place all columns of a row's foreign key in the redo log file if any column belonging to the foreign key is modified. To enable FOREIGN KEY logging at the database level, execute the following:

```
SQL> ALTER DATABASE ADD SUPPLEMENTAL LOG DATA (FOREIGN KEY) COLUMNS;
```

In many situations, database-wide supplemental logging may not be desirable as it would produce huge volumes of additional columns of data into the redo logs. Unless the goal is to set up a database-wide capture mechanism, this approach would not be the most desirable. Setting up supplemental logging at the table level is a controlled operation. By this method, better control can be exercised on the selection of tables and columns to be logged additionally.

The next sections provide table level logging examples.

Table-Level Identification Key Logging

When logging is specified at the table level, only the table level logging takes place. Identification key logging at the table level offers the same options as those provided at the database level: ALL, PRIMARY KEY, FOREIGN KEY, and UNIQUE index key. By specifying the right option, the logging level can be controlled.

As an example, the following statement specifies the table-level identification supplemental logging for table ALLINSURED. The implies that when any column in the ALLINSURED table is changed, the entire row, except LOB, LONGs, and ADTs, of the table is placed in the redo log file.

```
SQL> ALTER TABLE NYDATA1.ALLINSURED ADD SUPPLEMENTAL LOG DATA (ALL) COLUMNS;
```

Table-Level User-Defined Supplemental Log Groups

In addition to table-level identification key logging, Oracle supports table level user-defined supplemental log groups. Such log groups can be conditional or unconditional. Table level logging provides better control over configuration and will help to minimize the overall additional logging data.

To create user defined unconditional log groups, the ALWAYS clause is used. For example, to create a group called *allins_polno* for table ALLINSURED, use the following statement:

```
SQL> ALTER TABLE ALLINSURED ADD SUPPLEMENTAL LOG GROUP allins_polno (POL_NO, SALES_ID)
ALWAYS;
```

To create supplemental logging that uses user-defined conditional log groups at the table level, omit the ALWAYS clause from the ALTER TABLE statement. An example is shown next:

```
SQL> ALTER TABLE ALLINSURED
ADD SUPPLEMENTAL LOG GROUP allins_polno (POL_NO, SALES_ID);
```

The above statement creates a log group named *allins_polno* on table ALLINSURED. Since the ALWAYS clause was omitted, before-images of the columns will be logged only if at least one of the columns is updated.

In user-defined supplemental log groups, a column can belong to more than one supplemental log group; however, the before-image of the columns gets logged only once. If the same columns are specified to be logged both conditionally and unconditionally, the columns are logged unconditionally.

Staging and Propagation Process

Event propagation is the basis for the Streams methodology which does replication to other databases. Propagation of events always occurs between a source queue and a destination queue.

Although Propagation is always between two queues, a single queue may participate in multiple propagations. In other words, a single queue may send events to multiple queues and at the same time receive from many queues. However, only one Propagation configuration is allowed between a particular source and destination. As seen in the example shown in Figure 2.2, Type (A) shows the propagation from Queue at DB1 to queues at DB2, DB3, and DB4. Type (B) shows the queue at DB1 sending events to queue at DB2 and vice-versa. Configuring two propagations as shown in Type (C) is not allowed.

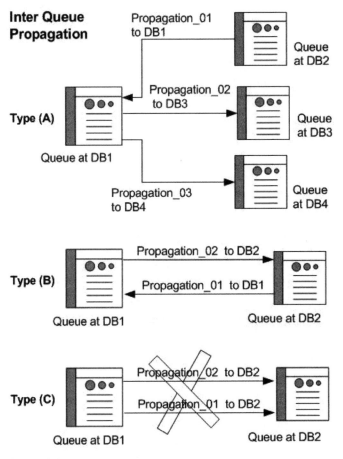

Figure 2.2 - *Propagation between the Queues*

The Propagation process uses the database links to the destination database from the source database. The Propagation process uses job processes and is scheduled to run continuously. Once a schedule is completed, it immediately begins the next schedule.

Propagation Rules

The Propagation process either propagates or discards events based on rules that are defined by the DBA.

For LCR events, each rule specifies the database objects and types of changes for which the rule evaluates to TRUE. These rules can be placed in a positive rule set for the propagation or a negative rule set for the propagation. Rules can be defined at table level, schema level, or database level. For Non-LCR events, DBAs can create their own rules.

Apply Process

The Apply process is an optional Oracle background process that dequeues LCRs and user messages from a specific queue. It then either applies each one directly or passes it as a parameter to a user-defined procedure, called a handler. The Apply process is basically a part of the consumer of or subscriber to the database changes. In other words, it is an end point in the data replication flow.

The Main Features of the Apply Process

The Apply process is implemented as an Oracle background process, whose process name is *Annn*, in which *nnn* is an Apply process number. The Apply process is the process which consumes the LCR events or user messages.

In other words, it is a dequeuing process. When dequeued by the Apply process, captured events, such as the LCRs, contain the DML changes or DDL changes that need to be applied to the destination database objects. The Apply process directly dequeues and implements the database changes. The apply user applies all row changes resulting from DML operations and all DDL changes.

A single Apply process can apply either captured events or user-enqueued events, but it cannot do both. If a queue at a destination database contains both captured and user-enqueued LCRs, the destination database must have at least two Apply processes to process the events. The Apply process can be associated with a SYS.AnyData queue, but it cannot be associated with a typed queue. The Apply process applies the changes based on the rules that are defined by the DBA. When the rule condition evaluates to TRUE, the changes are applied. Based on the rules evaluation, changes are either applied or discarded.

Apply process rules for the LCR events can be defined at various levels such as table level, schema level, and database level. For the non-LCR events, the DBA can create rules to control the consumption process.

Any typical Apply process can either handle captured events or user enqueued events. When the need exists to handle both of these types, two separate Apply processes must be created.

Direct Apply

Direct apply means that an Apply process applies an LCR without running a user procedure. This is likely the main method of applying changes to the destination database. It is also the simplest form of consuming the events at destination side.

The Apply process applies the change in the LCR to a database object unless a conflict or apply error is encountered. In the case of a conflict or apply error, the Apply process tries to resolve the error with a conflict handler or a user-specified procedure called an error handler.

Custom Apply and Apply Handlers

When an Apply process passes the LCR, as a parameter, to a user procedure for processing, it is known as Custom Apply. The user procedure can then process the LCR in a customized way by using a suitable stored procedure. These user-developed procedures are known as apply handlers. Each apply process can have multiple apply handlers.

Figure 2.3 illustrates the four types of apply handlers that are based on the type of events it deals with.

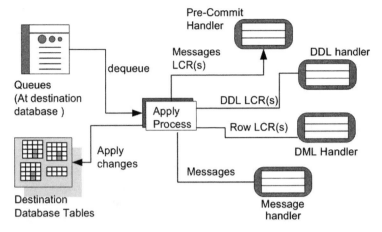

Figure 2.3 - *Apply Process and Apply Handlers*

DML Handler

A user procedure can be created that processes row LCRs resulting from DML statements. Such a procedure is called a DML Handler. For each table associated with an apply process, a separate DML handler can be set up to process each of the DML statements in row LCRs. DML statements include: INSERT, UPDATE, DELETE, and LOB_UPDATE.

DDL Handler

Another procedure that processes DDL LCRs resulting from the DDL statements can be created. Such a procedure is called a DDL Handler. An Apply process can have many DML handlers but only one DDL handler. Since the DDL is a special database activity that can be used to add or modify the database table structures, it often warrants more planning, coordination and control by administrators. The DDL handler can be used to keep an audit on DDL activities or even to make notifications in case a DDL command is executed.

Message Handler

A Message Handler defined at the apply process will process the user-enqueued event that does not contain an LCR. A message handler is a user-

---

defined procedure that can process non-LCR user messages in a customized way.

The message handler offers advantages in any environment that has applications that need to update one or more remote databases or perform some other remote action.

Pre-Commit Handlers

A pre-commit handler is a PL/SQL procedure that takes the commit SCN from an internal commit directive in the queue used by the Apply process. The pre-commit handler may use and process the commit information in any suitable way. For example, an auditing process can be developed using the commit information.

Logical Change Record Events

LCRs represent the redo changes that are converted into events. A Capture process reformats changes that are captured from the redo log into LCRs. The LCR is an object with a specific format that describes a database change.

The Capture process converts the database changes into events containing LCRs and subsequently enqueues them into a queue. A Capture process is always associated with a single SYS.AnyData queue and it only enqueues events into this queue. For improved performance, captured events are always stored in a buffered queue, which is SGA memory associated with a SYS.AnyData queue. Multiple queues can be created and a different Capture process can be associated with each queue.

A Capture process creates two types of LCRs: Row LCRs and DDL LCRs.

Row LCRs

A row LCR describes a change to the data in a single row or a change to a single LONG, LONG RAW, or LOB column in a row. The change in rows is caused by a DML statement or a piecewise update to a LOB.

A single DML statement may insert or merge multiple rows into a table, may update multiple rows in a table, or may delete multiple rows from a table. In this situation, a single DML statement would produce multiple row LCRs.

That is, a capture process creates an LCR for each row that is changed by the DML statement. Also an update to a LONG, LONG RAW, or LOB column in a single row may result in more than one row LCR.

Each row LCR is encapsulated in an object of *lcr$_row_record* type and contains the old and new values of the row. It also has many attributes that identify the source name, command type, SCN, and object name. A captured row LCR also contains transaction control statements such as the COMMIT and ROLLBACK. Such row LCRs are internal and are used by an Apply process to maintain transaction consistency between a source database and a destination database.

A full list of the attributes shown below:

- *source_database_name* - This is the name of the source database where the row change occurred.

- *command_type* - This is the type of DML statement that produced the change, either INSERT, UPDATE, DELETE, LOB ERASE, LOB WRITE, or LOB TRIM.

- *object_owner* - This is the schema name that contains the table with the changed row.

- *object_name* - This is the name of the table that contains the changed row.

- *tag* - This is a raw tag that can be used to track the LCR.

- *transaction_id* - This is the identifier of the transaction in which the DML statement was run.

- *scn* - This is the system change number (SCN) at the time when the change record was written to the redo log.

- *old_values* - These are the old column values related to the change. These are the column values for the row before the DML change. If the type of the DML statement is UPDATE or DELETE, these old values include some or all of the columns in the changed row before the DML statement. If the type of the DML statement is INSERT, there are no old values.

- *new_values* - These are the new column values related to the change. These are the column values for the row after the DML change. If the type of the DML statement is UPDATE or INSERT, these new values include some or all of the columns in the changed row after the DML statement. If the type of the DML statement is DELETE, there are no new values.

DDL LCRs

DDL LCRs contains the DDL changes. A DDL statement changes the structure of the database. For example, a DDL statement may create, alter, or drop a database object.

Each DDL LCR contains the following information:

- *source_database_name* - This is the name of the source database where the DDL change occurred.

- *command_type* - This is the type of DDL statement that produced the change, for example ALTER TABLE or CREATE INDEX.

- *object_owner* - This is the schema name of the user who owns the database object in which the DDL statement was run.

- *object_name* - This is the name of the database object on which the DDL statement was executed.

- *object_type* - This is the type of database object on which the DDL statement was run, for example TABLE or PACKAGE.

- *ddl_text* - This is the text of the DDL statement.

- *logon_user* - This is the logon user, which is the user whose session executed the DDL statement.

- *current_schema* - This is the schema that is used if no schema is specified for an object in the DDL text.

- *base_table_owner* - This is the base table owner. If the DDL statement is dependent on a table, the base table owner is the owner of the table on which it is dependent.

- *base_table_name* - This is the base table name. If the DDL statement is dependent on a table, the base table name is the name of the table on which it is dependent.

- *tag* - This is a raw tag that can be used to track the LCR.

- *transaction_id* - This is the identifier of the transaction in which the DDL statement was run.

- *scn* - This is the SCN when the change was written to the redo log.

Extra Attributes

The *include_extra_attribute* procedure in the *dbms_capture_adm* package can be used to instruct a Capture process to capture one or more extra attributes in addition to those presented earlier. The optional attributes are:

- *row_id* - This is the rowid of the row changed in a row LCR. This attribute is neither included in DDL LCRs, nor is it included in row LCRs for index-organized tables.

- *serial#* - This is the serial number of the session that performed the change captured in the LCR.

- *session#* - This is the identifier of the session that performed the change captured in the LCR.

- *thread#* - This is the thread number of the instance in which the change captured in the LCR was performed. Typically, the thread number is relevant only in a Real Application Clusters environment.

- *tx_name* - This is the name of the transaction that includes the LCR.

- *username* - This is the name of the user who performed the change captured in the LCR.

Rules Engine and Rules

Rules play an important role in configuring and conducting the streams data flow. A Rule is the Streams object which applies logic to determine if the change is to be captured or not, to be propagated or not and to be applied or not. In this manner, rules play a key role in filtering the changes. A faulty rule definition can create big administrative overhead that will require troubleshooting.

A rule is a database Streams object that enables the Streams client to perform an action when an event occurs and a particular condition is met. Rules Engine, which is built into Streams, evaluates the rules. When the rules are grouped, they are known as rule sets. Rule sets may be positive or negative. Stream tasks very much depend on the rules.

Stream Clients such as Capture, Apply, and Propagation processes utilize the rules to select or discard the events. For instance, capture rules dictate what events to be extracted and what events are discarded by a Capture process. The propagation rules specify dictate what events are to be sent out what events are discarded by a Propagation process. In the same way, apply rules determine what dictates, what events have applied, and what events have to be discarded by an Apply process.

Each rule has three distinct components:

- **Rule Condition** - The rule condition combines one or more expressions and conditions and returns a Boolean value which is a value of TRUE, FALSE or NULL. An expression is a combination of one or more values and operators.

- **Rule Evaluation Context** - This is an object that defines external data that can be referenced in the rule conditions. The external data can exist as variables, table data, or both.

- **Rule Action Context** - This is optional information associated with a rule that is interpreted by the Streams client of the rules engine when the rule is evaluated.

Rule Based Transformations

During the Apply process, it is also possible to modify certain attributes of the event and the data being applied. This is possible by employing the rule-based transformations. A rule-based transformation can, for example, modify the data type of a particular column in a table for an event. Thus, a rule-based transformation is any modification to an event that results when a rule in a positive set evaluates to TRUE.

Transformation can be configured at various levels in the Streams flow. They are as follows:

- During the enqueue of an event by the Capture process, the event can be formatted to make it appropriate for the destination database.

- When the events are propagated to a destination database queue, filtering can be introduced that will reduce the network traffic and increase the performance levels.

- When the events are dequeued by an Apply process or messaging clients, events can be modified to make them compatible with destination database.

Conclusion

In this chapter the basic components and overall data and event flow within a typical Streams environment have been presented.

The main points of this chapter include:

- The basic flow at the source database involves capture of database changes by scanning the redo log files and converting them into LCR events. LCR events are enqueued to a source database queue.

- The Propagation process sends the events to the specified queue in the destination database.

- From a destination queue, a typical Apply process or apply handler dequeues them and applies the changes to the destination database objects.

- Rules play an important role in controlling the selection and transportation of the required events. Information has also been presented on the nature of row LCRs and DDL LCRs.

In the next chapter, database replication using the Streams methodology will be introduced. The main steps for a typical replication flow will be examined. The information presented will also touch upon issues such as conflict detection and session tags.

Streams Replication

Maximizing Oracle Streams Replication can be a challenge

Introduction

In this chapter, information on how the Streams technology is put to use for database replication will be presented. There is no doubt that database replication, is the main beneficiary of the Streams technology. With the Streams technology, database replication became much more administratively simple and flexible. The impact of the replication process on the source database, when used with Streams technology, is quite minimal.

This chapter covers the basic methods and features of the Streams replication process. It highlights various issues related to the replication process such as the instantiation of objects, conflict detection, multi-way replication, supplemental logging, principles of the system change number, session tags, and downstream capture.

Database Changes

The database replication process is a method of keeping a copy of data at a remote location. In other words the primary or source data and the dependent remote secondary data is kept synchronized by a continuous data flow method. Any changes made at the source database are copied to the remote database system. This keeps the tables and the data synchronized. The source database system and the destination database system are peer systems and exist independently.

The source database is the where the Data Manipulation Language (DML) and the Data Definition Language (DDL) changes occur through database transactional activity. DML statements make changes to the data in the table through insert, update, and delete SQL statements. The table data rows are affected by DML statements. In contrast, the DDL statements make changes to the table definition or table structures. These changes are shared with the destination database. This process is called database replication.

The replicated configuration, in which changes occur on only one database and the remote database merely receives the changes is called One-Way Replication. When both of the participating databases make changes and those changes are shared with the other database, the configuration is called Two-Way Replication. When more than two databases participate, it is known as Multi-Way replication. Streams Replication allows all of these replication configuration types.

Source and Destination Database

The source database is where transaction changes are recorded into the redo log files. The Streams process then captures those changes and propagates them to the destination database. The Streams Capture and Propagation processes run primarily on the source database.

The Oracle background process, which acts as the Capture process, is the main means of extracting the changes from the redo log files and converting them into Logical Change Record (LCR) events. Such events are enqueued into a queue.

These changes can be either DML changes or DDL changes. If it is a DML operation, each LCR encapsulates a row change resulting from the DML operation to a shared table at the source database. If the change was a DDL operation, a LCR encapsulates the DDL change that was made to a shared database object at a source database. This process is basically a staging operation.

The Propagation process propagates the stages of the LCR to the queue of the destination database. At the destination database, an Apply process consumes the change by applying the LCR to the shared database object. An Apply process may dequeue the LCR and apply it directly, or it may dequeue the LCR and send it to an apply handler.

Sometimes the Propagation process can be optional. This is because an application can create and enqueue an LCR directly into a queue at a destination database. In addition, in a heterogeneous replication environment in which an Oracle database shares information with a non-Oracle database, an Apply process may apply changes directly to a non-Oracle database without propagating LCRs.

Local and Down Streams Capture

Typically, the capture is configured and executed at the source database where the actual database changes are effected. However, for the performance or administrative reasons, the Capture process can also be configured to run on an intermediate database, which is different from the source database where actual changes occur. The intermediate database acts as the host for the Capture process. This capture configuration is known as Down Streams Capture. This feature was made available in the 10g database release.

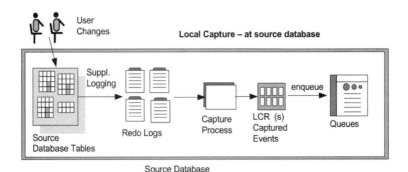

Figure 3.1 - *Local Capture Configured at Source Database*

Figure 3.1 presents a local capture configuration. In this method, the Capture process runs on the database where the redo logs are produced.

In the Down Streams Capture method, the archived redo log files from the source database are copied to the downstream database. The Capture process captures changes from these files at the downstream database. The archived redo log files can be copied to the downstream database using a variety of means. They include log transport services, the *dbms_file_transfer* package, a File Transfer Protocol (FTP), or some other mechanism.

The Down Streams database is not any particular database. It is another stand alone Oracle Instance in which the Capture process, queues, and other propagation processes are configured to run. Figure 3.2 shows the Down Streams capture configuration. This way, the Capture process overhead is effectively shifted from the primary database system.

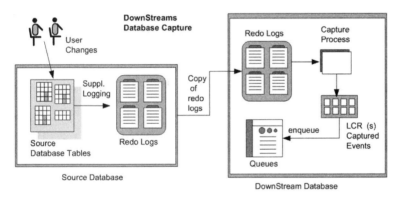

Figure 3.2 - *Capture Configured at a Down Streams Database*

There is an important distinction between local capture and the Down Streams method. In the local capture method, Capture reads the redo log files, and at times may read archived redo log files. In the case of Down Streams capture, it is always the archived redo files that are read by the Capture process. This is because the redo log files can be copied from the source database to the intermediate database only after they are archived. In this case, there will be a definite latency in the replication process.

Why use Down Streams Capture?

Down Streams Database Capture is a useful feature because the Capture process is shifted from the primary database. There is no utilization of additional resources in terms of process activity and memory resources on the source database. This way there is no overhead on the source database. Entire capture and enqueue activities are executed on the downstream database.

If multiple source databases are participating in the replication process, Capture processes for all of these multiple database sources can be centralized on a single database, the downstream database, for administrative convenience.

Since copying the redo log files to the downstream databases is an essential step, it provides improved protection against data loss. For example, the redo log files at the downstream database may be used for recovery of the source database in some situations.

The ability to configure multiple Capture processes at the downstream database provides more flexibility and improves scalability. Additional memory resources can be assigned without affecting the SGA of the source database.

Issues with Down Streams Capture

However, the use of Down Streams capture is not without its shortcomings. There is unavoidable delay in capturing the database changes since the Down Streams Capture process needs to wait for the log switching of the redo log file and the subsequent copying of the archive log file from the source database to the Down Streams database.

The Down Steams capture configuration requires an intermediate host and the database system, which is an additional expense. A new Oracle database instance has to be dedicated to host the Down Streams capture.

Configuration of Down Streams Capture

Operational Requirements

The source database needs to be at least the Oracle 10g release. At the same time, the downstream capture database should be of the same version as that of the source database.

The operating system on the source site and downstream capture site must be the same, but the operating system release does not need to be the same. For example, a 32-bit operating system is in use on the source database host, the same 32-bit operating system must be maintained at the downstream database host. Other hardware elements, such as the number of CPUs, memory size, and storage configuration, can be different between the source and downstream sites.

Database Link

When the downstream database is configured, it can be configured to have a database link to the source database. Though the database link creation between the downstream database and the source database is optional, there are many advantages to having one. The database link name and global name of the source database need to match.

Such a database link simplifies the creation and administration of a downstream Capture process. The DBA can specify that a downstream Capture process use a database link by setting the *use_database_link* parameter to TRUE when the *create_capture* or *alter_capture* is run on the downstream Capture process.

When the database link to the source database exists, certain administrative actions are automatically performed. For instance, the following actions are possible with a database link to the source database:

- It can run the *dbms_capture_adm.build* procedure at the source database to extract the data dictionary at the source database to the redo log when a Capture process is created.

- It can prepare source database objects for instantiation.

- It can obtain the first SCN for the downstream Capture process if the first SCN is not specified during the Capture process creation. The first SCN is needed to create a Capture process.

When there is no database link, the above actions need to be done manually.

As noted earlier, Data Replication is the main beneficiary of the Streams methodology. Streams based replication is a simple and yet flexible method that can be used to move data across the database systems. In the next section, the basic replication functionality and the related components of Streams replication will be presented.

Streams Replication Components

Data replication involves the setting up of data replicas at the remote database site. Replication can be set up at the table level, the schema level and even at the database level.

Types of Changes for Replication

When a Capture process is configured for replication purposes, database changes made by the following types of DML are extracted:

- INSERT

- UPDATE

- DELETE

- MERGE

- Piecewise updates to LOBs

In case of MERGE, the Capture process converts each MERGE change translated into either an INSERT or UPDATE change. MERGE is not a valid command type in a row LCR.

A Capture process does not capture CALL, EXPLAIN PLAN, or LOCK TABLE statements. Since these SQL statements have no bearing on data rows, they are not relevant to the Capture process. At the same time, the DML changes made to a temporary table are also not captured by the Capture process either. This is because the DML activities on a temporary table are merely staging operations and the rows are lost the moment the session is finished.

The sequence values used for individual rows at the databases may vary. Changes to actual sequence values are not captured. For example, if a user references a NEXTVAL or sets the sequence, a Capture process does not capture changes resulting from these operations.

Types of DDL Changes Ignored

A Capture process captures the DDL changes that satisfy its rule sets; however, the following types of DDL changes are never captured. These are very specific to the individual database.

- ALTER DATABASE
- CREATE CONTROLFILE
- CREATE DATABASE
- CREATE PFILE
- CREATE SPFILE

This is very important because these above shown SQL statements are database level operations and have no bearing on data rows in the tables. Since the database operations are exclusive and peculiar to that particular database, they are never sent to the destination database, which is a peer system and its own full fledged database system

A Capture process can capture DDL statements, but not the results of DDL statements, unless the DDL statement is a CREATE TABLE AS SELECT statement. A good example can be seen in an execution of ANALYZE SQL statement on the source database. When a Capture process captures an ANALYZE statement, it does not capture the statistics generated by the ANALYZE statement. Note that the ANALYZE command writes a considerable amount of information to the data dictionary tables.

When a statement such as CREATE TABLE AS SELECT is executed on the source database, the Capture process extracts the statement as the INSERT row LCRs. The CREATE TABLE AS SELECT statement actually involves an INSERT statement. Therefore, it is natural that the Streams capture process extracts the DML changes.

In addition, the following types of changes are also ignored by a Capture process:

- The session control statements ALTER SESSION and SET ROLE, etc. which are very specific to the application environment in which they are used.

- The system control statement: ALTER SYSTEM.

- Invocations of PL/SQL procedures. However, the invocation is not captured if the execution, such as the PL/SQL procedure, makes changes to the tables. Such changes are captured by the Capture process.

Note: Online table redefinition, using the *dbms_redefinition* package, is not supported on a table or schema for which a Capture process captures the changes.

Effect of *nologging* and *unrecoverable*

nologging or *unrecoverable* operations are often used by administrators and application users to increase performance levels and to load large data sets into the database tables in a relatively short time. DBAs are willing to take the risk of re-loading such data in case a media recovery is performed and the non-logged operations are not played back during the recovery.

When no logging operations are executed at the source database by using the *nologging* or *unrecoverable* keyword for a SQL operation, the changes resulting from the SQL operation cannot be captured by a Capture process. This is because the *nologging* operations do not create REDO entries.

Note: If the object for which the logging attributes are specified resides in a database or tablespace in FORCE LOGGING mode, Oracle ignores any *nologging* or *unrecoverable* setting until the database or tablespace is taken out of FORCE LOGGING mode.

If the *unrecoverable* clause is used in the SQL*Loader operation for a direct path load, the table changes resulting from the direct path load cannot be captured by a Capture process. Specifying the unrecoverable clause in the Control File is one example, as noted below.

```
UNRECOVERABLE
LOAD DATA
INFILE 'myfile.dat'
INTO TABLE salesperson
(sname VARCHAR2(40), salesid NUMBER(4));
```

Therefore, if the changes resulting from a direct path load should be captured by a Capture process, the *unrecoverable* clause should not be used.

If a data or index segment has the SQL *nologging* parameter set, the full image redo logging is disabled for that segment, and the invalidation redo is generated. Use of the *nologging* parameter allows a finer degree of control over the objects that are not logged. This operation does affect the Capture process and subsequently the Replication process. When such *nologging* and *unrecoverable* operations are performed at the source database, they need to be repeated at the destination database in order to maintain data synchronization.

Supplemental Logging

The process of logging extra columns of information to the redo log files is called Supplemental Logging. It is not a default behavior. It has to be enabled either at the database level or at the object level. When Supplemental Logging is enabled, selected columns or all columns are specified for extra logging. They are called a supplemental log group, which is nothing but a set of additional columns that are being logged.

Supplemental Logging is necessary for certain columns at a source database in order for changes to those columns to be applied successfully at a destination database. With the help of the values from these additional columns, Oracle decides the rows which need to be updated on the destination side. In this way, supplemental logging is a crucial requirement in most data replication situations.

The Capture process captures this additional information and places it in LCRs. Supplemental Logging is always configured at a source database, regardless of location of the Capture process that captures the changes that occur in the source database. Even if the capture process is configured at the downstream database, the source database needs to specify the Supplemental Logging. In the case of Streams replication, the Apply process uses the additional information in the LCRs to properly apply DML changes and DDL changes that are replicated from a source database to a destination database.

There are two types of supplemental log groups: Unconditional Supplemental Log Groups and Conditional Supplemental Log Groups.

- Unconditional Supplemental Log Groups - The before images of specified columns are logged any time a row is updated, regardless of whether or not the update affected any of the specified columns. This can be referred to as an ALWAYS log group.

- Conditional Supplemental Log Groups - The before images of all specified columns are logged only if at least one of the columns in the log group is updated.

Supplemental Logging can be enabled at database level or at table level. Figure 3.3 shows the types of Supplemental Logging options at the table level.

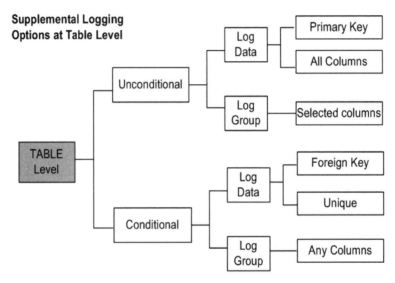

Figure 3.3 - *Supplemental Logging Options at the Table Level*

Unconditional Supplemental Groups

To specify an unconditional supplemental log group that only includes the primary key column(s) for a table, use an ALTER TABLE statement with the PRIMARY KEY option in the ADD SUPPLEMENTAL LOG DATA clause. The log group will have a system-generated name. For example, to add the primary key column of the NYDATA1.ALLINSURED table to an unconditional log group, use the statement:

```
ALTER TABLE nydata1.allinsured
ADD SUPPLEMENTAL LOG DATA (PRIMARY KEY) COLUMNS;
```

To specify an unconditional supplemental log group that includes all columns for a table, use an ALTER TABLE statement with the ALL option in the ADD SUPPLEMENTAL LOG DATA clause. The log group will have a system-generated name. For example, to add all the columns of the NYDATA1.ALLINSURED table to an unconditional log group use the statement:

```
ALTER TABLE nydata1.allinsured
ADD SUPPLEMENTAL LOG DATA (ALL) COLUMNS;
```

To specify an unconditional supplemental log group that contains columns that are selected by the DBA, use an ALTER TABLE statement with the ALWAYS specification. These log groups may also include key columns, if needed. For example, to add the POL_NO and SALESID column of the NYDATA1.ALLINSURED table to an unconditional log group named *log_group_pol_salesid* use the following statement:

```
ALTER TABLE nydata1.allinsured
ADD SUPPLEMENTAL LOG GROUP log_group_pol_salesid
(pol_no , salesid ) ALWAYS;
```

The ALWAYS specification makes this log group an unconditional log group.

Conditional Supplemental Groups

In this method, the before images of all specified columns are logged only if at least one of the columns in the log group is updated. To create a conditional group, the LOG DATA or LOG GROUP options are used.

The following options can be used in the ADD SUPPLEMENTAL LOG DATA clause of an ALTER TABLE statement.

- The FOREIGN KEY option creates a conditional log group that includes the foreign key column(s) in the table.

- The UNIQUE option creates a conditional log group that includes the unique key column(s) in the table. If more than one option is specified in a single ALTER TABLE statement, a separate conditional log group is created for each option. For example, the following statement creates two conditional log groups:

  ```
  ALTER TABLE nydata1.allinsured ADD SUPPLEMENTAL LOG DATA (UNIQUE, FOREIGN KEY)
  COLUMNS;
  ```

The LOG GROUP clause allows the specification of any columns. To specify a conditional supplemental log group that includes any columns that the DBA chooses to add, the ADD SUPPLEMENTAL LOG GROUP clause can be used in the ALTER TABLE statement. To make the log group conditional, do not include the ALWAYS specification.

For example, the SALES_ID and SUM_ASSURED columns in the NYDATA1.ALLINSURED table are included in a column list for conflict resolution at a destination database. The following statement adds the SALES_ID and SUM_ASSURED columns to a conditional log group named *log_group_sales*:

```
ALTER TABLE nydata1.allinsured ADD SUPPLEMENTAL LOG GROUP log_group_sales (sales_id,
sum_assured);
```

So far, the data types and supplemental logging requirements for data replication have been presented. Another important requirement of the Streams environment is Object Instantiation. The following section will provide and introduction to this concept.

Object Instantiation and Streams

When data replication is set up for any object, the source object needs to be instantiated. In other words, the DBA specifies that the source database object is ready to allow the changes to be propagated and applied on to the destination database object. Object Instantiation is an essential requirement in the Streams environment.

It is important to note that when the plan is to have a table replication to the destination site, the table must exist at the destination database. It may be possible that the source table already has many rows and once the Streams process begins, it can only capture the changes subsequent to the configuration time. What about the existing rows? That is where the instantiation of the table, schema, or database becomes important. The Instantiation process is the method used for creating a copy of the source object at the destination database and setting up appropriate System Change Number (SCN) values for replication.

There are three basic steps in instantiating objects with Streams:

- Prepare the object for instantiation at the source database.

- Ensure that a copy of the same object with the existing data or rows is created at the destination database. This can be achieved using export/import, the transportable tablespace method, or the RMAN utility.

- Set the instantiation SCN for the database object at the destination database. The instantiation SCN provides a directive to the Apply process running at the destination database. It implies that only the database changes committed after this SCN at the source database need to be applied at the destination database. Instantiation is required whenever an Apply process dequeues captured LCRs, even if the Apply process sends the LCRs to an apply handler that does not execute them.

Steps one through three are automatically achieved when rules are added with the *dbms_streams* package. The export/import method also sets up the instantiation automatically.

In order to replicate changes to a database object, the object must be prepared for instantiation at the source database and the instantiation SCN is set for the object at the destination database. By preparing an object for instantiation, the lowest SCN is being set for which changes to the object may need to be applied at destination databases. This SCN is called the ignore SCN. The setup of the instantiation has to be done after the Capture process is configured.

dbms_capture_adm has three procedures which achieve the instantiation of objects. They are:

- *prepare_table_instantiation* – This procedure prepares a single table for instantiation. This procedure is used while configuring the individual tables. This gives fine control over tables that are chosen for replication and those that are not.

- *prepare_schema_instantiation* – This procedure prepares all of the database objects in a schema and all database objects added to the schema in the future for instantiation. This method is useful when the goal is to maintain a total replicated schema at the destination database. In a single instantiation step, all the existing objects are instantiated

- *prepare_global_instantiation* – This procedure prepares all of the database objects in a database and all database objects added to the database in the future for instantiation.

The chapters of this book on configuration contain additional details and examples, including the syntax of the procedures and arguments.

These procedures record the SCN value below which changes to an object cannot be applied at the destination database. The above methods need to be used appropriately before the SCN number is recorded and specified to the Apply process at the destination database. Rules must be added to the positive rule set for the Capture process before the database objects are prepared for instantiation.

As noted earlier, Oracle provides multiple methods for performing instantiation. These other methods include the traditional export/import method, newly available data pump export/import method, transportable tablespace method and the RMAN utility. Each of these methods works very well. However, all of these methods may not work in all situations. The following some general considerations to follow when selecting a method for instantiation:

- If replication is being setup between databases located on different operating systems or character sets, the export/import becomes the choice tool. For example, by using export/import, an object can be dumped or exported from the source database residing on a Solaris host and imported into the destination database residing on a Linux host.

- Export and import using the Data Pump utility is recommended as it is faster and more efficient than the traditional export and import method. However, the Data Pump utilities cannot be used when dealing with replication between 10g release database and 9i release database.

- The RMAN duplicate command cannot be used when the data is being moved to a database residing on a different operating system. However, when the RMAN utility can be used, the instantiation process is generally faster than using the export/import method. This becomes important when there are large data volumes to be dealt with.

The following section provides an overview of these methods.

Instantiation by the Data Pump Export and Import Method

In this method, Data Pump export can be used to export table(s) or schema(s) from the source database. Typically, the *expdp* utility is used to export the schema or objects. The *flashback_scn* export parameter is specified in the *expdp* command line. The current SCN of the source database is specified as the *flashback_scn*.

Copy the dump file to the destination database and import the tables or schema using the *impdp* utility. Once the tables or schema are imported, the data is synchronized between the source and destination databases. The destination is now ready to accept the changes above this SCN value.

Traditional export and import can also be used to set up the tables at the destination database and set up the instantiation. In this case, the *streams_instantiation* parameter should be used with a value of 'Y'.

Instantiation Using the Transportable Tablespace

In this method, the tablespace has to be self-contained and should contain only the objects that are of interest for replication. This is usually a very fast method, which makes it an appropriate option for dealing with large tables.

First make the tablespace read-only; then export the metadata with the parameter *transport_tablespace* set to the desired tablespace. Copy both the data file supporting the tablespace and the Meta data dump to the destination database. At the destination site, import the Meta data dump files and attach the data file in order to access the tablespace and the objects at the destination database.

More details of the instantiation, with examples, are covered in later chapters. The next section presents details about the session tags that control the replication process.

Streams Tags

Streams Tags are useful components of the Streams replication process because they control the behavior of the Streams clients. With the help of these tags, the DBAs will be able to exercise fine control over the replication process. The tags help to exclude data changes from propagation and from the apply activity.

Tags are always associated with entries in the redo log file. The data type of the tag is RAW. By default, when a user or application generates redo entries, the value of the tag is NULL for each entry. A NULL tag consumes no space in the redo entry. For entries that are not NULL, the size limit for a tag value is 2,000 bytes.

The following section presents information on how the tags are used in the Streams process.

How Tags are used in Streams

In Streams, the DBA may define rules that may have conditions relating to tag values, and these can be used to control the behavior of Streams clients.

For instance, a tag can be used to determine whether an LCR contains a change that originated in the local database or at a different database. In this way, change cycling, or the return of a LCR back to the database where it originated, can be avoided. A tag can also be used to specify the set of destination databases for each LCR. Tags may be used for other LCR tracking purposes as well.

When there is bi-directional table replication, even Oracle uses the tag values internally to determine where the redo is generated, if it is done at local database or at the remote database. Once it determines local or remote, it can avoid the cyclic propagation of table changes.

Streams tags can be specified for redo entries that are generated by a particular session. These tags become part of the LCRs captured by a Capture process. Based on the value of the tag, a decision can be made to apply or discard a change at the destination database.

The value of the tags generated by the current session or by an Apply process can be set or retrieved. The *set_tag* procedure in the *dbms_streams* package sets the tag for all redo entries generated by the current session.

For example, the following procedure can be used to set the tag to the hexadecimal value of 2A in the current session:

```
BEGIN
DBMS_STREAMS.SET_TAG(tag => HEXTORAW('2A')  );
END;
/
```

After running this procedure, each redo entry generated by DML or DDL statements in the current session will have a tag value of 2A. Running this procedure affects only the current session.

The tag for all redo entries generated by the current session can be retrieved by using the *get_tag* procedure in the *dbms_streams* package. For example, to get the hexadecimal value of the tags generated in the redo entries for the current session, use the following SQL block:

```
SET SERVEROUTPUT ON
DECLARE
raw_tag RAW(2000);
BEGIN
raw_tag := DBMS_STREAMS.GET_TAG();
DBMS_OUTPUT.PUT_LINE('Session Tag Value = ' || RAWTOHEX(raw_tag));
END;
/
```

The tag value for the current session can be displayed by querying the *dual* view:

```
SELECT DBMS_STREAMS.GET_TAG FROM DUAL
/
```

Since an Apply process is typically an SQL session that makes the transactional changes on the destination database, it does generate the redo entries. Such redo entries will have Non-NULL tags in order to avoid further capture. By default, the non-NULL value is system dependent. However, if the goal is to create a specific non-NULL tag value, the *alter_apply* procedure of the *dbms_apply_adm* procedure can be used to set up desired non-NULL tag value.

In another situation, the default tag for all redo entries generated by an Apply process can also be set when the Apply process is created. In this case, the *create_apply* procedure in the *dbms_apply_adm* package will be used.

For example, to set the value of the tags generated in the redo log by an existing apply process named *nydata1_apply* to the hexadecimal value of 6, run the following SQL block:

```
BEGIN
DBMS_APPLY_ADM.ALTER_APPLY(
apply_name => 'nydata1_apply', apply_tag => HEXTORAW('6'));
END;
/
```

In a Streams-based replication configuration, there is often a need to define bi-directional or multi-way replication of specific tables. Though the configuration of such multi-way replication is fairly simple, the management of data flows within this environment gets complicated due to conflicts. The following section provides information on multi-way replication issues and the conflict resolution methods.

Multi-Way Replication and Conflict Resolution

In a bi-directional configuration, a typical table is replicated in both ways. For example, table ORDERS at the NY site is replicated to London site. And again, any changes made on the ORDERS table at the London site are replicated to the ORDERS table at the NY site. When this is extended to additional sites, it is known as multi-way replication.

An important issue that must be dealt with in multi-way Streams replication is conflict resolution. Oracle Streams provides many useful built-in features that are intended to detect, avoid, and resolve the conflict.

Before examining the conflict resolution methods, it will be useful to detail what kinds of conflicts are possible in a typical bi-directional or multi-way replication.

- **Update Conflict**: This occurs when a specific row is updated with different values in two sites at almost the same time. When the row LCR arrives to the destination, it finds that the column's old value does not match that of the source. This transaction typically gets into an error queue. This situation is called an update conflict.

- **Uniqueness Conflict**: This occurs when a row with an identical primary key value or unique key value is inserted at almost the same time in two sites. When the row LCR reaches the destination, it finds that the row with the same primary key or unique key is already present. It becomes an integrity violation and results in an error. Now both the sites have different rows. This kind of conflict is called a uniqueness conflict.

- **Delete Conflict**: There are some situations where at Site-A, a row is updated and on Site-B, the same row is deleted. Both of these transactions are performed at almost the same time. When Site-A's row LCR goes to the destination Site-B, it does not find the row to update. In the same way, when the Site-B's row LCR reaches the destination of Site-A, it has different values. In another situation, the same row may be deleted in both the sites at almost the same time. In this situation, both of the row LCRs will fail to execute the delete operation on the destination site. This situation is called a delete conflict.

- **Foreign Key Conflict:** In a situation where there is dependency between the parent and child table, the apply process may fail to execute an update, or update just because the row parent key does not exist at the destination. For example, when a row is inserted into ALLINSURED table with *polno* of 452289, it has *sales_id* value of 165. *sales_id* is the foreign key. Salesman is the parent table, where a row for *sales_id* of 165 is inserted. When the row LCR containing the *sales_id* arrives later than the ALLINSURED row LCR to the destination database, the apply transaction for row insertion into ALLINSURED fails with foreign integrity failure. This happens because the row with *sales_id* of 165 does not exist when there is an attempt to insert row into ALLINSURED table at that destination. This kind of situation is called a foreign key conflict.

All the mentioned scenarios are automatically detected by the Streams Apply process. By default, it will place them into an error queue. Unless an error handler or any other type of handler is provided to the apply procedure, they will remain in error conditions.

Then, how are they dealt with and how are conflict issues avoided? There are two ways of resolution to this tricky problem. One is to design the bi-directional or multi-way replication in such a way that there is minimum scope for conflict generation. The second one is to use the Oracle provided pre-built update conflict handlers to resolve the conflicts. Information will be provided next that will examine how they can be used.

Design Considerations

There are many design techniques and considerations which help avoid conflict situations. When multi-site replication exists for a table, one site should be designated as 'in-charge' and only that site can insert and update rows during a particular time frame. Another way to handle the issue is to make each site in-charge of a subset of the data. For example, the London site performs transactions on all the rows with *region_id* of EUROPE, and the Singapore site takes care of all rows with *region_id* of APAC. The remainder of the rows are handled by the NewYork site. In this way, partial ownership of the table avoids some potential DML conflicts.

Of course, this method may be too restrictive for business and application systems. In such cases, there are some design considerations which may help avoid conflicts.

For instance, to avoid the uniqueness conflicts, a sequence number can be created and combined with the region code or site-code. This composite value can be used as the primary key and it helps to insert rows freely without getting into uniqueness conflicts. Instead of using a combined key, a different series of values can be viewed for a different site.

In another example, delete conflicts can be avoided by a simple strategy. Instead of deleting the rows, the rows can simply be marked for deletion. One specified site can then take charge and delete them. In this way, a potential delete conflict issue can be avoided.

Pre-built update conflict handlers

Before moving on to an examination of the conflict handlers, it is important to understand what a column list is and what the resolution columns are. The column list indicates the set of columns for which the update conflict handler is called when there is an update conflict. The resolution columns are the columns which will be used to identify an update handler. Also in some cases, resolution columns will be used to resolve the conflict.

Oracle provides four types of pre-built update conflict handlers. They are OVERWRITE, DISCARD, MAXIMUM and MINIMUM. The following example will illustrate the use of these handlers.

A row in the ALLINSURED table with *polno* 452366 is updated at the NY site and at the same time at London site. The update at the NY site changes the value of the SUM_ASSURED column to 45000 from 35000, but the London site changes the value to 62000 from 35000. When the row LCR from NY reaches the London site, it finds the old value of 62000 instead of expected 35000.

When used, the OVERWRITE handler, in the above situation, will overwrite the value at the London site value with 45000 and the conflict is resolved.

The DISCARD handler behaves differently. When conflict arises, it ignores the source database values. As a result, in the above example, the value of 62000 at the London site will remain.

When the MAXIMUM handler is used, the new value and the old values are compared and the higher values is retained or applied. In the above example, 62000 would be retained since it is higher than 45000. In the same way, if the MINIMUM conflict handler had been used, the value of 45000 would have been applied.

Conclusion

In this chapter, the focus has been on the principle components of the Streams process that are relevant for the replication process. The main points of this chapter include:

- The Capture processes can be configured on the source database where transactions are effected as well as on an intermediate database which is known as the Down Streams capture database.

- Object instantiation methods and supplemental logging methods are essential for data replication. Instantiation prepares the objects for replication. Supplemental logging adds extra data values to the redo entries.

- Session Tags help to develop better control over what can be replicated and what can not. Administrators can use the tags to solve data mismatch issues, etc.

- In multi-way replication, conflicts do arise. There are specific design considerations that can be used to resolve them. There are also Oracle provided pre-built conflict update handlers that can be used help to resolve conflicts.

In the next chapter, the configuration details of the two main Streams clients will be presented. These two main clients are the Capture process and the Propagation process.

Capture and Propagate Configuration

A good Oracle professional is always on the lookout for data to capture.

Introduction

In this chapter, the configuration details of the Streams clients will be examined. The three main Streams clients have been introduced in a previous chapter. They are Capture, Propagation and Apply. The next step is to focus on the methodology used to create and manage these Streams processes. Examples will be included in order to show how the data flow, in terms of replication, moves from the producer to the consumer.

In the environment set up section, information will be presented on the methods used to set up the user/schema that acts as the Streams administrator. This setup includes the assignment of the appropriate privileges and the adjustment of the initialization parameters needed for the Streams process. Initialization parameters configure the necessary queue and job processes for the database instance.

In the section that deals with Streams clients, various methods that can be used to create the Capture and Propagate processes will be introduced. In the next chapter, the information will be expanded to cover the other Streams client known as the Apply process. The Apply process by itself is a distinct and independent process that runs on a destination database instance.

Before getting into the detailed explanation, it will be useful to review the information from earlier chapters about the Streams clients.

The Capture process is an Oracle background process that scans the database redo log files that are used to extract the Data Manipulation Language (DML) and the Data Definition Language (DDL) changes that were done on the source database objects. Those changes are converted into Logical Change Record (LCR) events and then enqueued into queues at the source database. The Propagation process then sends the events from the source queue to the destination queue. The Propagation process either propagates or discards events based on user defined rules.

The Apply process is an optional Oracle background process that dequeues LCRs and user messages from a specific queue. The Apply process then either applies each one directly or passes it as a parameter to a user-defined procedure called a handler.
The general information on the Capture process does not cover creating user messages. User messages and the method of enqueue for them will be examined in more detail in later chapters.

For each of these processes, rules have been defined either automatically or manually. Rules control the filtering of changes. Whether the changes are taken up or discarded is highly dependent on the rule that is in effect at the time that the Streams client process runs. When the Capture or Propagation processes are created, rules are automatically generated.

Environment Set up

Figure 4.1 shows One-Way Replication where the Instance DNYTST10 will replicate data to the DNYOIP20 Instance.

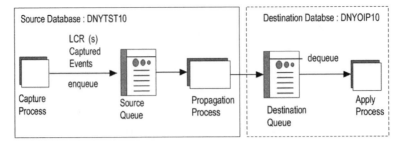

Figure 4.1 *One Way replication and the main processes.*

In this section, the Streams environment will be prepared and set up at both the source and destination databases. The environment set up process includes the following:

- Setting the required *init.ora* parameters

- Streams pool considerations

- Setting up a separate tablespace for the LogMiner

- Creating a user who acts as Streams Administrator

- Creating the schema or user whose objects are to be replicated

- Configuring the Supplemental Logging at table level

- Creating Database Links between the source and destination databases.

- Proper use of the System Change Number (SCN)

- Setting up the Queues to stage and propagate the events

The next section will cover the essential initialization parameters that are needed for Streams configuration

Initialization parameters

The essential initialization parameters are:

compatible: This parameter specifies the release of the Oracle Database software with which the Oracle server must maintain compatibility. To use the new Streams features introduced in Oracle Database 10g, this parameter must be set to 10.1.0 or higher. For example, to use downstream capture, this parameter must be set to 10.1.0 or higher at both the source database and the downstream database. Failure to set this parameter would disable the 10g features.

global_names: This parameter specifies whether or not the database link is required to have the same name as the database to which it connects. In order to use Streams to share information between databases, this parameter should be set to TRUE at each database that is participating in the Streams environment. When setting a TRUE value for this parameter, a database link whose name matches with the destination database name must be created.

job_queue_processes This parameter specifies the number of job queue processes for each instance. The numbers range from J000 to J999. Job queue processes handle requests created by *dbms_job*. This parameter must be set to at least 2 at each database that is propagating events in the Streams environment. It should be set to the same value as the maximum number of jobs that can run simultaneously, plus two. This is an important parameter. If this parameter is not set, Oracle will not spawn any job processes and the Streams propagation process never starts.

open_link This parameter specifies the maximum number of concurrent open connections to remote databases that are allowed in one session. These connections include database links as well as external procedures and cartridges, each of which uses a separate process. In a Streams environment, this parameter should be set to the default value of 4 or higher. Especially, when multi-way replication is configured, many database links will be used for data transfer. Setting the correct number of links in the *open_link* parameter ensures that all of those links will be successful.

streams_pool_size This parameter specifies, in bytes, the size of the Streams pool. The Streams pool contains captured events. The Streams pool is part of the System Global Area (SGA). In addition, the Streams pool is also used for internal communication during parallel capture and applies. By setting this parameter, a new pool of memory within the SGA called Streams pool is dedicated to the use of Streams buffers.

If the size of the Streams pool is greater than zero, any SGA memory used by Streams is allocated from the Streams pool. If the Streams pool size is set to zero, the SGA memory used by Streams is allocated from the shared pool and it may use up to 10% of the shared pool only. When Streams buffers are allocated from the shared pool, there will be a limitation on how much memory can be used.

This parameter can be modified; however, if it is set to zero when an instance starts, increasing it beyond zero has no effect on the current instance because it is already using the shared pool for Streams buffer allocations. If this parameter is set to a value greater than zero when an instance starts and is then reduced to zero when the instance is running, Streams processes and jobs will not run. Oracle recommends that the size of the Streams pool be adjusted for each of the following factors:

- 10 MB for each Capture process parallelism

- 1 MB for each Apply process parallelism

- 10 MB or more for each Queue staging captured events

- The DBA must ensure that enough buffers can be created. Failure to do so may cause memory contention.

timed_statistics This parameter specifies whether or not statistics related to time are collected. To collect elapsed time statistics in the dynamic performance views related to Streams, this parameter should be set to TRUE. The views that include elapsed time statistics include:

- *v$streams_capture*

- *v$streams_apply_coordinator*

- *v$streams_apply_reader*

- *v$streams_apply_server*

The collection of timing details yields information that is useful to the DBA for monitoring and analyzing the performance load issues.

The next section introduces information on the creation of the Streams pool in the SGA and its true nature.

Streams Pool in the SGA

Unlike a persistent AQ queue, which stages all events in a queue table on disk, a Streams queue has a queue buffer that is used to stage captured events in shared memory. A queue buffer is memory associated with a SYS.AnyData queue that contains only the captured events. The queue buffering mechanism enables the database to optimize captured events by buffering them in the SGA instead of always storing them in a queue table on disk.

By default in earlier releases of the Oracle database, the memory used by Streams was allocated from the Shared Pool. The size was limited to 10% of the Shared pool which was controlled by the parameter *shared_pool_size*. In many instances, the buffer would overflow due to speedier capture activity.

A queue buffer would normally overflow if there were not enough *shared_pool_size* available to hold captured events. Captured events that overflow a queue buffer are stored in the appropriate *aq$_<queue_table_name>_p* table on disk. When queue buffers spill over to the physical table, the system will normally experience performance issues. There will also be additional overhead of processing.

When the number of Capture processes was increased or the parallelism for Capture or Apply process was introduced, there was a need for additional buffers. Since the size of the SGA that can be used by the Streams was limited to 10% of the Shared pool, in the total Shared pool size had to be increased considerably in order to enhance the buffer capacity needed for Streams.

With the 10g release, Oracle provides a great relief by allowing the configuration of a separate Streams pool which is controlled by the *streams_pool_size* initialization parameter. The limitation of using the shared pool is lifted by using the separate Streams pool area. Figure 4.2 shows the memory components in a typical Oracle instance.

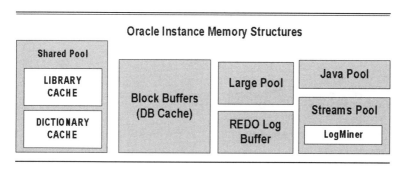

Figure 4.2 *Oracle Instance Memory Structures*

The *streams_pool_size* parameter is dynamic. If this parameter is set to zero when an instance starts, increasing it beyond zero has no effect on the current instance because the instance is already using the Shared pool for Streams allocations. In other words, if the *streams_pool_size* is set to a value greater than zero at the start of the instance, the dynamic adjustment becomes meaningful.

The memory required by persistent LogMiner sessions, such as those used by Data Guard SQL Apply, are also now automatically allocated from the Streams pool, if the Streams pool is configured.

LogMiner TableSpace

Every Capture process spawns a LogMiner process. The LogMiner process and its environment use many objects which are also essential for managing Streams. Some of the LogMiner objects are used by the Streams Capture process. By default, all LogMiner tables are created to use the SYSAUX tablespace; however, it may be desirable to have LogMiner tables use an alternate tablespace. To use an alternate tablespace, it is recommended that the separate tablespace be created and LogMiner related objects moved to this tablespace. Oracle provides the *dbms_logmnr_d.set_tablespace* procedure to achieve this.

As an example, a tablespace called LOGMNR_TBS should be created. After the tablespace has been created, the *dbms_logmnr_d.set_tablespace* procedure should be used to move the objects to the alternate tablespace.

```
-- To create the tablespace
CREATE TABLESPACE LOGMNR_TBS
DATAFILE 'logmnr_tbs.dbf' SIZE 25M
AUTOEXTEND ON MAXSIZE UNLIMITED
/
-- To move all the objects, execute
BEGIN
DBMS_LOGMNR_D.SET_TABLESPACE('LOGMNR_TBS');
END;
/
```

Creating the Streams Administrator

A user will have to be created to act as the Streams administrator. Any name can be given to the user, as there is no restriction on naming conventions. However, it is recommended that a new tablespace be created for the use of the Streams administrator account. By using a separate tablespace, a place is created for all of the related objects in this tablespace. This separate tablespace makes it easy to manage and monitor the growth of the tablespace.

The following SQL statements show the steps for the creation of the tablespace, creation of the Streams administrator account, and the granting of necessary privileges to that administrator account.

🖫 setup_streams.sql

```
-- **************************************************
-- Copyright © 2005 by Rampant TechPress
-- This script is free for non-commercial purposes
-- with no warranties.  Use at your own risk.
--
-- To license this script for a commercial purpose,
-- contact info@rampant.cc
-- **************************************************

spool setup_strmadm.log

PROMPT (1) ** Creating tablespace strm_tbs
CREATE TABLESPACE strm_tbs DATAFILE '/app/oracle/DNYTST10/data/strmtbs_01.dbf' SIZE 500M
EXTENT MANAGEMENT LOCAL UNIFORM SIZE 4M
/

PROMPT (2) ** Creating  User strmadm
CREATE USER strmadm IDENTIFIED BY strmadm
DEFAULT TABLESPACE strm_tbs QUOTA UNLIMITED ON strm_tbs
/

PROMPT 3) ** Grant the privilege
GRANT CONNECT, RESOURCE, DBA TO strmadm
/

PROMPT 4) ** Use the AUTH package function to grant privilege
BEGIN
DBMS_STREAMS_AUTH.GRANT_ADMIN_PRIVILEGE(
grantee             => 'strmadm',
grant_privileges => true);
END;
/
SPOOL OFF
```

With the above code, the STRMADM user has been created. By using the *dbms_streams_auth.grant_admin_privilege* procedure, in a single operation, all of the necessary privileges were granted to the STRMADM user.

Alternately, a series of SQL statements can be generated that grant various privileges. Using this method gives the DBA better control over the kinds of privileges that are granted. For example, the main Streams administrator account may be created with all of the privileges of database administrators. However, for another application group or user, it may be desirable to create additional Streams administrator accounts with selected privileges only.

The next example shows how to generate the script file containing the SQL statements that grants various privileges to the Streams administrator account. By careful selection of required privileges, the DBA is able create multiple users with different degree of privileges.

```
-- First ensure we have a Directory Object

CREATE DIRECTORY admin_dir AS '/app/oracle/DNYTST10/data'
/

-- generate the Script File
BEGIN
DBMS_STREAMS_AUTH.GRANT_ADMIN_PRIVILEGE(
grantee                 => 'strmadm',
grant_privileges => false,
file_name          => 'grant_strms_privs.sql',
directory_name   => 'admin_dir');
END;
/
```

Create the Schema at Source Database

The next step is to create schema/users named NY1, NY2, NY3, and NY4 where tables will be created. After the schema/users have been created, the objects will be used to demonstrate the replication process using the Streams technology. *Setup_NY1.sql*, which is available in the code depot, lists SQL statements that create the necessary tablespace, schema, tables and sequence for the Schema NY1. Similarly, objects can also be created in NY2, NY3, and NY4.

The creation of tables will be repeated later in the additional schemas NY2, NY3 and NY4 to demonstrate some other options with which the Streams flow can be configured.

Set up the Supplemental Logging

As presented earlier, the process of logging extra columns to the redo log files is called supplemental logging. It is not a default behavior. It has to be enabled at either the database level or at the object level.

Using the primary key for the supplemental logging causes the database to place all columns of a row's primary key in the redo log file whenever a row containing a primary key is updated. This will occur even if no value in the primary key has changed.

The following SQL statements show the set up of supplemental logging at the table level for the table named ALLINSURED1, using the primary key.

```
-- Unconditional Primary Key only
alter table ny1.allinsured1
add supplemental log data (primary key) columns ;
```

The ALL columns option specifies that when a row is updated, all columns of that row, except for LOBs, LONGs, and ADTs, are placed in the redo log file. To enable ALL column logging at the table level for ALLINSURED1, the following SQL statement should be executed:

```
-- unconditional ALL columns
ALTER TABLE ny1.allinsured1
ADD SUPPLEMENTAL LOG DATA (ALL) COLUMNS;
```

The *dba_log_groups* view can be queried to verify the supplemental logging setup. The following SQL statement can be used to query:

```
SELECT log_group_name, owner, table_name,
DECODE(always, 'ALWAYS', 'Unconditional',
NULL, 'Conditional') ALWAYS
FROM DBA_LOG_GROUPS
/
```

To drop a conditional or unconditional supplemental log group, use the DROP SUPPLEMENTAL LOG GROUP clause in the ALTER TABLE statement. For example, to drop a supplemental log group named *log_grp_allins1*, the following statement should be run:

```
ALTER TABLE ny1.allinsured1 DROP SUPPLEMENTAL LOG GROUP  log_grp_allins1
/
```

When does the supplemental log group get dropped? It gets dropped when the DBA decides to cease replication for a table. At that point, the DBA may even want to remove the additional logging for that table, so that unnecessary extra values are not created into the redo log.

Creating the Database Links

The next step would be to create the database links. In order to propagate events from a source queue at a database to a destination queue at another database, a private database link must be created between the database containing the source queue and the database containing the destination queue.

In the following example, a database link will be created from the STRMADM schema of the source database of DNYTST10 to the destination schema of STRMADM of DNYOIP20 and vice-versa.

```
-- At source database, creater the DB link
CONNECT strmadm/strmadm@DNYTST10.world

CREATE DATABASE LINK DNYOIP20.world CONNECT TO strmadm IDENTIFIED BY strmadm USING
'DNYOIP20.world'
```

```
/
-- At Target Database, create database link
CONNECT strmadm/strmadm@DNYOIP20.world

CREATE DATABASE LINK DNYTST10.world CONNECT TO strmadm IDENTIFIED BY strmadm USING
'DNYTST10.world'
/
```

Understanding the SCN values

The System Change Number (SCN) is the main controlling function that is used to keep track of database transactional activity. SCN is a stamp that defines a committed version of a database at a particular point in time. Oracle assigns every committed transaction a unique SCN. To support the multi-version read-consistency capabilities, Oracle keeps records of all database changes with the help of SCN numbers. SCN is a running number for the database changes.

SCN is a vital tool utilized by the Streams Methodology. The processes of reading, propagating and applying database changes make use of the SCN numbers. SCN values provide a time-based tracking number that can be used to coordinate the various Streams processes. Based on SCN numbers, various Streams processes are able to restart from where they left off when a particular process is interrupted and has to be restarted.

Oracle provides a DBMS procedure that is used to query the SCN that was in effect at any point. As shown in the following SQL statement, the *get_system_change_number* procedure shows the current SCN value of the database.

```
Select DBMS_FLASHBACK.GET_SYSTEM_CHANGE_NUMBER() from dual
/
```

During the database checkpoint, Oracle records the SCN number into the control files and also all data files. The same SCN number is recorded in all the files.

Most of the Streams-related dynamic performance views show the SCN number. This helps the DBA understand the progress of the Streams process. This also helps in troubleshooting and monitoring. For example, the *dba_capture* view records the following SCN values which helps track the Capture process progress.

- **captured_scn**: The *captured_scn* is the one that corresponds to the most recent change scanned in the redo log by a Capture process. This value keeps incrementing to a higher number as the database transactional activity goes on. As long as the Capture process is running, this value should change gradually.

- **applied_scn**: The *applied_scn* for a Capture process is the SCN of the most recent event dequeued by the relevant Apply processes. It indicates that all events with SCNs lower than this one have been dequeued by all Apply processes that apply changes captured by the Capture process. The *applied_scn* for a Capture process is equivalent to the low-watermark SCN for such an Apply process.

- **first_scn**: The *first_scn* is the lowest SCN in the redo log from which a Capture process can capture changes. If a *first_scn* is specified during creation of the Capture process, the database must be able to access redo log information from the specified SCN and those with higher values.

- **start_scn**: The *start_scn* is the SCN from which a Capture process begins to capture changes.

- **required_checkpoint_scn**: This value indicates the lowest checkpoint SCN for which the Capture process requires redo information. At very regular intervals, the Capture process records a checkpoint where it records its current state persistently in the data dictionary of the database running the Capture process. The redo log file that contains the required checkpoint SCN, and all subsequent redo log files must be available to the Capture process. If a Capture process is stopped and restarted, it starts scanning the redo log from the SCN that corresponds to its *required_checkpoint_scn*.

- **max_checkpoint_scn**: This is the SCN value at which the last checkpoint was taken by the Capture process. The Capture process has its own check point schedule.

At the same time, the *v$streams_capture* view provides additional information about the Capture process SCN values. As a supplement to the above shown information, the *v$log* and *v$archived_log* will show the SCN numbers.

A glance at various SCN values helps the DBA monitor and keep tight control over the Streams performance issues, if any. Analysis of the time lags helps in monitoring latency levels between the creation of a transaction, flushing to the redo log file, enqueue of the event and the dequeue process.

In summary, from the *dba_capture* view, the following columns can be seen:

```
START_SCN
CAPTURED_SCN
APPLIED_SCN
```

```
FIRST_SCN
MAX_CHECKPOINT_SCN
REQUIRED_CHECKPOINT_SCN
```

From the *v$streams_capture* view, the following columns can be seen:

```
ENQUEUE_MESSAGE_NUMBER  (Last Enqueued Msg#)
AVAILABLE_MESSAGE_NUMBER (Last redo SCN flushed to log)
CAPTURE_MESSAGE_NUMBER (Most recently captured message)
TOTAL_MSG_CAPT (From last start of Capture process)
TOTAL_MESSAGES_CAPTURED
ENQUEUE_MESSAGE_NUMBER ('Last EnqueSCN )
```

A script called *show_capture_details.sql*, which can be obtained from the code depot, has been developed based on some selected columns of the following dictionary views:

```
SELECT [columns] from dba_capture
SELECT [columns] from v$streams_capture
SELECT DBMS_FLASHBACK.GET_SYSTEM_CHANGE_NUMBER from DUAL
SELECT CHECKPOINT_CHANGE# from v$database
SELECT [columns] from v$log where status in ('ACTIVE', 'CURRENT')
```

The typical output from the script shows all the relevant SCNs in one place:

```
DNYTST10 SQL>@show_capture_details

CAPTURE_PROFILE
--------------------------------------------------------------
Capture_name (dba_capture)  ---> : NY3_CAPTURE
Queue Name                       : NY3_QUEUE
RULE_SET_NAME                    : RULESET$_156
Capture_User and Type            : STRMADM Type : LOCAL
START_SCN                        : 13089644
Captured_SCN                     : 13089673
Applied_SCN                      : 13089644
FIRST_SCN                        : 13089644
MAX_CHECKPOINT_SCN               : 13091418
Reqd CKPT SCN                    : 13089644
Total Delta SCN Captured         : 20814
Delta SCN Applied    (Delta)     : 20843
Error Number                     :
Error Message ..                 :

Now Time             ------> : 16:20:24 10/15/2004
Current SCN (from DBMS_FLASHBACK): 13110487
CKPT SCN (from v$database)       : 13105814
Current Redo Log Begin SCN       : 13107332
Redo Group Number and Status     : 1   CURRENT
Last Capt.SCN(v$streams_capture) : 13093098  At 16:19:06 10/15/2004
Last EnqueSCN (v$streams_capture): 13093098  At 16:19:06 10/15/2004

Now Time             ------> : 16:20:24 10/15/2004
Current SCN (from DBMS_FLASHBACK): 13110488
CKPT SCN (from v$database)       : 13105814
Current Redo Log Begin SCN       : 13105814
Redo Group Number and Status     : 3   ACTIVE
Last Capt.SCN (v$streams_capture): 13093098 At 16:19:06 10/15/2004
Last EnqueSCN (v$streams_capture): 13093098 At 16:19:06 10/15/2004

Process SID (v$streams_capture)  : 1
CAPTURE_NAME  ..                 : NY3_CAPTURE
State                            : PAUSED FOR FLOW CONTROL
TOTAL_MESSAGES_CREATED           : 17622
TOTAL_FULL_EVALUATIONS           : 5138
Tot Msg Enqueued from start      : 5157
Last Enqueued Messg #            : 13093098
```

```
Last redo SCN flushed to the Log : 13110487
Most recently captured message   : 13093098
Time when most recent msg captd  : 16:20:18 10/15/2004
TOTAL_MSG_CAPT(from last start)  : 7328

DNYTST10 SQL>
```

Creating Queues and Queue tables

Steams data flow is totally integrated with the queues. Both the source database and destination database need to have queues to manage events. Events are stored or staged in a queue. These events may be captured events or user-enqueued events. The Capture process enqueues events into a SYS.AnyData queue. A SYS.AnyData queue can stage events of different types. The queue and its associated queue table can be created by using the procedure *set_up_queue* of the *dbms_streams_adm* package.

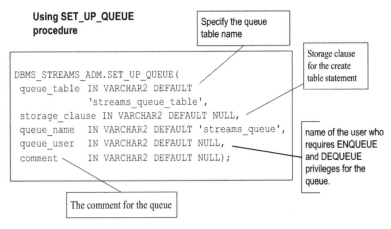

Figure 4.3 *Procedure for creating the queue*

As shown in Figure 4.3, the queue name and queue table name must be supplied as arguments. In order to specify the storage characteristic features such as the tablespace, the *storage_clause* argument can be used.

The following SQL statement can be used to view the queues:

```
set linesize 132

COLUMN OWNER          HEADING 'Owner'      FORMAT A14
COLUMN NAME           HEADING 'Queue Name' FORMAT A30
COLUMN QUEUE_TABLE    HEADING 'Queue Table' FORMAT A25
COLUMN USER_COMMENT   HEADING 'Comment' FORMAT A25

SELECT q.OWNER, q.NAME, t.QUEUE_TABLE, q.USER_COMMENT
  FROM DBA_QUEUES q, DBA_QUEUE_TABLES t
```

```
WHERE t.OBJECT_TYPE = 'SYS.ANYDATA' AND
q.QUEUE_TABLE = t.QUEUE_TABLE AND
q.OWNER = t.OWNER
/
```

A buffered queue consists of following two storage areas:

- System Global Area (SGA) memory associated with a SYS.AnyData queue that contains only captured events

- Part of a queue table for a SYS.AnyData queue that stores captured events that have spilled from memory

A buffered queue helps to optimize the capture of events by buffering them in the SGA instead of always storing them in a queue table. This buffering of captured events occurs at both the source database and the destination database. Captured events are always stored in a buffered queue, but user-enqueued LCR events and user-enqueued non-LCR events are always stored in queue tables rather than in buffered queues.

To determine whether there are captured events in a buffered queue, the *v$buffered_queues* and *v$buffered_subscribers* dynamic performance views can be queried. The latter view shows the Streams clients who subscribe to this queue to receive the messages. Sometimes it is possible that more than one destination database will receive the captured events. In other words, there exists more than one subscriber to the queues messages.

To determine whether there are user-enqueued events in a queue, the queue table for the queue can be queried. The following SQL statements show the messages in the buffered queues:

🖫 show_buffered_queues.sql

```
-- ***************************************************
-- Copyright © 2005 by Rampant TechPress
-- This script is free for non-commercial purposes
-- with no warranties.  Use at your own risk.
--
-- To license this script for a commercial purpose,
-- contact info@rampant.cc
-- ***************************************************
COLUMN QUEUE_SCHEMA      HEADING 'Queue Owner' FORMAT A15
COLUMN QUEUE_NAME        HEADING 'Queue Name' FORMAT A15
COLUMN MEM_MSG           HEADING 'LCRs in Memory' FORMAT 99999999
COLUMN SPILL_MSGS        HEADING 'Spilled LCRs' FORMAT 99999999
COLUMN NUM_MSGS          HEADING 'Total Captured LCRs|in Buffered Queue' FORMAT 99999999

SELECT QUEUE_SCHEMA,
       QUEUE_NAME,
       (NUM_MSGS - SPILL_MSGS) MEM_MSG,
       SPILL_MSGS, NUM_MSGS
  FROM V$BUFFERED_QUEUES
/
```

The CNUM_MSGS column shows the cumulative total number of messages enqueued into the buffered queue since the buffered queue was created. This information is useful for monitoring the Capture process activity and to examine the load patterns etc.

Configuration Flow

In general, a simple Streams configuration of Capture, Propagation and Apply involves the creation of certain entities, as shown below:

At the Source database:

- A SYS.AnyData queue
- Supplemental Logging specifications to the objects
- Capture process
- Propagation process and schedule
- Rule sets for the Capture process and the propagation
- Each shared object prepared for instantiation

At the Destination Database:

- A SYS.AnyData queue
- Instantiation SCN set for each shared object
- An Apply process for the source database
- Rule sets for the Apply process

Next, the configuration details on how to create the Capture, Propagation and Apply Process and how to manage them will be presented. As the process details are introduced, a simple example will also be provided. The example will cover scenarios where the goal is to replicate data:

- from a set of tables
- from a subset of the table
- from a schema

In each scenario, different procedures will be used to create the necessary client processes such as Capture, Propagate and Apply.

The next section examines the architecture and components for a typical capture process.

Capture Architecture

Internally, the Capture mechanism or architecture has four main components: Reader server; Preparer server; Builder server; and Capture process.

Each Reader server, Preparer server, and Builder server is a parallel execution server. The Capture process (Cnnn) is an Oracle background process.

- **Reader Server**: Reads the redo log file and divides the log into multiple regions.

- **One or more Preparer Servers**: Scan the regions defined by the Reader server in parallel and sends information about objects and schema changes to the rules engine.

- **Builder Servers**: Merges redo records from the preparer servers and evaluates them. It does initial evaluation.

The following section presents details on how the Capture process works.

Capture Process

After receiving the merged records from the preparer servers, the Capture process:

- formats the merged records into LCR(s)

- sends the messages to the rules for full evaluation in instances where the initial evaluation was inconclusive.

- receives the results of the full evaluation of the LCR, if it was performed

- enqueues the LCR into the queue associated with the Capture process if the LCR satisfies the rules in the positive rule set for the Capture process, or it discards the LCR if it satisfies the rules in the negative rule set for the Capture process or if it does not satisfy the rules in the positive rule set

Capture Process Rule Evaluation

The Capture process either captures or discards the changes based on the rules that the DBA defines. The rules of extraction are defined in either a negative or positive rule set. There are basically three levels at which rules and rules sets are defined:

- A Table rule captures or discards either row changes resulting from DML changes or DDL changes to a specified table. As a part of the table, sub set rules act on a specific set of rows within a table.

- A Schema rule captures or discards either row changes resulting from DML or DDL changes to the objects in a particular schema.

- Global rule captures or discards either all row changes from DML changes or all DDL changes in the database.

The Capture Process never captures changes in SYS, SYSTEM or CTXSYS schemas. Since the SYS and SYSTEM maintain the data dictionary for the whole instance and they are also specific to that instance, the tables are never part of the Capture process.

When *nologging* or *unrecoverable* SQL operations are used, the resulting changes are never captured by the Capture process. This is because the *nologging* operations do not create the redo entries.

When the changes are extracted from the redo log file by the Capture process, the changes are put thorough a series of rule evaluation steps. The Capture process evaluates a change against the negative rule set first. When one or more rules in the negative rule set evaluate to TRUE for the change, the change is discarded. When one or more rules in the positive rule set evaluate to TRUE for the change, the change satisfies the positive rule set and it is retained for enqueue.

The first step is to perform Pre-Filtering in which a Capture process evaluates rules in its rule sets at the object level and schema level. The goal is to place changes found in the redo log into two categories: changes that should be converted into LCRs and changes that should not be converted into LCRs.

The Pre-Filtering process is done with incomplete information. A change is converted into a LCR when the change satisfies the rule sets. In case of MAYBE evaluations against both the positive and negative rule sets, the change is converted to an LCR for further evaluation.

Next, LCR-Filtering is performed. This is when a Capture process evaluates rules against information in each LCR to separate the LCRs into two categories: LCRs that should be enqueued, and LCRs that should be discarded.

The Capture process then discards the LCRs that should not be enqueued and enqueues the LCRs that have qualified into the Queue associated with the Capture process.

Figure 4.4 shows the evaluation process graphically.

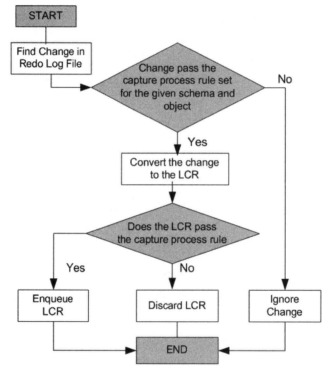

Figure 4.4 *Rule Evaluation Flow*

LogMiner Data Dictionary

The Capture process makes use of a data dictionary, which is different from the source database data dictionary. This special data dictionary is called the

LogMiner Data Dictionary. The Capture process requires a LogMiner data dictionary because the information in the primary data dictionary may not match the changes being captured from the redo log. These changes may have occurred minutes, hours, or even days before they are captured by a Capture process. This is important in the sense that when the actual capture takes place, it needs to have the right dictionary information. Since the timing of the Capture process and timing of the actual database table change can be different, the maintenance of the log dictionary, which can provide time sensitive dictionary information, becomes significant.

The first time a Capture process is started at the database, Oracle uses the extracted data dictionary information in the redo log to create a LogMiner data dictionary. This dictionary is separate from the primary data dictionary for the source database. Additional Capture processes may use this existing LogMiner data dictionary, or they may create new LogMiner data dictionaries.

Since the Capture process can have its own timing, when it does extract and create the LCRs, the object's structure in the primary dictionary may not match. The Capture process cannot depend on the primary data dictionary, especially when it is stopped for some time. This is the reason that the LogMiner Data Dictionary is maintained.

The *dbms_capture_adm.build* procedure extracts data dictionary information to the redo log. The extracted data dictionary information in the redo log is consistent with the primary data dictionary at the time when the *dbms_capture_adm.build* procedure is run. The build procedure is automatically run when the Capture process is created.

The amount of information extracted to a redo log, when the *dbms_capture_adm.build* procedure is run, depends on the number of database objects in the database. The *dbms_capture_adm.build* procedure generates a corresponding valid first SCN value that can be specified when the new Capture process is created. A First SCN generated by the *dbms_capture_adm.build* procedure can be found by running the following query:

```
SELECT DISTINCT FIRST_CHANGE#, NAME FROM V$ARCHIVED_LOG WHERE DICTIONARY_BEGIN = 'YES';
```

Propagation and Apply processes use a Streams data dictionary to keep track of the database objects from a particular source database. A Streams data dictionary is populated whenever one or more database objects are prepared for instantiation at a source database. When a database object is prepared for instantiation, it is recorded in the redo log. When a Capture process scans the redo log, it uses this information to populate the local Streams data dictionary for the source database. After an object has been prepared for instantiation, the local Streams data dictionary is updated whenever a DDL statement on the object is processed by a Capture Process.

Capture Process Creation

A Capture process that captures changes to the local source database can be created, or a Capture process that handles the database changes that occur at a remote site can be created. The *atter* method is known as Down Streams capture. If a Capture process runs on a Down Streams database, redo log files from the source database are copied to the Down Streams database, and the Capture process captures changes in these redo log files at the downstream database. Configuration of Down Streams capture is covered in later chapter.

Oracle provides many procedures that can be used to create the capture process. Any of the following procedures can be used to create a local Capture process:

- *dbms_streams_adm.add_table_rules*

- *dbms_streams_adm.add_subset_rules*

- *dbms_streams_adm.add_schema_rules*

- *dbms_streams_adm.add_global_rules*

- *dbms_capture_adm.create_capture*

Each one of these methods will be examined as will the circumstances in which each one is appropriate.

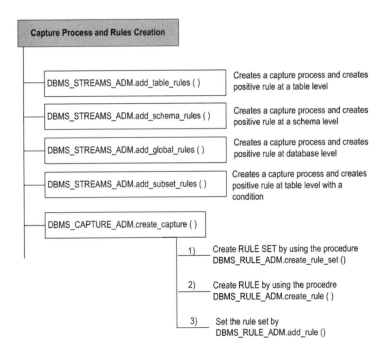

Figure 4.5 *Methods of Creating the Capture Process*

As shown in Figure 4.5, there are three procedures in the package *dbms_streams_adm*, each one of these can create a Capture process with the specified name if it does not already exist. They also create either a positive or negative rule set for the Capture process if the Capture process does not already have such a rule set. They can also add table, schema, or global rules to the rule set.

When the *create_capture* procedure of *dbms_capture_adm* is used to create a Capture process, it does not create a rule set or rules for the Capture process. The rules and the rule set need to be created manually. In this way the DBA gets precise control over the definition of rules and creation of capture. Also, the *create_capture* procedure enables the specification of a first SCN and a start SCN for the Capture process. By setting up the first SCN and start SCN values manually, it becomes possible to go back in time to begin capture changes. This becomes necessary when a Capture process is re-created or for some reason some old data needs to be replicated again. However, it is also important to ensure that the necessary archive logs are not deleted from the file system.

To create a Capture process that performs downstream capture, the *create_capture* procedure will be used.

Using *add_table_rules* to create Capture process

In this method, the procedure *add_table_rules* of *dbms_streams_adm* is used to specify the table whose changes are captured by the Capture process. *steams_name* specifies the Capture process name and it creates the Capture process if it does not exist. If the Capture process is already present, it adds the additional table to the Capture process. The *streams_type* parameter has to be specified as CAPTURE.

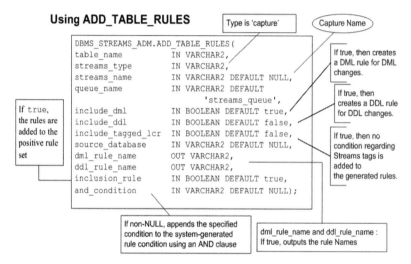

Figure 4.6 *Parameters for add_table_rules procedure*

Figure 4.6 gives a glance at all of the parameters that are needed for the *add_table_rules* procedure. The procedure has two OUT variables, *dml_rule_name* and *ddl_rule_name*, to show the rules it generates.

As an example, Figure 4.7 shows a graphical view of the steps involved in a typical Streams replication configuration. This figure shows the use of the *add_table_rules()* procedure to create the Capture process and the Apply process.

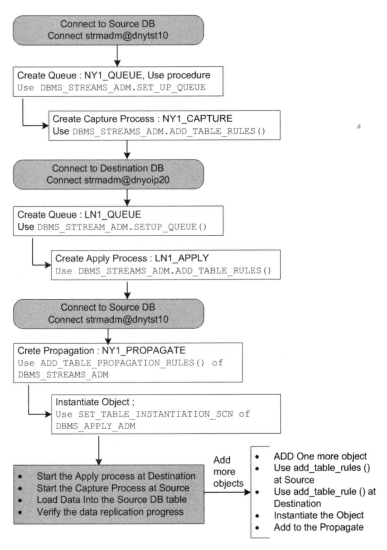

Figure 4.7 *Steps in configuring the Streams replication*

The steps that are used to configure all of the necessary processes are presented in the following section.

```
Source DB            : DNYTST10
Destination DB       : DNYOIP20
```

From previous examples, a couple of tables have been created in the NY1 schema. These will be configured for replication. The NY1 schema exists on both source and destination databases.

The first method is to configure One Way Replication for tables ALLINSURED1 and SALESPERSON1. First, the queue to stage the database changes is created. The following SQL statement can be used to create a queue named NY1_QUEUE.

```
connect strmadm/strmadm@dnytst10
PROMPT ** Creating the Queue NY1_QUEUE at Source DNYTST10
BEGIN
DBMS_STREAMS_ADM.SET_UP_QUEUE(
queue_table     => 'strmadm.ny1_queue_table',
queue_name               => 'strmadm.ny1_queue');
END;
/
```

The queues that were created above can be verified by the following SQL block which queries the *dba_queues*.

```
SELECT q.NAME, t.QUEUE_TABLE , q.USER_COMMENT
 FROM DBA_QUEUES q, DBA_QUEUE_TABLES t
 WHERE t.OBJECT_TYPE = 'SYS.ANYDATA' AND
 q.QUEUE_TABLE = t.QUEUE_TABLE AND
 q.OWNER = t.OWNER and q.owner = 'STRMADM'
/

Queue Name                            Queue Table              Comment
-----------------------------   -------------------   ----------------
AQ$_NY1_QUEUE_TABLE_E           NY1_QUEUE_TABLE       exception queue
NY1_QUEUE                       NY1_QUEUE_TABLE
```

Now at the source database, the Capture Process called 'NY1_CAPTURE' can be created by using the *add_table_rules* procedure. In the following example, the first SQL block creates the Capture process and the rules for table NY1.ALLINSURED1. The second SQL block adds another rules table for the same Capture process.

```
PROMPT Creating the first table and its rules at Source DNYTST10
BEGIN
DBMS_STREAMS_ADM.ADD_TABLE_RULES(
table_name      => 'ny1.allinsured1',
streams_type    => 'capture',
streams_name    => 'ny1_capture',
queue_name      => 'ny1_queue',
include_dml     => true,
include_ddl     => true,
include_tagged_lcr => false,
source_database => NULL,
inclusion_rule  => true);
END;
/
-- Add second table rules
BEGIN
DBMS_STREAMS_ADM.ADD_TABLE_RULES(
table_name      => 'ny1.salesperson1',
streams_type    => 'capture',
streams_name    => 'ny1_capture',
```

```
queue_name        => 'ny1_queue',
include_dml       => true,
include_ddl        => true,
include_tagged_lcr => false,
source_database => NULL,
inclusion_rule  => true);
END;
/
```

In the above example,

- A Capture process was created with the name NY1_CAPTURE. This process captures the changes for the tables ALLINSURED1 and SALESPERSON1 of the schema NY1. The *streams_type* shows that a streams process of type CAPTURE is being created.

- The procedure also associates the Capture process with an existing queue named NY1_QUEUE. This queue was created previously by using the procedure *dbms_streams_adm.set_up_queue.*

- The procedure creates a positive rule set and associates it with the Capture process. Since the *inclusion_rule* parameter has been set to TRUE, the rules are added to the positive rule set.

- The procedure prepares the NY1.ALLINSURED1 and NY1.SALESPERSON1 tables for instantiation by running the *prepare_table_instantiation* procedure in the *dbms_capture_adm* package internally.

When the Capture process is created using the *add_table_rules* procedure, two rules are created for each table. For example, one rule evaluates to TRUE for DML changes to the NY1.ALLINSURED1 table, and the other rule evaluates to TRUE for DDL changes to the NY1.ALLINSURED1 table. The same thing happens to the other table, NY1.SALESPERSON1. The rule names are specified by the system. These two rules are added to the positive rule set associated with the Capture process. Since the *inclusion_rule* parameter has been set to TRUE, the rules are added to the positive rule set.

After creating the above Capture process, the capture prepared tables can be seen from the *dba_capture_prepared_tables* view. The following SQL block shows the tables prepared for the capture.

```
SELECT table_owner, table_name, to_char(SCN) SCN, to_char(timestamp, 'DD-MON-YY HH24:MI')
Time_Stamp FROM DBA_CAPTURE_PREPARED_TABLES

TABLE_OWNER      TABLE_NAME      SCN             TIME_STAMP
---------------  --------------  --------------  ---------------
NY1              ALLINSURED1     13302862        18-OCT-04 11:06
NY1              SALESPERSON1    13302886        18-OCT-04 11:06
```

The next step is to view the capture rules that were defined automatically when the *add_table_rules* procedure was executed. The rules and rule sets names are arrived at by combining the auto-generated sequence number and the object name. The following SQL block shows the rules created for NY1_CAPTURE.

```
select RULE_SET_NAME, RULE_SET_TYPE, RULE_NAME, STREAMS_RULE_TYPE, OBJECT_NAME, RULE_TYPE
from DBA_STREAMS_RULES
where STREAMS_NAME = 'NY1_CAPTURE'
/
gives the output as shown below ..

                                    Streams
Rule Set     Rule Set Rule          Rule   Object        Rule
Name         Type     Name          Level  Name          Type
------------ -------- -------------- ------ ------------- ----
RULESET$_164 POSITIVE SALESPERSON1165 TABLE SALESPERSON1  DML
RULESET$_164 POSITIVE SALESPERSON1166 TABLE SALESPERSON1  DDL
RULESET$_164 POSITIVE ALLINSURED1162  TABLE ALLINSURED1   DML
RULESET$_164 POSITIVE ALLINSURED1163  TABLE ALLINSURED1   DDL
```

As an example, SQL statements can be used to view the full details of the rules generated by querying the *dba_rules* view. The following SQL statement shows the *rule_condition* for the DML rule ALLINSURED1162. As seen in this example, the rule condition, when the tag is null, the schema is NY1, and table is ALLINSURED1, evaluates to TRUE.

```
SQL>SELECT              dbms_lob.substr(rule_condition,dbms_lob.getlength(rule_condition),1)
rule_condition FROM dba_rules  where rule_name = 'ALLINSURED1162'
/

RULE_CONDITION
-------------------------------------------------------------
(((:dml.get_object_owner () = 'NY1' and :dml.get_object_name () = '
ALLINSURED1')) and :dml.is_null_tag() = 'Y' )
```

The following SQL statement shows *rule_condition* for DDL rule ALLINSURED1163.

```
SQL>SELECT              dbms_lob.substr(rule_condition,dbms_lob.getlength(rule_condition),1)
rule_condition FROM dba_rules  where rule_name = 'ALLINSURED1163'
/

RULE_CONDITION
-------------------------------------------------------------
(((:ddl.get_object_owner () = 'NY1' and :ddl.get_object_name () = '
ALLINSURED1')or (:ddl.get_base_table_owner () = 'NY1' and :ddl.get
_base_table_name () = 'ALLINSURED1')) and :ddl.is_null_tag () = 'Y' )
```

It is important to note the difference between the DML and DDL rule conditions. The *get_base_table_owner* member function is also used in the DDL LCR rule. This is because the *get_object_owner* function may return NULL if a user who does not own an object performs a DDL change on the object. Therefore, the rule condition for DDL includes an extra variable in the condition clause.

The following SQL shows the Capture process that has been created. At this time, the CAPTURED_SCN value is shown as a blank.

```
SELECT capture_name, queue_name, rule_set_name,
status, to_char(CAPTURED_SCN) CAPTURED_SCN FROM DBA_CAPTURE
/

Capture Name      QUEUE_NAME       Name          STATUS   CAPTURED_SCN
--------------    ----------------  ------------  -------- ------------
NY1_CAPTURE       NY1_QUEUE        RULESET$_164  DISABLED
```

At this time, the Capture process is not yet started. When the Capture process is created, it is placed initially in disabled status.

To complete the whole replication process, Queue and Apply process will be created at the destination database by using the following SQL statements.

🖫 Queue_and_Apply.sql

```
-- ****************************************************
-- Copyright © 2005 by Rampant TechPress
-- This script is free for non-commercial purposes
-- with no warranties.  Use at your own risk.
--
-- To license this script for a commercial purpose,
-- contact info@rampant.cc
-- ****************************************************

connect strmadm/strmadm@dnyoip20

PROMPT ** Creating Queue Table at Destination
BEGIN
DBMS_STREAMS_ADM.SET_UP_QUEUE(
  queue_table => 'strmadm.ln1_queue_table',
  queue_name => 'strmadm.ln1_queue');
END;
/
PROMPT ** Creating Apply Side Table rules at destination
BEGIN
DBMS_STREAMS_ADM.ADD_TABLE_RULES(
 table_name => 'ny1.allinsured1',
 streams_type => 'apply',
 streams_name => 'ln1_apply',
 queue_name => 'ln1_queue',
 include_dml => true,
 include_ddl => true,
 source_database => 'DNYTST10.world',
 inclusion_rule => true);
END;
/
BEGIN
DBMS_STREAMS_ADM.ADD_TABLE_RULES(
 table_name => 'ny1.salesperson1',
 streams_type => 'apply',
 streams_name => 'ln1_apply',
 queue_name => 'ln1_queue',
 include_dml => true,
 include_ddl => true,
 source_database => 'DNYTST10.world',
 inclusion_rule => true);
END;
/
```

To view the Apply process created by above SQL statements, the following query can be used:

```
SELECT apply_name, queue_name, rule_set_name,
apply_captured, APPLY_USER, status FROM DBA_APPLY
/

APPLY_NAME    QUEUE_NAME  Rule Set    Captrd  APPLY_USER   STATUS
-----------   ----------- ---------   ------  -----------  --------
LN1_APPLY     LN1_QUEUE   RULESET$_55 YES     STRMADM      DISABLED
```

At this stage, the Apply process is in a disabled condition. It is yet to receive any events. Next, the propagation rule and propagation schedule will be created at the source database. The name of the propagation will be NY1_PROPAGATE. The following SQL statements create the propagate process and add the propagation rules for the two tables named NY1.ALLINSURED1 and NY1.SALESPERSON1.

🖫 Propagate.sql

```
-- **************************************************
-- Copyright © 2005 by Rampant TechPress
-- This script is free for non-commercial purposes
-- with no warranties.  Use at your own risk.
--
-- To license this script for a commercial purpose,
-- contact info@rampant.cc
-- **************************************************

connect strmadm/strmadm@dnytst10

PROMPT ** Now create propagate rules for for Table AllInsured1
BEGIN
DBMS_STREAMS_ADM.ADD_TABLE_PROPAGATION_RULES(
  table_name            => 'ny1.allinsured1',
  Streams_name          => 'ny1_propagate',
  source_queue_name     => 'strmadm.ny1_queue',
  destination_queue_name => 'strmadm.ln1_queue@DNYOIP20.world',
  include_dml           => true,
  include_ddl           => true,
  include_tagged_lcr    => false,
  source_database       => 'DNYTST10.world',
  inclusion_rule        => true);
END;
/
BEGIN
DBMS_STREAMS_ADM.ADD_TABLE_PROPAGATION_RULES(
  table_name            => 'ny1.salesperson1',
  Streams_name          => 'ny1_propagate',
  source_queue_name     => 'strmadm.ny1_queue',
  destination_queue_name => 'strmadm.ln1_queue@DNYOIP20.world',
  include_dml           => true,
  include_ddl           => true,
  include_tagged_lcr    => false,
  source_database       => 'DNYTST10.world',
  inclusion_rule        => true);
END;
/
```

To view the brief details of the propagation that were just created, execute the following SQL statement:

```
SELECT p.propagation_name propagation_name,
TO_CHAR(s.start_date, 'HH24:MI:SS MM/DD/YY') START_DATE,
s.propagation_window DURATION, s.latency, s.schedule_disabled,
TO_CHAR(s.next_run_date, 'HH24:MI:SS MM/DD/YY') NEXT_TIME,
process_name, total_number, failures
FROM dba_queue_schedules S , dba_propagation P
WHERE p.propagation_name = 'NY1_PROPAGATE'
/

START_DATE DURATION LATENCY Disabl NextWindow   PROC TOTAL# FAILURES
------------------ -------- ------ ---------    -------- ----- ------
15:40:43 10/18/04     3      N                  J000    0      0
```

The next step is to instantiate the tables ALLINSURED1 and
SALESPERSON1 and set the SCN value at the destination database. The
instantiation process sets the SCN value for the Apply process and this SCN
specifies that changes after this are applied at destination database.

```
-- Run this SQL block at Source DB i.e. DNYTST10

set serveroutput on
DECLARE
  iscn NUMBER;  -- Variable to hold instantiation SCN value
BEGIN
  iscn := DBMS_FLASHBACK.GET_SYSTEM_CHANGE_NUMBER();
  dbms_output.put_line ('Instantiation SCN : ' || iscn ) ;
  DBMS_APPLY_ADM.SET_TABLE_INSTANTIATION_SCN@DNYOIP20.world (
  source_object_name    => 'ny1.allinsured1',
  source_database_name  => 'DNYTST10.world',
  instantiation_scn     => iscn  );
  DBMS_APPLY_ADM.SET_TABLE_INSTANTIATION_SCN@DNYOIP20.world (
  source_object_name    => 'ny1.salesperson1',
  source_database_name  => 'DNYTST10.world',
  instantiation_scn     => iscn  );
END;
/
Instantiation SCN : 13310426

PL/SQL procedure successfully completed.
```

In the above SQL block, the SCN value 133104426 is set at the destination.
This indicates that any changes effected after this value are to be applied to
the destination database tables.

Everything is now in place to start the Apply and Capture processes at the
destination and source databases. The following SQL statements start these
processes:

```
connect strmadm/strmadm@dnyoip20
PROMPT Starting the Apply Process at DNYOIP20 ..
begin
dbms_apply_adm.start_apply (apply_name => 'LN1_APPLY ' ) ;
end ;
/

PROMPT Now Connect to Source DB (DNYTST10)
connect strmadm/strmadm@dnytst10

PROMPT Starting the Cature Prcoess at DNYTST10
begin
```

```
dbms_capture_adm.start_capture (capture_name => 'NY1_CAPTURE' ) ;
end ;
/
```

The next step is to create some transactional activity at the source database tables. Before loading data into these source tables, it would be useful to look at the SCN and other details with the script *show_capture_details.sql*. This script is located in the code depot and can be used to view all possible SCN values and the states of various processes in a single glance.

```
CAPTURE_PROFILE
--------------------------------------------------------
Capture_name (dba_capture)----> : NY1_CAPTURE
Queue Name                      : NY1_QUEUE
RULE_SET_NAME                   : RULESET$_164
Capture_User and Type           : STRMADM Type : LOCAL
START_SCN                       : 13300225
Captured_SCN                    : 13320462
Applied_SCN                     : 13302861
FIRST_SCN                       : 13300225
MAX_CHECKPOINT_SCN              : 13320508
Reqd CKPT SCN                   : 13302861
Total Delta SCN Captured        : 6128
Delta SCN Applied    (Delta)    : 23729
Error Number                    :
Error Message ..                :

Now Time              ------> : 16:07:29 10/18/2004
Current SCN (from DBMS_FLASHBACK): 13326590
CKPT SCN (from v$database)       : 13318551
Current Redo Log Begin SCN       : 13320557
Redo Group Number and Status     : 2   CURRENT
Last Capt.SCN(v$streams_capture) : 13326584  At 16:07:19 10/18/2004
Last EnqueSCN (v$streams_capture): 13326478  At

SID of (v$streams_capture) ----> : 34
CAPTURE_NAME and State ..        : NY1_CAPTURE     CAPTURING CHANGES
TOTAL_MESSAGES_CREATED           : 9038
TOTAL_FULL_EVALUATIONS           : 5
Tot Msg Enqueued from start      : 132
Last Enqueued Messg #            : 13326478
Last redo SCN flushed to the log : 13326590
Most recently captured message   : 13326584
Time when most recent msg captd  : 16:07:28 10/18/2004
TOTAL_MSG_CAPT(from last start)  : 8902
```

A look into the *v$propagation_sender* view yields details about the bytes transferred to the destination. Execute the following SQL statement to view the bytes propagated.

```
SELECT p.PROPAGATION_NAME,
  s.QUEUE_NAME, s.DBLINK,  s.TOTAL_MSGS,  s.TOTAL_BYTES
  FROM DBA_PROPAGATION p, V$PROPAGATION_SENDER s
  WHERE p.DESTINATION_DBLINK = s.DBLINK AND
  p.SOURCE_QUEUE_OWNER = s.QUEUE_SCHEMA AND
  p.SOURCE_QUEUE_NAME = s.QUEUE_NAME
/
```

Propagation	Queue Name	Database Link	Total Events	Total Bytes
NY1_PROPAGATE	NY1_QUEUE	DNYOIP20.WORLD	31	27,761

The following SQL statement shows the number of rows in the source and destination. Initially, the source table has 50,000 rows and the destination has no rows.

```
select  (select count(*) from ny1.allinsured1) at_source,
(select count(*) from ny1.allinsured1@dnyoip20) at_dest  from dual
/

AT_SOURCE    AT_DEST
---------- ----------
     50000          0
```

The next step is to add rows to the source table. The *load_ny1_allinsured1.sql* script, a complete listing of which can be found in the code depot, inserts 30,000 rows into the source table ALLINSURED1. It commits for every 1000 records inserted.

```
SQL>@CONFIG1/load_ny1_allinsured1.sql
Start Time =18-OCT-2004 16:31
Before Loading, the SCN : 13327900
Job ENDED.....Success
End Time =18-OCT-2004 16:31
Total Output Records = 30000
Total Commits        = 30
After Loading the SCN : 13332294

PL/SQL procedure successfully completed.
```

Use the *show_capture_details.sql* to view the capture details. The output is shown below:

```
SQL>@show_capture_details

CAPTURE_PROFILE
------------------------------------------------------------
Capture_name (dba_capture)-----> : NY1_CAPTURE
Queue Name                       : NY1_QUEUE
RULE_SET_NAME                    : RULESET$_164
Capture_User and Type            : STRMADM Type : LOCAL
START_SCN                        : 13300225
Captured_SCN                     : 13331427
Applied_SCN                      : 13329886
FIRST_SCN                        : 13300225
MAX_CHECKPOINT_SCN               : 13331428
Reqd CKPT SCN                    : 13320508
Total Delta SCN Captured         : 1345
Delta SCN Applied   (Delta)      : 2886
Error Number                     :
Error Message ..                 :

Now Time            ------> : 16:32:14 10/18/2004
Current SCN (from DBMS_FLASHBACK): 13332773
CKPT SCN (from v$database)       : 13329513
Current Redo Log Begin SCN       : 13331156
Redo Group Number and Status     : 2    CURRENT
Last Capt.SCN(v$streams_capture) : 13332763  At 16:32:10 10/18/2004
Last EnqueSCN (v$streams_capture): 13332293  At 16:31:16 10/18/2004

SID of (v$streams_capture) ----> : 34
CAPTURE_NAME and State ..        : NY1_CAPTURE     CAPTURING CHANGES
TOTAL_MESSAGES_CREATED           : 110254
TOTAL_FULL_EVALUATIONS           : 30005
Tot Msg Enqueued from start      : 30163
Last Enqueued Messg #            : 13332293
```

```
Last redo SCN flushed to the log : 13332772
Most recently captured message   : 13332763
Time when most recent msg captd  : 16:32:12 10/18/2004
TOTAL_MSG_CAPT(from last start)  : 50087
```

After the transactions are propagated and applied at the destination, 30000
rows will be visible at the destination table, as shown in the next output.

```
select (select count(*) from ny1.allinsured1) at_source,
(select count(*) from ny1.allinsured1@dnyoip20) at_dest from dual
/
AT_SOURCE   AT_DEST
---------- ----------
    80000      30000
```

The view of the bytes and events shows 30,063 events propagated.

```
SQL>@show_prop_bytes_sent

                Queue     Database             Total   Total
Propagation     Name      Link                 Events  Bytes
------------    --------  -------------------  ------  ---------
NY1_PROPAGATE   NY1_QUEUE DNYOIP20.WORLD       30,063  34,032,871
```

The examples above show the data flow and also show the dictionary views
that can be used to monitor the processes.

The next step is to add a new object to the same replication configuration.
Remember, capture, propagation, queue etc. have already been created. The
following actions just add another object that is used to support the
processes.

Addition of new objects to the existing configuration

While adding new objects, in order not to lose any events or get into error
conditions, a certain methodology will have to be followed. At the source
database where extra objects are being added, supplemental logging should be
specified for the objects, as appropriate. Follow the configuration flow as
shown below:

Step-1: Stop the Streams Processes

Stop the Capture process, disable one of the propagation jobs, or stop the
Apply processes:

- Use the *stop_capture* procedure in the *dbms_capture_adm* package to stop a
  Capture process.

- Use the *disable_propagation_schedule* procedure in the *dbms_aqadm* package to disable a propagation job.

- Use the *stop_apply* procedure in the *dbms_apply_adm* package to stop an Apply process.

Step-2: Define the Rules for Apply

At the apply side, add the relevant rules to the rule sets for the Apply processes. To add rules to the rule set for an Apply process, one of the following procedures can be used:

- *dbms_streams_adm.add_table_rules*

- *dbms_streams_adm.add_subset_rules*

These procedures can add rules to the positive or negative rule set for an Apply process. The *add_subset_rules* procedure can add rules only to the positive rule set for an Apply process.

Step-3: Define the Rules for Propagation

Add the relevant rules to the rule sets for the propagations. To add rules to the rule set for a propagation, one of the following procedures can be used:

- *dbms_streams_adm.add_table_propagation_rules*

- *dbms_streams_adm.add_subset_propagation_rules*

These procedures can add rules to the positive or negative rule set for a propagation; however, the *add_subset_propagation_rules* procedure can add rules only to the positive rule set for a propagation.

Step-4: Define the Rules for Capture

Add the rules to the rule sets used by the Capture process. To add rules to a rule set for an existing Capture process, one of the following procedures can be used and the existing Capture process name must be specified:

- *dbms_streams_adm.add_table_rules*

- *dbms_streams_adm.add_subset_rules*

These procedures can add rules to the positive or negative rule set for a Capture process; however, the *add_subset_rules* procedure can add rules only to the positive rule set for a Capture process.

At the destination database, either instantiate or set the instantiation SCN for each database object added to the Streams environment. In case the database objects do not exist at a destination database, instantiate them using export/import, transportable tablespaces, or RMAN. In the case of database objects being present at the destination database, set the instantiation SCNs for them manually.

In order to set the instantiation SCN for a table manually, run the procedure *set_table_instantiation_scn* procedure in the *dbms_apply_adm* package at a destination database. Finally, the Streams process that was stopped earlier must be started or enabled.

To start the Streams process:

- Use the *start_capture* procedure in the *dbms_capture_adm* package to start a Capture process.

- Use the *enable_propagation_schedule* procedure in the *dbms_aqadm* package to enable a propagation job.

- Use the *start_apply* procedure in the *dbms_apply_adm* package to start an Apply process.

So far, the basic configurations of the Capture and Propagation processes have been presented. The next step is to see how to manage them and how to understand different attributes for those processes

Capture Process States

The state of a Capture process describes what the Capture process is doing currently. The state of a Capture process can be viewed by querying the STATE column in the *v$streams_capture* dynamic performance view. This is a useful piece of information to monitor in the Capture process. For example, the state PAUSED FOR FLOW CONTROL reveals that there are some bottlenecks in the Capture process. Typically, the state should be CAPTURING CHANGES.

The following Capture process states are possible:

- **INITIALIZING**: The process is starting up

- **WAITING FOR DICTIONARY REDO** – The process is waiting for redo log files containing the dictionary build related to the first SCN to be added to the Capture process session. A Capture process cannot begin to scan the redo log files until all of the log files containing the dictionary build have been added.

- **DICTIONARY INITIALIZATION** – The process is processing a dictionary build.

- **MINING** – The process is mining a dictionary build at the SCN shown in the message.

- **LOADING** – The process is processing information from a dictionary build.

- **CAPTURING CHANGES** – The process is scanning the redo log for changes that evaluate to TRUE against the Capture process rule sets

- **WAITING FOR REDO** – The process is waiting for new redo log files to be added to the Capture process session. This message is shown when the Capture process has finished processing the entire redo log files added to its session. This indicates that there is no activity at a source database. For a downstream Capture process, this state is possible if the Capture process is waiting for new log files to be added to its session.

- **EVALUATING RULE** – The process is evaluating a change against a Capture process rule set.

- **CREATING LCR** – The process is converting a change into an LCR.

- **ENQUEUING MESSAGE** – The process is enqueuing a LCR that satisfies the Capture process rule sets into the Capture process queue.

- **PAUSED FOR FLOW CONTROL** – The process is unable to enqueue LCRs either because of low memory or because propagations and Apply processes are consuming messages slower than the Capture process is creating them. This state indicates flow control that is used to reduce spilling of captured LCRs when propagation or apply has fallen behind. This potentially can happen when there is huge transactional activity on the source database tables.

- **SHUTTING DOWN** – The process is stopping.

Next information on how to manage various parameters for a Capture process will be presented.

Setting Up the Capture Parameters

Even though a simple format of the Capture process can be created by using the *add_table_rules, add_schema_rules* or *add_subset_rules*, certain extra parameters can be set up only by executing the *set_parameter* procedure of the *dbms_capture_adm* package. Capture process parameters control the way a Capture process operates.

What are the parameters that are allowed to be altered? Table 4.1 shows all of the parameters that can be set.

disable_on_limit	If set to Y, the Capture process is disabled if the Capture process terminates because it reached a value specified by the *time_limit* parameter or *message_limit* parameter. If set to N, the Capture process is restarted immediately after stopping because it reached a limit. The default is N.
maximum_scn	Sets the SCN value beyond which Capture process becomes disabled. If set to INFINITE, then the Capture process runs regardless of the SCN value. The default is INFINITE.
message_limit	Imposes limit on the number of messages. Capture process stops after capturing the specified number of messages. If set to INFINITE, the Capture process continues to run regardless of the number of messages captured. The default is INFINITE.
parallelism	Sets the number of parallel execution servers that may concurrently mine the redo log.
startup_seconds	The maximum number of seconds to wait for another instantiation of the same Capture process to finish.
time_limit	The Capture process stops as soon as possible after the specified number of seconds since it started. The default is INFINITE.
trace_level	Set this parameter only under the guidance of Oracle Support Services.
write_alert_log	If set to Y, the Capture process writes a message to the alert log on exit. The message specifies the reason the Capture process stopped. The default is INFINITE.

Table 4.1 *List of Parameters that can be set in the Capture process*

The following is the syntax of the procedure that can be used to set parameters:

```
DBMS_CAPTURE_ADM.SET_PARAMETER(
 capture_name   IN VARCHAR2,
 parameter               IN VARCHAR2,
 value                   IN VARCHAR2);
```

For example, the following procedure sets the *parallelism* parameter for a Capture process named NY1_CAPTURE to 3.

```
BEGIN
DBMS_CAPTURE_ADM.SET_PARAMETER(
 capture_name   => 'NY1_CAPTURE',
 parameter               => 'parallelism', value => '3');
END;
/
```

Use the *dba_captures_parameters* view to list the parameters set for a particular Capture process.

The following SQL statement displays the current setting for each Capture process parameter in a database:

```
SELECT CAPTURE_NAME,
 PARAMETER,
 VALUE,
 SET_BY_USER FROM DBA_CAPTURE_PARAMETERS
/
```

Shows the following output:

```
CAPTURE_NAME       PARAMETER            VALUE         SET_BY_USER
----------------   --------------------  -----------   -----------
NY1_CAPTURE        PARALLELISM          3             YES
NY1_CAPTURE        STARTUP_SECONDS      0             NO
NY1_CAPTURE        TRACE_LEVEL          0             NO
NY1_CAPTURE        TIME_LIMIT           INFINITE      NO
NY1_CAPTURE        MESSAGE_LIMIT        INFINITE      NO
NY1_CAPTURE        MAXIMUM_SCN          INFINITE      NO
NY1_CAPTURE        WRITE_ALERT_LOG      Y             NO
NY1_CAPTURE        DISABLE_ON_LIMIT     N             NO
```

The following section will present information on how to manage the extra attributes for a Capture process.

Capturing Extra Information

Typically, when the source database table change information is captured, it has enough information for the replication to the destination. Row and DDL LCRs constructed from the Capture process can also include some useful extra information. However, the inclusion of this extra information is optional. These extra attributes help track certain useful information for auditing and other purposes. Based on the extra attributes, certain filtering can also be done at the destination database. This gives an added facility for the apply handlers to manipulate the data.

With the help of the *dbms_capture_adm.include_extra_attribute* procedure, the following attributes can be included into LCRs captured by the Capture process. Once the Capture process is created at the source database, the procedure *include_extra_attribute* can be used to add the required attributes.

Here is the syntax of the procedure:

```
DBMS_CAPTURE_ADM.INCLUDE_EXTRA_ATTRIBUTE(
  capture_name           IN VARCHAR2,
  attribute_name         IN VARCHAR2,
  include                IN BOOLEAN DEFAULT true);
```

The argument include, when set to TRUE, is included in LCRs captured by the Capture process. When set to false, the specified attribute is excluded from LCRs captured by the Capture process.

The following values are allowed as *attribute_name*:

- **row_id**: The rowid of the row changed in a row LCR. This attribute is neither included in DDL LCR nor in row LCRs for index-organized tables.

- **serial#:** The serial number of the session that performed the change.

- **session#:** The identifier of the session that performed the change.

- **thread#:** The thread number of the instance in which the change captured. The thread number is relevant only in a Real Application Clusters Environment.

- **tx_name**: The name of the transaction that includes the LCR.

- **username**: The name of the user who performed the change captured in the LCR.

The following example adds an extra attribute to include the *username* to the LCR:

```
BEGIN
DBMS_CAPTURE_ADM.INCLUDE_EXTRA_ATTRIBUTE(
 capture_name => 'NY1_CAPTURE',
 attribute_name => 'USERNAME',
 include => TRUE );
END;
/
```

The following example removes the extra attribute *tx_name* to include the *username* to the LCR:

```
BEGIN
DBMS_CAPTURE_ADM.INCLUDE_EXTRA_ATTRIBUTE(
  capture_name   => 'NY1_CAPTURE',
  attribute_name => 'TX_NAME',
  include => FALSE );
END;
/
```

How can the DBA see what extra information is set to the Capture process? Use the *dba_capture_extra_attributes* view to list the attributes set for a particular Capture process.

The following SQL statement lists such attributes:

```
SELECT CAPTURE_NAME, ATTRIBUTE_NAME, INCLUDE
FROM DBA_CAPTURE_EXTRA_ATTRIBUTES
ORDER BY CAPTURE_NAME;

Shows the output below:

CAPTURE_NAME              ATTRIBUTE_NAME                    INC
-----------------------  ------------------------------  ---
NY1_CAPTURE              THREAD#                          NO
NY1_CAPTURE              ROW_ID                           NO
NY1_CAPTURE              SESSION#                         NO
NY1_CAPTURE              SERIAL#                          NO
NY1_CAPTURE              USERNAME                         YES
NY1_CAPTURE              TX_NAME                          YES
```

Next, how to start, stop and drop the capture process will be examined.

Starting, Stopping, and Dropping a Capture Process

Unlike Oracle's other back ground process, the Capture process is not a mandatory process. It should be in a RUN state only when the goal is to have capture activity. Therefore the capture process can be stopped and started as needed. It can also be dropped when it is not needed. When a Capture process is created, it remains in a disabled condition. It has to be started manually even for the first time.

To Start a Capture Process:

The *start_capture* procedure in the *dbms_capture_adm* package can be executed to start an existing Capture process. For example, to start the Capture process NY1_CAPTURE, the following SQL statement should be used:

```
BEGIN
DBMS_CAPTURE_ADM.START_CAPTURE( capture_name => 'NY1_CAPTURE');
END;
/
```

Once the Capture process is started successfully, the status in *dba_capture* shows ENABLED. The start status is persistently recorded. If the status is ENABLED, the Capture process is started upon database instance startup.

To Stop a Capture Process:

The *stop_capture* procedure in the *dbms_capture_adm* package can be used to stop the Capture process. For example, to stop the Capture process NY1_CAPTURE, the following SQL statement should be used:

```
BEGIN
DBMS_CAPTURE_ADM.STOP_CAPTURE( capture_name => 'NY1_CAPTURE');
END;
/
```

Once Capture process is stopped successfully, the status in *dba_capture* shows DISABLED. The start status is persistently recorded. If the status is DISABLED, the Capture process will remain in the stopped condition upon database instance startup.

To Drop a Capture Process

The *drop_capture* procedure in the *dbms_capture_adm* package can be used to drop an existing Capture process.

The following is the syntax for the procedure:

```
DBMS_CAPTURE_ADM.DROP_CAPTURE(
capture_name            IN VARCHAR2,
drop_unused_rule_sets   IN BOOLEAN DEFAULT false);
```

The argument, *drop_unused_rule_sets*, when set to TRUE, drops any rule sets, positive or negative, used by the specified Capture process provided they are not used by any other Streams client, including Capture processes, Propagations, Apply processes, and messaging clients. If this procedure drops a rule set, this procedure also drops any rules in the rule set that are not in another rule set.

If *drop_unused_rule_sets* is set to FALSE, it does not drop the rule sets used by the specified Capture process, and the rule sets retain their rules.

For example, the following SQL block drops a Capture process named NY1_CAPTURE and all the associated rule sets:

```
BEGIN
DBMS_CAPTURE_ADM.DROP_CAPTURE(
capture_name              => 'NY1_CAPTURE',
drop_unused_rule_sets     => true);
END;
/
```

Earlier, information was presented on a variety of SCN values. In the next section, information will be presented on how to set them manually to an existing Capture process.

Setting SCN Values for an Existing Capture Process

When the goal is to capture changes in the redo log from a point in time in the past a particular *first_scn* value which corresponds to a previous data dictionary build can be specified. The build procedure in the *dbms_capture_adm* package performs a data dictionary build in the redo log.

If the specified *first_scn* is higher than the current *start_scn* for the Capture process, the start SCN is automatically set to the new value of the *first_scn*.

The *first_scn* for an existing Capture process can be set using the *alter_capture* procedure in the *dbms_capture_adm* package. However, the specified *first_scn* must meet the following requirements:

- It must be greater than the current *first_scn* for the Capture process.

- It must be less than or equal to the current *applied_scn* for the Capture process. This requirement does not apply if the current *applied_scn* for the Capture process is zero.

- It must be less than or equal to the *required_checkpoint_scn* for the Capture process.

The current *first_scn, applied_scn*, and *required_checkpoint_scn* for each Capture process in a database can be determined using the following query:

```
SELECT CAPTURE_NAME, FIRST_SCN, APPLIED_SCN, REQUIRED_CHECKPOINT_SCN FROM DBA_CAPTURE
/
```

When a situation exists where a point-in-time recovery must be performed on one of the destination databases that receives changes from the Capture process, the appropriate *start_scn* for an existing Capture process will have to be set. This can be done using the *alter_capture* procedure in the *dbms_capture_adm* package.

The specified *start_scn* must be greater than or equal to the *first_scn* for the Capture process. When a *start_scn* for a Capture process is reset, make sure the required redo log files are available to the Capture process.

So far, the creation of the Capture process through the *add_table_rules* procedure has been presented. The following section presents the creation of the Capture process by other procedures.

Capture Creation - Using *add_subset_rules*

The *add_subset_rules* procedure adds rules whose rule condition evaluates to TRUE for DML changes made to a subset of rows in a specified table.

This procedure creates the specified Capture process if it does not exist. Running this procedure generates three rules for the specified Capture process; one for INSERT statements; one for UPDATE statements; and one for DELETE statements. For INSERT and DELETE statements, only DML changes that satisfy the condition specified for the *dml_condition* parameter are captured, applied, or dequeued.

How does this help? This procedure helps configure the part of the table for data replication.

Note : The *add_subset_rules* procedure can also create an Apply process or messaging client when the *streams_type* is specified as APPLY and DEQUEUE, respectively.

Figure 4.8 shows the *add_subset_rules* procedure arguments that can be used to create the Capture process.

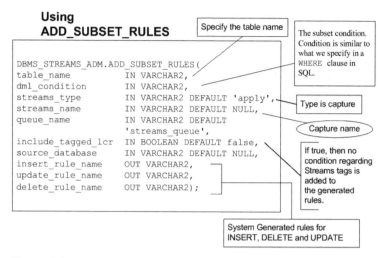

Figure 4.8 *Parameters for add_subset_rules procedure*

As seen in the Figure 4.8, the *streams_type* parameter specifies the type of Streams client. For the Capture process creation, the type to use is CAPTURE.

The *dml_condition* parameter specifies the subset condition. This condition similar to the way conditions are specified in a WHERE clause in a SQL statement.

For example, to specify rows in the NY3.ALLINSURED1 table where the *sales_id* is greater than 120, use the following as the condition: *sales_id* > 120 . The following SQL block creates the Capture process NY3_CAPTURE where rows with *sales_id* > 120 are captured.

```
BEGIN
DBMS_STREAMS_ADM.ADD_SUBSET_RULES(
  table_name      => 'ny3.allinsured1',
  streams_type    => 'capture',
  streams_name    => 'ny3_capture',
  queue_name      => 'ny3_queue',
  dml_condition   => ' sales_id > 120 ',
  include_tagged_lcr => false,
  source_database => NULL ) ;
END;
/
```

The creation of the NY3_CAPTURE Capture process creates three rules automatically: INSERT; DELETE; and UPDATE DML.

The following section presents information on the capture creation using the *add_schema_rules* procedure.

Capture Creation - Using *add_schema_rules* procedure

In the previous sections, detailed information was presented on the creation of the Capture process using the *add_table_rules* procedure and the *add_subset_rules* procedure. Selected tables were added one by one to the replication configuration. In this method, the procedure *add_schema_rules* is used to specify the schema whose tables participate in the Capture process. This procedure is quite handy and it helps administratively to configure the whole schema for propagation. Besides the initial creation, even future objects will be covered once the schema instantiation is done.

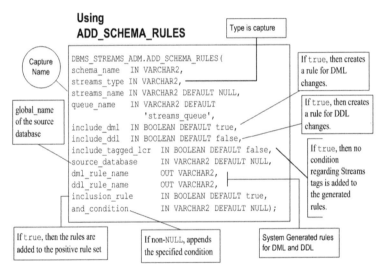

Figure 4.9 *Parameters for add_schema_rules procedure*

As shown in Figure 4.9, the *add_schema_rules* procedure prepares all the objects in the schema specified for instantiation. It also creates DML and DDL rules with system generated names. The rules are added to the positive rule set when the *inclusion_rule* parameter is set to TRUE.

When the *include_tagged_lcr* parameter is set to FALSE, it specifies that the Capture process captures a change in the redo log only if the change has NULL tag.

Next, a simple illustration of using the *add_schema_rules* procedure to configure replication of the objects from the NY2 schema of DNYTST10 to NY2 schema of DNYOIP20 database will be presented.

This method has following steps:

- Create the queue at the source database

- Create Capture process using the *add_schema_rules* procedure

- Create the Queue at the destination database

- Create the Apply process using the *add_schema_rules* procedure

- Create the Propagation process at source database

- Data pump export the schema from the source database

- Data pump import the schema into the destination database

- Instantiate the schema objects

- Start the Apply and Capture process at the source and destination databases, respectively

The first step is to create the queue named NY2_QUEUE and then create the Capture process using the *add_schema_rules* procedure.

```
connect strmadm/strmadm@dnytst10
PROMPT Step (1) Create Queue at source database
BEGIN
DBMS_STREAMS_ADM.SET_UP_QUEUE(
  queue_table    => 'strmadm.ny2_queue_table',
  queue_name     => 'strmadm.ny2_queue');
END;
/
```

The next step will create the schema rule for the NY2 schema using following SQL block.

```
PROMPT Step (2) Create Capture process using add_schema_rules
BEGIN
DBMS_STREAMS_ADM.ADD_SCHEMA_RULES(
  schema_name            => 'ny2',
  streams_type           => 'capture',
  streams_name           => 'ny2_capture',
  queue_name             => 'ny2_queue',
  include_dml            => true,
  include_ddl            => true,
  include_tagged_lcr     => false,
  source_database        => NULL,
```

```
    inclusion_rule          => true);
END;
/
```

Since the *inclusion_rule* parameter has been set to TRUE, a positive rule set is created and associated with the Capture process. The following rule set and rules are created:

```
SELECT STREAMS_NAME,
 STREAMS_TYPE,
 RULE_NAME,
 RULE_SET_NAME ,
 RULE_SET_TYPE,
 STREAMS_RULE_TYPE,  ·
 OBJECT_NAME,
 RULE_TYPE
 FROM DBA_STREAMS_RULES where SCHEMA_NAME = 'NY2'
/
```

Streams Name	Streams Type	Rule Name	Rule Set name	RuleSet Type	Object Name	Rule Type
NY2_CAPTURE	CAPTURE	NY2172	RULESET$_174	POSITIVE	SCHEMA	DML
NY2_CAPTURE	CAPTURE	NY2173	RULESET$_174	POSITIVE	SCHEMA	DDL

The rule condition for the above rules can be seen by using the *show_rule_details.sql* script, which can be found in the code depot.

```
SQL>@show_rule_details shows the following:

Rule Condition of rule NY2172

((:dml.get_object_owner () = 'NY2') and :dml.is_null_tag() = 'Y' )

Rule Condition of Rule NY2173

((:ddl.get_object_owner () = 'NY2' or :ddl.get_base_table_owner () = 'NY2') and
:ddl.is_null_tag() = 'Y' )
```

The *get_base_table_owner* member function is used in the DDL LCR rule because the *get_object_owner* function may return a value of NULL if a user who does not own an object performs a DDL change on the object.

As a result of the execution of the *add_schema_rules* procedure, all of the objects of the schema are prepared automatically for the Capture process. The following SQL statement shows this:

```
SELECT table_owner, table_name, to_char(SCN) SCN,
to_char(timestamp, 'DD-MON-YY HH24:MI') Time_Stamp FROM DBA_CAPTURE_PREPARED_TABLES where
TABLE_OWNER = 'NY2'
/
```

TABLE_OWNER	TABLE_NAME	SCN	TIME_STAMP
NY2	TEST1	13335321	18-OCT-04 17:11
NY2	ALLINSURED2	13335322	18-OCT-04 17:11
NY2	SALESPERSON2	13335323	18-OCT-04 17:11

Next, the queue and the Apply Process will be created at the destination database, as shown in the following SQL block:

```
connect strmadm/strmadm@dnyoip20

Prompt Connected to Target DNYREP10
Prompt Step(3) Creating A new Queue (LN2_QUEUE) at destination
BEGIN
DBMS_STREAMS_ADM.SET_UP_QUEUE(
queue_table      => 'strmadm.ln2_queue_table',
queue_name       => 'strmadm.ln2_queue');
END;
/
PROMPT Step(4) Create APPLY process schema rules at destination
BEGIN
DBMS_STREAMS_ADM.ADD_SCHEMA_RULES(
 schema_name     => 'ny2',
 Streams_type    => 'apply',
 Streams_name    => 'ln2_apply',
 queue_name      => 'ln2_queue',
 include_dml     => true,
 include_ddl     => true,
 include_tagged_lcr       => false,
 source_database          => 'dnytst10.world',
 inclusion_rule                => true);
END;
/
```

At the source database, propagation rules are created for schema using *add_schema_propagation_rules* procedure:

```
connect strmadm/strmadm@dnytst10
PROMPT Step(5) Create schema propagation process at source database
BEGIN
DBMS_STREAMS_ADM.ADD_SCHEMA_PROPAGATION_RULES(
schema_name              => 'ny2',
streams_name             => 'ny2_propagate',
source_queue_name        => 'strmadm.ny2_queue',
destination_queue_name => 'strmadm.ln2_queue@dnyoip20.world',
include_dml              => true,
include_ddl              => true,
include_tagged_lcr       => false,
source_database          => 'dnytsts10.world',
inclusion_rule           => true);
END;
/
```

Next, the data pump export and import method will be used to create the NY2 schema objects, load the initial data and then instantiate the schema. This will copy the source table and its rows to the destination database. Once the same data exists on both sides, the replication process will focus on future changes. This ensures that the data is consistent in both locations.

At the source database, find the SCN value by using the following SQL statement and record the SCN values:

```
SELECT DBMS_FLASHBACK.GET_SYSTEM_CHANGE_NUMBER FROM DUAL;
```

Then, create the directory object where the data pump export dump file will be written.

```
CREATE DIRECTORY DPUMP_DIR AS '/app/home/oracle/work'
/
```

The data pump export is then performed by using the *expdp* command, which creates the NY2_SCHEMA.dmp file. Executing the following command at the operating system level on the source database hosts performs the data pump export:

```
>expdp    strmadm/strmadm    SCHEMAS=NY2    DIRECTORY=DPUMP_DIR    DUMPFILE=NY2_SCHEMA.dmp
FLASHBACK_SCN=11638722
```

The SCN value obtained from the *get_system_change_number* procedure has been specified to the data pump export parameter of *flashback_scn*.

The log file of the data pump export process looks like:

```
Export: Release 10.1.0.2.0 - 64bit Production on Thursday, 30 September, 2004 23:54

Copyright (c) 2003, Oracle.  All rights reserved.

Connected to: Oracle Database 10g Enterprise Edition Release 10.1.0.2.0 - 64bit Production
With the Partitioning, OLAP and Data Mining options
FLASHBACK automatically enabled to preserve database integrity.
Starting     "STRMADM"."SYS_EXPORT_SCHEMA_01":        strmadm/********     SCHEMAS=NY2
DIRECTORY=DPUMP_DIR DUMPFILE=NY2_SCHEMA.dmp FLASHBACK_SCN=11638722
Estimate in progress using BLOCKS method...
Processing object type SCHEMA_EXPORT/TABLE/TABLE_DATA
Total estimation using BLOCKS method: 2 MB
Processing object type SCHEMA_EXPORT/USER
Processing object type SCHEMA_EXPORT/SYSTEM_GRANT
Processing object type SCHEMA_EXPORT/ROLE_GRANT
Processing object type SCHEMA_EXPORT/DEFAULT_ROLE
Processing object type SCHEMA_EXPORT/SE_PRE_SCHEMA_PROCOBJACT/PROCACT_SCHEMA
Processing object type SCHEMA_EXPORT/SEQUENCE/SEQUENCE
Processing object type SCHEMA_EXPORT/TABLE/PROCACT_INSTANCE
Processing object type SCHEMA_EXPORT/TABLE/TABLE
. . exported "NY2"."ALLINSURED2"          1.128 MB     6000 rows
. . exported "NY2"."BRANCH2"                 2 KB       12 rows
. . exported "NY2"."SALESPERSON2"            3 KB       15 rows
. . exported "NY2"."TEST1"                   1 KB        2 rows
Master table "STRMADM"."SYS_EXPORT_SCHEMA_01" successfully loaded/unloaded
******************************************************************
Dump file set for STRMADM.SYS_EXPORT_SCHEMA_01 is:
  /app/home/oracle/work/NY2_SCHEMA.dmp
Job "STRMADM"."SYS_EXPORT_SCHEMA_01" successfully completed at 23:55
```

Now, by using the FTP or remote copy, send the exported dump file to the destination database host. Then, at the destination database, use data pump to import the exported dump file NY2_SCHEMA.dmp as shown below:

```
>impdp strmadm/strmadm DIRECTORY=DPUMP_DIR DUMPFILE=NY2_SCHEMA.dmp
```

The log of the data pump import looks like:

```
Import: Release 10.1.0.2.0 - Production on Friday, 01 October, 2004 0:29
Copyright (c) 2003, Oracle.  All rights reserved.

Connected to: Oracle Database 10g Enterprise Edition Release 10.1.0.2.0 - Production
With the Partitioning, OLAP and Data Mining options
Master table "STRMADM"."SYS_IMPORT_FULL_01" successfully loaded/unloaded
Starting    "STRMADM"."SYS_IMPORT_FULL_01":        strmadm/********    DIRECTORY=DPUMP_DIR
DUMPFILE=NY2_SCHEMA.dmp
Processing object type SCHEMA_EXPORT/USER
Processing object type SCHEMA_EXPORT/SYSTEM_GRANT
Processing object type SCHEMA_EXPORT/ROLE_GRANT
Processing object type SCHEMA_EXPORT/DEFAULT_ROLE
Processing object type SCHEMA_EXPORT/SE_PRE_SCHEMA_PROCOBJACT/PROCACT_SCHEMA
Processing object type SCHEMA_EXPORT/SEQUENCE/SEQUENCE
Processing object type SCHEMA_EXPORT/TABLE/PROCACT_INSTANCE
Processing object type SCHEMA_EXPORT/TABLE/TABLE
Processing object type SCHEMA_EXPORT/TABLE/TABLE_DATA
. . imported "NY2"."ALLINSURED2"          1.128 MB      6000 rows
. . imported "NY2"."BRANCH2"                  2 KB        12 rows
. . imported "NY2"."SALESPERSON2"             3 KB        15 rows
. . imported "NY2"."TEST1"                    1 KB         1 rows
Job "STRMADM"."SYS_IMPORT_FULL_01" successfully completed at 00:29
```

The next step is the instantiation of the schema and its objects using the procedure *set_schema_instantiation_scn*:

```
PROMPT Step(8) Instantiate the Schema Objects
DECLARE
  iscn  NUMBER;         -- Variable to hold instantiation SCN value
BEGIN
 iscn := DBMS_FLASHBACK.GET_SYSTEM_CHANGE_NUMBER();
 dbms_output.put_line ('Instantiation SCN : ' || iscn ) ;
DBMS_APPLY_ADM.SET_SCHEMA_INSTANTIATION_SCN@DNYOIP20.world (
    source_schema_name    => 'ny2',
    source_database_name  => 'DNYTST10.world',
    instantiation_scn     => iscn ,
    recursive => true
    );
END;
/
```

Start both the Apply and Capture processes at the destination and source databases, respectively:

```
connect STRMADM/STRMADM@dnyoip20

PROMPT Connected to Destination (DNYOIP20)
PROMPT Starting the Apply Process at Destination
begin
dbms_apply_adm.start_apply (apply_name => 'LN2_APPLY ' ) ;
end ;
/

connect STRMADM/STRMADM@dnytst10
PROMPT Connected to Source (DNYTST10)
PROMPT Starting the Capture Process at source DNYTST10
begin
dbms_capture_adm.start_capture (capture_name => 'NY2_CAPTURE' ) ;
end ;
/
```

The source schema is now ready for replication to the destination schema.

The next section will present yet another method by which the Capture process can be created.

Capture Creation - Using add_schema_rules procedure

129

Capture Creation – Using *create_capture* procedure

In this method, the *create_capture* procedure of *dbms_capture* package is used to configure the Capture process. This method provides a flexible method of creation and configuration.

Why use this method when there is such simple creation procedure as the ones presented in earlier sections? It is because the *create_capture* procedure:

- gives the Streams administrators fine control over the process of capture creation and setting up of *start_scn* and *first_scn* values.

- helps to design custom made rules and rules sets.

- helps to specify required *start_scn* and *first_scn* for the Capture stream.

- helps to configure the Capture process at the Down Streams database also.

On the down side, it requires more manual creation of necessary rules and rules sets. Since much of the work is manual, it requires careful planning.

Figure 4.10 shows the list of arguments for the *create_capture* procedure.

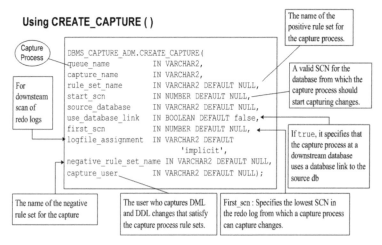

Figure 4.10 *Parameters for the create_capture procedure*

The following guidelines are used for running the *create_capture* procedure:

- The name of the positive rule set which already exists must be specified. The positive rule set contains the rules that instruct the Capture process to capture changes. The rule set should be specified as [SCHEMA_NAME.]RULE_SET_NAME. If the schema is not specified, the current user is the default.

- A rule set can be created and rules added to it using the *dbms_streams_adm* package or the *dbms_rule_adm* package prior to running this procedure.

- For *start_scn*, a valid SCN must be specified for the database from which the Capture process should start capturing changes. If the specified value is lower than the *current_scn* of the source database, either the *first_scn* should be specified or the SCN value specified for *start_scnmust* be greater than or equal to the *first_scn* of an existing Capture process which has taken at least one checkpoint.

- If the *start_scn* is NULL and no value is specified for the *first_scn*, the database's *current_scn* is used as the *start_scn*. If the *start_scn* is NULL and *first_scn* is non-NULL, the First_SCN value is used. If a value is specified for both the *start_scn* and the *first_scn*, the *start_scn* value must be greater than or equal to the *first_scn* value. An error is returned if an invalid SCN is specified.

- For the *first_scn*, the lowest SCN in the redo log from which a Capture process can capture changes is specified. A non-NULL value for this parameter is valid only if the *dbms_capture_adm.build* procedure has been run at least once at the source database.

- The *logfile_assignment* parameter is relevant for Down Streams capture configuration. If set to IMPLICIT, which is the default, the Capture process at a Down Streams database scans all redo log files added by log transport services or manually from the source database to the Down Streams database. If set to EXPLICIT, a redo log file is scanned by a Capture process at a Down Streams database only if the Capture process name is specified in the for *logminer_session_name* clause when the redo log file is added manually to the Down Streams database.

The following section presents an example that is used to illustrate the local capture creation using the *create_capture* procedure.

The first step is to create the rule set and add a rule to the rule set. For creating the rule, the *create_rule* procedure can be used. For creating the rule

---

set, the *create_rule_set* procedure of the *dbms_rule_adm* package can be used. The following SQL creates a rule, a rule set and adds the rule to the rule set.

```
--(1) First Create Rule Set
BEGIN
DBMS_RULE_ADM.CREATE_RULE_SET(
  rule_set_name            => 'strmadm.ny4_set1',
  evaluation_context       => 'SYS.STREAMS$_EVALUATION_CONTEXT');
END;
/
-- (2) Then Create a Rule
BEGIN
DBMS_RULE_ADM.CREATE_RULE(
  rule_name => 'strmadm.ny4_rule1_dml',
  condition => ' :dml.get_object_owner () = ''NY4'' AND ' || ' :dml.is_null_tag() = ''Y'' '
);
END;
/
-- (3) Add the rules to the rule set
BEGIN
DBMS_RULE_ADM.ADD_RULE(
rule_name => 'strmadm.ny4_rule1_dml',
rule_set_name => 'strmadm.ny4_set1');
END;
/
```

The next example shows how the *create_capture* procedure in the *dbms_capture_adm* package is used to create a local Capture process. It uses the rule set that was created in the previous step.

```
BEGIN
DBMS_CAPTURE_ADM.CREATE_CAPTURE(
queue_name               => 'ny4_queue',
capture_name             => 'ny4_capture',
rule_set_name            => 'strmadm.ny4_set1',
start_scn                => NULL,
source_database          => NULL,
use_database_link        => false,
first_scn                => NULL);
END;
/
```

This procedure performs the following actions:

- It creates a Capture process called NY4_CAPTURE. A Capture process with the same name must not exist.

- It associates the Capture process with an existing queue named NY4_QUEUE

- It associates the Capture process with an existing rule set named NY4_SET1. This is the positive rule set for the Capture process.

- It creates a Capture process that captures local changes to the source database because the *source_database* parameter is set to NULL. For a local Capture process, the global name of the local database for this parameter may also be specified.

Because both the *start_scn* and the *first_scn* are set to NULL, Oracle database determines the *start_scn* and *first_scn* for the Capture process.

If no other Capture processes that capture local changes are running on the local database, the build procedure in the *dbms_capture_adm* package is run automatically. Running this procedure extracts the data dictionary to the redo log, and a LogMiner data dictionary is created when the Capture process is started for the first time.

The next step is to examine the final method by which the Capture process can be created.

Capture Creation – Using *add_global_rules* procedure

Using the *add_global_rules* procedure of the *dbms_streams_adm* package is another way that the database level changes can be configured.

The global Capture process captures changes from all of the schema objects: however, it does not capture changes made in the SYS, SYSTEM, or CTXSYS schemas. This procedure would be used for maintaining a total copy of the database at a remote site.

The *add_global_rules* procedure creates two rules: one for row LCRs containing the results of DML changes and another one for DDL LCRs.

Below is the rule condition used by the row LCR rule:

```
(:dml.is_null_tag() = 'Y' )
```

Below is the rule condition used by the DDL LCR rule:

```
(:ddl.is_null_tag() = 'Y' )
```

The following SQL block shows the signature of the *add_global_rules* procedure:

```
DBMS_STREAMS_ADM.ADD_GLOBAL_RULES(
  Streams_type          IN VARCHAR2,
  Streams_name          IN VARCHAR2 DEFAULT NULL,
  queue_name            IN VARCHAR2 DEFAULT 'Streams_queue',
  include_dml           IN BOOLEAN DEFAULT true,
  include_ddl           IN BOOLEAN DEFAULT false,
  include_tagged_lcr    IN BOOLEAN DEFAULT false,
  source_database            IN VARCHAR2 DEFAULT NULL,
```

```
dml_rule_name          OUT VARCHAR2,
ddl_rule_name          OUT VARCHAR2,
inclusion_rule                  IN BOOLEAN DEFAULT true,
and_condition          IN VARCHAR2 DEFAULT NULL);
```

In order to copy the source database initially, the RMAN DUPLICATE command can be used to instantiate the source database at the destination database. The UNTIL SCN clause can be used to specify an SCN for the duplication.

Once the destination database has been created successfully, the Streams configuration at the destination must be removed in order to facilitate a fresh configuration. The *remove_streams_configuration()* procedure of the package *dbms_streams_adm* can be used to accomplish this.

At the destination database, the instantiation SCN is set for the entire database and all of the database objects by using the *set_global_instantiation_scn* of the package *dbms_apply_adm* procedure.

At the source database, a propagation can be created that propagates all changes from the source queue by using the *add_global_propagation_rules* procedure. By using the *add_global_rules* procedure, the Apply process can be configured at the destination database.

So far, quite a lot ground has been covered on Capture process creation, capture management, etc. In the next section, the configuration of Propagation will be presented as well as how it is managed.

Propagation Process

Once the changes to the database tables are captured, they are staged to the specified queue of type SYS.AnyData. Only the changes which qualify after the rule engine evaluation process make their way into the staging queue in the form of LCRs for further propagation.

The main objective of the Propagation process is to send the enqueued message to the destination queue from the source queue. A propagation is always between the source queue and the destination queue. However, a single queue may participate in many propagations. A single source queue may propagate events to multiple destination queues, and a single destination queue may receive events from multiple source queues. However, only one propagation is allowed between a particular source queue and a particular destination queue. A single queue may be a destination queue for some propagations and a source queue for other propagations.

Propagation Rules

The Propagation process also follows user defined rules. Rules control those events which need to be propagated and those which need to be discarded. These rules are defined at three levels: Table, Schema and Global:

- A Table rule propagates or discards either row changes resulting from DML changes or DDL changes to a particular table. Subset rules are table rules that include a subset of the row changes to a particular table.

- A Schema rule propagates or discards either row changes resulting from DML changes or DDL changes to the database objects in a particular schema.

- A Global rule propagates or discards either all row changes resulting from DML changes or all DDL changes in the source queue.

When a particular captured change is configured for propagation to multiple destinations with relevant Apply processes, the staged event remains at the source queue until all the configured destination queues receive the events. When all destination queues receive and acknowledge, the source event is dropped successfully.

Prior to propagation, all the events are buffered into buffered queues which reside partly in the SGA and partly in the queue table. The buffering of events helps optimize the Propagation process.

Creation of Propagation Process

The propagation of events uses the *dbms_job* package and internally makes use of the job queue processes (Jnnn). A single propagation job propagates all events that use a particular database link even if the database link is used by more than one propagation to propagate events to multiple destination queues.

When a propagation is created, a *dbms_job* schedule which has the following properties is created:

- The start time is *sysdate()*, which says that it is to start immediately.

- The duration is NULL, which means infinite. The process keeps running until it is dropped

- The next time is NULL, which means that propagation restarts as soon as it finishes its current duration

- The latency is 3 seconds, which is the wait time between when a queue becomes empty and the propagation job is resubmitted.

To create the propagation, any of the following procedures can be used:

- *dbms_streams_adm.add_table_propagation_rules*

- *dbms_streams_adm.add_subset_propagation_rules*

- *dbms_streams_adm.add_schema_propagation_rules*

- *dbms_streams_adm.add_global_propagation_rules*

- *dbms_propagation_adm.create_propagation*

Each of the procedures in the *dbms_streams_adm* package creates propagation with the specified name if it does not already exist. It creates either a positive or negative rule set for the propagation if the propagation does not have such a rule set. It may also add Table, Schema, or Global rules to the rule set.

The *create_propagation* procedure creates a propagation, but it does not create rules or a rule set for the propagation. The *create_propagation* procedure enables the specification of an existing rule set that can be associated with the propagation, either as a positive or a negative rule set. All propagations are started automatically upon creation. Creation of propagation in this manner gives a manual yet flexible method for administration.

The next section will present details on the creation of the Propagation process.

Using *add_table_propagation_rules*

The *add_table_propagation_rules* procedure is most often used for configuring a table level propagation. It is fairly simple to use and it creates rule sets and rules automatically.

This procedure adds table rules to the positive or negative rule set for a propagation. It will create the specified propagation if it does not exist.

Figure 4.11 shows the parameters that the DBA can specify for the procedure.

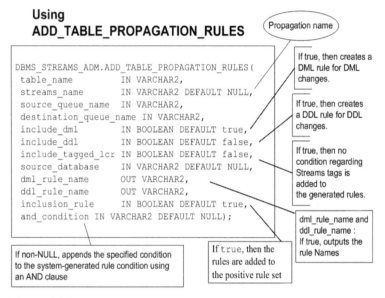

Figure 4.11 *Parameters for add_table_propagation_rules*

The following is an example that runs the *add_table_propagation_rules* procedure in the *dbms_streams_adm* package to create a propagation:

```
BEGIN
DBMS_STREAMS_ADM.ADD_TABLE_PROPAGATION_RULES(
table_name              => 'ny1.allinsured1',
streams_name            => 'ny1_propagate',
source_queue_name       => 'strmadm.ny1_queue',
destination_queue_name  => 'strmadm.ln1_queue@DNYOIP20.world',
include_dml             => true,
include_ddl             => true,
include_tagged_lcr      => false,
source_database         => 'DNYTST10.world',
inclusion_rule          => true);
END;
/
```

The above procedure performs the following:

- It creates a propagation named NY1_PROPAGATE.

- It specifies that the LCRs are to be propagated from NY1_QUEUE in the current database to LN1_QUEUE in the DYNOIP20.WORLD database

- It specifies that the propagation uses the DNYOIP20.WORLD database link to propagate the LCRs because the *destination_queue_name* parameter contains DNYOIP20.WORLD.

- It creates a positive rule set and associates it with the propagation because the *inclusion_rule* parameter is set to TRUE. The rule set uses the evaluation context *sys.streams$_evaluation_context*. The rule set name is specified by the system.

- It creates two rules. One rule evaluates to TRUE for row LCRs that contain the results of DML changes to the NY1.ALLINSURED1 table. The other rule evaluates to TRUE for DDL LCRs that contain DDL changes to the NY1.ALLINSURED1 table. The rule names are specified by the system.

- It adds the two rules to the positive rule set associated with the propagation since the *inclusion_rule* is set to TRUE.

The following SQL statement can be executed to view the propagation details:

```
SELECT p.propagation_name propagation_name,
 TO_CHAR(s.start_date, 'HH24:MI:SS MM/DD/YYYY') START_DATE,
 s.propagation_window DURATION, s.latency, s.schedule_disabled,
 TO_CHAR(s.next_run_date,'HH24:MI:SS MM/DD/YYYY') NEXT_TIME,
 process_name, total_number, failures
 FROM dba_queue_schedules S, dba_propagation P
 WHERE p.propagation_name in
(select propagation_name from DBA_PROPAGATION)
/
```

There is another useful SQL query that can be used to view the propagation details including the bytes transferred etc. *v$propagation_sender* displays information about buffer queue propagation schedules on the source side. Columns such as TOTAL_MSGS, TOTAL_BYTES, and HIGH_WATER_MARK are helpful in showing the progress and load on the Propagation process. The following SQL block queries the *v$propagation_sender* view.

```
-- to see the bytes transferred etc
SELECT p.PROPAGATION_NAME,
 s.QUEUE_NAME,
 s.DBLINK,
 s.TOTAL_MSGS,
 s.TOTAL_BYTES
 FROM DBA_PROPAGATION p, V$PROPAGATION_SENDER s
 WHERE p.DESTINATION_DBLINK = s.DBLINK AND
 p.SOURCE_QUEUE_OWNER = s.QUEUE_SCHEMA AND
 p.SOURCE_QUEUE_NAME = s.QUEUE_NAME
/
```

The above SQL statement gives the following sample output:

```
               Queue      Database       Total    Total
Propagation    Name       Link           Events   Bytes
---------------  ------------------------  --------  --------------
NY1_PROPAGATE    NY1_QUEUE  DNYOIP20.WORLD  50,077  56,696,005
```

To list the rules associated with the Propagation process, the following SQL statement can be used:

```
SELECT Streams_name, table_owner || '.'|| table_name Table_N_Owner,
source_database, rule_type ,
rule_name, rule_owner, include_tagged_lcr
FROM DBA_STREAMS_TABLE_RULES
WHERE Streams_name in
(select propagation_name from DBA_PROPAGATION)
/
```

A more detailed view of the propagation can be obtained by running the following SQL statement:

```
set linesize 140
COLUMN propagation_name FORMAT A26
COLUMN start_date                    FORMAT a20
COLUMN propagation_window FORMAT 99999
COLUMN next_time HEADING 'Next Window' FORMAT A12
COLUMN latency                       FORMAT 99999
COLUMN schedule_disabled HEADING 'Disabl' FORMAT A6
COLUMN process_name HEADING PROC FORMAT A8
COLUMN failures                      FORMAT 999
COLUMN total_num                     FORMAT 99999999
col propagate_schedule_profile format a60

SELECT
'Propagtion name    : ' || p.propagation_name || chr(10) ||
'start_date         : ' || TO_CHAR(s.start_date, 'HH24:MI:SS MM/DD/YY') || chr(10) ||
'propagation_window : ' || s.propagation_window || chr(10) ||
'latency            : ' || s.latency || chr(10) ||
'schedule_disabled  : ' || s.schedule_disabled || chr(10) ||
'next_run_date      : ' || TO_CHAR(s.next_run_date, 'HH24:MI:SS MM/DD/YY') || chr(10) ||
'process_name       : ' || process_name || chr(10) ||
'total_number       : ' || total_number || chr(10) ||
'failures           : ' || failures || chr(10) ||
'TOTAL_TIME         : ' || TOTAL_TIME   || chr(10) ||
'TOTAL_NUMBER(MSGS) : ' || TOTAL_NUMBER || chr(10) ||
'TOTAL_BYTES        : ' || TOTAL_BYTES  || chr(10) ||
'MAX_NUMBER(MSGS)   : ' || MAX_NUMBER   || chr(10) ||
'MAX_BYTES          : ' || MAX_BYTES
propagate_schedule_profile
FROM dba_queue_schedules S , dba_propagation P
WHERE p.propagation_name in (select propagation_name from DBA_PROPAGATION)
/
```

The following is the output:

```
PROPAGATE_SCHEDULE_PROFILE
----------------------------------------------------------
Propagtion name    : NY1_PROPAGATE
start_date         : 16:18:55 10/15/04
propagation_window :
latency            : 3
schedule_disabled  : N
next_run_date      :
process_name       : J000
total_number       : 50077
failures           : 0
TOTAL_TIME         : 748
```

```
TOTAL_NUMBER(MSGS)  :  50077
TOTAL_BYTES         :  56696005
MAX_NUMBER(MSGS)    :  0
MAX_BYTES           :  0
```

Using *add_schema_propagation_rules*

The section will present information on using the *add_schema_propagation_rules* procedure to create a Propagation process. This method helps to configure the schema level propagation, and as such, all the objects in the schema will be covered for propagation.

The *add_schema_propagation_rules* procedure in the *dbms_streams_adm* package can be used to configure the Streams propagation to propagate row LCRs and DDL LCRs relating to the specified schema from a queue at source database to a queue at the destination database.

As an example, the replication of NY2 schema will be configured using the following SQL statement.

```
BEGIN
DBMS_STREAMS_ADM.ADD_SCHEMA_PROPAGATION_RULES(
schema_name               => 'ny2',
streams_name              => 'ny2_propagate',
source_queue_name         => 'strmadm.ny2_queue',
destination_queue_name => 'strmadm.ln2_queue@dnyoip20.world',
include_dml               => true,
include_ddl               => true,
include_tagged_lcr        => false,
source_database           => 'dnytsts10.world',
inclusion_rule            => true);
END;
/
```

In the above example, the destination queue of LN2_QUEUE at the DNYOIP20 database has been specified. NY2 schema objects are configured to be propagated to the destination.

If the goal is to use schema rules but there is concern about changes to database objects in a schema that are not supported by Streams, the rules can be used to discard unsupported changes. The *dbms_rules_adm* package can be used to achieve this.

Using *dbms_propagation_adm* to create propagation

The following is an example that uses the *create_propagation* procedure of the *dbms_propagation_adm* package to create a propagation:

```
BEGIN
DBMS_PROPAGATION_ADM.CREATE_PROPAGATION(
propagation_name                    => 'ny4_propagate',
source_queue            => 'strmadm.ny4_queue',
destination_queue             => 'strmadm.ln4_queue',
destination_dblink             => 'dnyoip20.world',
rule_set_name           => 'strmadm.ny4_rule_set1');
END;
/
```

The above example creates the NY4_PROPAGATE propagation to send events from the queue named NY4_QUEUE to the LN4_QUEUE located at DNYOIP20 database.

This method does not create the propagation rules automatically. The pre-created rule set must be specified and associated with this propagation. In the above example, the propagation is associated with an existing rule set named NY4_RULE_SET1. This rule acts as the positive rule set for the propagation.

Managing the Propagation Job

Enabling and Disabling the Propagation Job

By default the propagation jobs are enabled when propagation is created. If a propagation job is disabled for any specific reason and subsequently it needs to be enabled, the *enable_propagation_schedule* procedure in the *dbms_aqadm* package can be used to enable it.

For example, to enable a propagation job that propagates events from the NY4_QUEUE source queue using the DNYOIP20.world database link, the following SQL block should be run:

```
BEGIN
DBMS_AQADM.ENABLE_PROPAGATION_SCHEDULE(
queue_name => 'strmadm.NY4_QUEUE',
destination => 'DNYOIP20.world');
END;
/
```

To disable the propagation job that stops the event propagation, use the following SQL block:

```
BEGIN
DBMS_AQADM.DISABLE_PROPAGATION_SCHEDULE(
queue_name => 'strmadm.NY4_QUEUE',
destination => 'DNYOIP20.world');
END;
/
```

Dropping the Propagation

The *drop_propagation* procedure in the *dbms_propagation_adm* package can be used to drop an existing propagation. Why would there be a need to drop a propagation? For example, if a particular site is no longer maintaining a data replica, it may be desirable to remove a propagation for that site.

For example, the following procedure drops a propagation named NY4_PROPAGATE:

```
BEGIN
DBMS_PROPAGATION_ADM.DROP_PROPAGATION(
propagation_name => 'NY4_PROPAGATE',
drop_unused_rule_sets => TRUE);
END;
/
```

Since the *drop_unused_rule_sets* parameter is set to TRUE, this procedure also drops any rule sets used by the propagation NY4_PROPAGATE, unless the rule set is used by another Streams client. If this procedure drops a rule set, it also drops any rules in the rule set that do not exist in another rule set.

The next section presents information on how to alter the settings and properties of the Propagation process.

Altering the Propagation Settings

The *alter_propagation* procedure of *dbms_propagation_adm* package can be used to add, alter, or remove a rule set for a propagation.

The following is the syntax of the *alter_propagation* procedure:

```
DBMS_PROPAGATION_ADM.ALTER_PROPAGATION(
propagation_name              IN VARCHAR2,
rule_set_name                 IN VARCHAR2 DEFAULT NULL,
remove_rule_set               IN BOOLEAN DEFAULT false,
negative_rule_set_name    IN VARCHAR2 DEFAULT NULL,
remove_negative_rule_set  IN BOOLEAN DEFAULT false);
```

If the *remove_rule_set* parameter is set to TRUE, it removes the positive rule set for the specified propagation. When a positive rule set for a propagation is removed and the propagation does not have a negative rule set, the propagation will propagate all events.

If the *remove_negative_rule_set* parameter is set to TRUE, it removes the negative rule set for the specified propagation.

Conclusion

This Chapter presented detailed information on the configuration of the Capture process and the Propagation process. Examples have been used to illustrate the replication flow.

The main points of this chapter include:

- There are multiple methods for configuration of the Capture process. Each configures at various levels within the database. These levels are: Table level; A subset of Table level: Schema level; and Database level.

- There are different sets of procedures that can be used to manage the Capture process. To stop, start and drop the capture and for adding extra attributes to the captured LCR(s), appropriate procedures were introduced.

- By using the *create_capture* procedure, a flexible type of Capture process can be created where the administrators are able to specify the *start_scn* and *first_scn* values for the capture. This gives better control over the capture mechanism.

- Propagation rules can also be configured at various levels such as Global, Schema and Table levels.

In the next chapter, the configuration details of the Apply process will be examined.

Apply Process Configuration

Always apply the appropriate technology

Introduction

In this chapter, the configuration details of the Apply Process will be presented. In earlier chapters, the Streams clients of Capture and Propagation were examined. The examples that started in those chapters will be extended to show the details of the Apply process.

The Apply process is an optional Oracle background process. It dequeues Logical Change Records (LCRs) and user messages from a specific queue and then either applies each one directly or passes it as a parameter to a user-defined procedure called a handler.

The database changes are captured at the source database by the Capture process, then the Propagation process sends them to destination queue where the Apply process takes over. All of these processes fit the producer and consumer model very well.

The rules that are defined for the Apply process control the application of database table changes. Whether the changes are taken up or discarded depends on the rule that is in effect as part of the Streams Apply process. Rules are defined either automatically when the Apply process is created or they are created manually. In the case of the manual process, the rule set will have to be associated with the Apply process.

Apply Process

The Apply process is an optional Oracle background process. It dequeues the LCR(s) and user messages from a destination queue. When the Apply process dequeues, the events may be applied to database objects directly as transactions or they may be passed on as parameters to user defined procedures, which are also called user-defined Apply handlers. The database changes may include the DML or DDL changes.

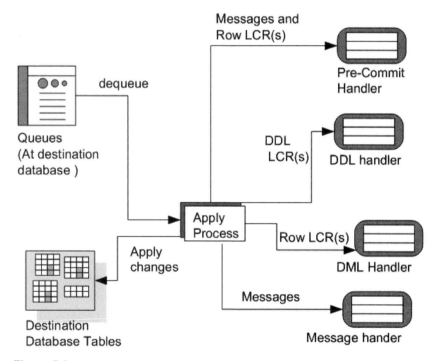

Figure 5.1 *Apply Process and Apply Handlers*

As shown in Figure 5.1, Apply handlers typically include Message handler, DML Handler, DDL Handler, and Pre-Commit handlers. The following is a brief description of the handlers:

Message Handler Procedure: This is a user-defined procedure that can process non-LCR user messages in a customized way. A message handler for an Apply process can be specified using the *message_handler* parameter in the *create_apply* or the *alter_apply* procedure in the *dbms_apply_adm* package.

DML and DDL Handlers: This is a user procedure that processes row LCRs resulting from DML statements. It is called a DML handler. A user procedure that processes DDL LCRs resulting from DDL statements is called a DDL handler. An Apply process can have many DML handlers but only one DDL handler. The DDL handler processes all DDL LCRs dequeued by the Apply process. These handlers provide a mechanism to use the LCR information and execute custom operations on the database tables.

Pre-Commit Handler procedure: - This is a user-defined PL/SQL procedure that can receive the commit information for a transaction and process it in a customized way. It can deal with LCRs and Messages. It helps track the transactional history and helps in audit process.

More details and examples about the Apply handlers will be presented in the next Chapter.

Apply Process Rules

The rules defined for the Apply process dictate what is applied or what is not applied to the destination databases. Rules can be placed in a positive rule set or negative rule set. If a rule evaluates to TRUE for a change and the rule is in the positive rule set for an Apply process, the Apply process applies the change. If a rule evaluates to TRUE for a change but the rule is in the negative rule set for an Apply process, the Apply process discards the change. If an Apply process has both a positive and a negative rule set, the negative rule set is always evaluated first and acts as the first level filter.

Apply process rules for LCR events can be specified at the following three levels:

- A Table rule applies or discards either row changes resulting from DML changes or DDL changes to a particular table. The subset rules which configure the table rules that impact the subset of the rows of a particular table can also be specified. .

- A Schema rule applies or discards either row changes resulting from DML changes or DDL changes to the database objects in a specified schema.

- A Global rule applies or discards either all row changes resulting from DML changes or all DDL changes in the queue associated with an Apply process.

Understanding and setting up the right rule condition is very important for proper data replication flow. Otherwise, data can be ignored or not applied at all.

The following section presents information on the apply mechanism and architecture.

Apply Process Components

Apply architecture has three main parts:

- The reader server

- The coordinator process

- One or more Apply servers

The following sections present these parts in more detail.

Reader Server:

This is the main component that mainly serves to dequeue the events. This is a parallel execution server that works out the dependencies between LCRs and assembles the events into transactions. It then returns the assembled transactions to the coordinator process, which assigns them to idle Apply servers.

The state of the reader server and other useful progress information for an Apply process can be viewed by querying the *v$streams_apply_reader* view. The STATE column shows the current activity being performed by the reader server. The STATE column can have any one of the following values:

- IDLE - Performing no work

- DEQUEUE MESSAGES - Dequeuing events from the queue

- SCHEDULE MESSAGES – Working out the dependencies between events and assembling events into transactions

The following SQL block shows some useful Apply reader details for a given specific Apply process that helps with monitoring.

```
COL FROM_STREAMS_APPLY_READER format a60

select
 'Session SID          : ' || SID || chr(10) ||
 'APPLY Name           : ' || APPLY_NAME|| chr(10) ||
 'Current State        : ' || STATE || chr(10) ||
 'TOT MSGs Dequed      : ' || TOTAL_MESSAGES_DEQUEUED || chr(10) ||
 'Time last msg received: ' || to_char(DEQUEUE_TIME,
                               'YYYY-MM-DD HH24:MI') || chr(10) ||
 'Last DeQued MSG NUM  : ' || DEQUEUED_MESSAGE_NUMBER || chr(10) ||
 'CRT-Time at SRCDB of Last MSG : ' ||
                        to_char(DEQUEUED_MESSAGE_CREATE_TIME,
                        'YYYY-MM-DD HH24:MI') || chr(10) ||
 'SGA Used so far      : ' || SGA_USED || chr(10) ||
 'Last browse SCN      : ' || LAST_BROWSE_NUM || chr(10) ||
 'Oldest SCN           : ' || OLDEST_SCN_NUM
FROM_STREAMS_APPLY_READER
from V$STREAMS_APPLY_READER
/
```

The following is the output:

```
FROM_STREAMS_APPLY_READER
------------------------------------------------------------
Session SID           : 27
APPLY Name            : LN1_APPLY
Current State         : DEQUEUE MESSAGES
TOT MSGs Dequed       : 30069
Time last msg received: 2004-10-18 17:12
Last DeQued MSG  NUM  : 13335488
CRT-Time at SRCDB of Last MSG : 2004-10-18 17:12
SGA Used so far       : 800
Last browse SCN       : 0
Oldest SCN            : 13335488
```

With the help of the above information, the DBA can keep track of the messages and the transaction load for the Apply process.

Coordinator Process:

The coordinator process is an Oracle background process. It gets the transactions from the reader server and passes them to Apply servers. The coordinator process name is Annn, where nnn is a coordinator process number.

The state of a coordinator process describes what the coordinator process is doing currently. The state of a coordinator process can be viewed by querying the *v$streams_apply_coordinator* dynamic performance view. The following coordinator process states are possible:

- INITIALIZING - Starting up

- APPLYING - Passing transactions to Apply servers

- SHUTTING DOWN CLEANLY - Stopping without an error

- ABORTING - Stopping because of an Apply error

The following SQL block, for example, shows the activity of the Apply coordinator:

```
COL APPLY_NAME HEADING 'Apply Process Name' FORMAT A25
COL TOTAL_RECEIVED HEADING 'Total|Trans|Received' FORMAT 99999999
COL TOTAL_APPLIED HEADING 'Total|Trans|Applied' FORMAT 99999999
COL TOTAL_ERRORS HEADING 'Total|Apply|Errors' FORMAT 9999
COL BEING_APPLIED HEADING 'Total|Trans Being|Applied' FORMAT 9999999
COL TOTAL_IGNORED HEADING 'Total|Trans|Ignored' FORMAT 99999999
--
SELECT APPLY_NAME,
 TOTAL_RECEIVED,
 TOTAL_APPLIED,
 TOTAL_ERRORS,
 TOTAL_ASSIGNED - (TOTAL_ROLLBACKS + TOTAL_APPLIED) BEING_APPLIED,
 TOTAL_IGNORED
FROM V$STREAMS_APPLY_COORDINATOR
/
```

The following is the output:

Apply Process Name	Total Trans Received	Total Trans Applied	Total Apply Errors	Total Trans Being Applied	Total Trans Ignored
LN1_APPLY	30	30	0	0	0

Apply Servers:

Each Apply server is a parallel execution server. The Apply servers apply LCRs to database objects as DML or DDL statements or pass the LCRs to the appropriate handlers. For non-LCR messages, the Apply servers pass the events to the message handler. If an Apply server encounters an error, it then tries to resolve the error with a user-specified conflict handler or error handler. If an Apply server cannot resolve an error, it rolls back the transaction and places the entire transaction, including all of its events, in the error queue. This is, in fact, the end point of the apply mechanism. At this stage, either the transactions have to be executed, also called applied, or they are moved to the error queue.

When an Apply server commits a completed transaction, this transaction is treated as applied. When an Apply server places a transaction in the error queue and commits, this transaction is also treated as applied.

The STATE of an Apply server describes what the Apply server is doing currently. The STATE of each Apply server for an Apply process can be seen by querying the *v$streams_apply_server* dynamic performance view. The following Apply server states are possible:

- IDLE - Performing no work

- RECORD LOW-WATERMARK - Performing an administrative action that maintains information about the Apply progress, which is used in the *all_apply_progress* and *dba_apply_progress* data dictionary views

- ADD PARTITION - Performing an administrative action that adds a partition that is used for recording information about in-progress transactions

- DROP PARTITION - Performing an administrative action that drops a partition that was used to record information about in-progress transactions

- EXECUTE TRANSACTION - Applying a transaction

- WAIT COMMIT - Waiting to commit a transaction until all other transactions with a lower commit SCN are applied. This state is possible only if the *commit_serialization* Apply process parameter is set to a value other than NONE and the *parallelism* Apply process parameter is set to a value greater than 1.

- WAIT DEPENDENCY - Waiting to apply an LCR in a transaction until another transaction, on which it has a dependency, is applied. This state is possible only if the *parallelism* Apply process parameter is set to a value greater than 1.

- WAIT FOR NEXT CHUNK - Waiting for the next set of LCRs for a large transaction

- TRANSACTION CLEANUP - Cleaning up an applied transaction, which includes removing LCRs from the Apply process queue

The following SQL block shows the details from the apply server.

```
COL FROM_STREAMS_APPLY_SERVER format a60

select
 'SID (streams_apply_server): ' || SID || chr(10) ||
```

```
'APPLY Name              : '  || APPLY_NAME|| chr(10) ||
'Current State           : '  || STATE || chr(10) ||
'Tot Trans Assgned       : '  || TOTAL_ASSIGNED  || chr(10) ||
'Tot Admin               : '  || TOTAL_ADMIN || chr(10) ||
'TOT MSGs APPLIED         : '  || TOTAL_MESSAGES_APPLIED||chr(10)||
'Time last msg applied   : '  || to_char(APPLY_TIME,
                               'YYYY-MM-DD HH24:MI')  || chr(10) ||
'Last APPLIED_MSG_NUM    : ' ||APPLIED_MESSAGE_NUMBER ||chr(10)||
'CRTTime at SRC of Last APPL_MSG : ' || to_char(
 APPLIED_MESSAGE_CREATE_TIME,'YYYY-MM-DD HH24:MI') || chr(10) ||
'ELAPSED_DEQUEUE_TIME : ' ||ELAPSED_DEQUEUE_TIME * 100 ||chr(10)||
'ELAPSED_APPLY_TIME   : ' || ELAPSED_APPLY_TIME
FROM_STREAMS_APPLY_SERVER
from V$STREAMS_APPLY_SERVER
/
```

The following is the output:

```
FROM_STREAMS_APPLY_SERVER
-------------------------------------------------------------
SID (streams_apply_server): 32
APPLY Name                 : LN1_APPLY
Current State              : IDLE
Tot Trans Assgned          : 30
Tot Admin                  : 35
TOT MSGs APPLIED           : 30030
Time last msg applied      : 2004-10-18 16:32
Last APPLIED_MSG_NUM       : 13332293
CRTTime at SRC of Last APPL_MSG : 2004-10-18 16:31
ELAPSED_DEQUEUE_TIME       : 201500
ELAPSED_APPLY_TIME         : 2822
```

The next step is to examine the creation of the Apply process. The following section presents information on all of the procedures that can be used to create the Apply process.

Apply Process Creation

To create an Apply process, any of the following procedures can be used.

- *dbms_streams_adm.add_table_rules*

- *dbms_streams_adm.add_subset_rules*

- *dbms_streams_adm.add_schema_rules*

- *dbms_streams_adm.add_global_rules*

- *dbms_streams_adm.add_message_rule*

- *dbms_apply_adm.create_apply*

Once the events and messages are propagated to the destination queue, they are ready to be dequeue by the Apply process. The active Apply process applies the changes to the destination objects.

As shown in Figure 5.2, When an Apply process is created using *add_subset_rules*, *add_table_rules*, *add_schema_rules*, or *add_global_rules* procedures of the *dbms_streams_adm* package, the Apply process applies only the captured events. When an Apply process is created using the *add_message_rule* procedure of the *dbms_streams_adm* package, the Apply process applies only user-enqueued events.

However, when an Apply process is created using the *create_apply* procedure in the *dbms_apply_adm* package, the *apply_captured* parameter can be used to specify whether the Apply process applies captured or user-enqueued events. By default, the *apply_captured* parameter is set to FALSE for an Apply process created with this procedure. Therefore, by default, an Apply process created with the *create_apply* procedure in the *dbms_apply_adm* package applies user-enqueued events.

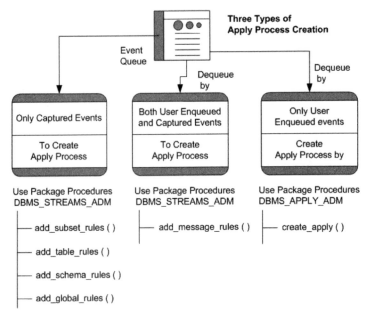

Figure 5.2 *Apply Process Creation Procedures*

The next section will provide details on how to create an Apply process and the associated rules using the various methods available.

Using *add_table_rules*

This is the simplest of all methods and it provides a way to define Apply rules table-by-table at the destination database and helps in the creation of the Apply process. In a single procedural call, all the necessary rules are defined for the Apply process.

Figure 5.3 gives a view of all the parameters that needed to pass to the *add_table_rules* procedure to create the Apply process. The procedure has two OUT variables, *dml_rule_name* and *ddl_rule_name*, to show the rules that are generated. The *streams_type* parameter needs to be specified as APPLY.

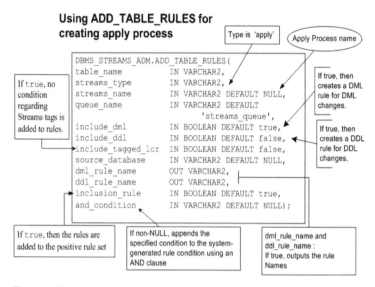

Figure 5.3 *add_table_rules procedure parameters*

In the *add_table_rules* procedure, various parameters provide necessary attributes as shown below:

- *include_dml*: If TRUE, the procedure creates a DML rule for DML changes. If FALSE, the procedure does not create a DML rule. NULL is not permitted.

- *include_ddl*: If TRUE, the procedure creates a DDL rule for DDL changes. If FALSE, the procedure does not create a DDL rule. NULL is not permitted.

- *include_tagged_lcr*: If TRUE, no condition regarding Streams tags is added to the generated rules. Therefore, these rules can evaluate to TRUE regardless of whether a redo entry or LCR has a non-NULL tag.

- *inclusion_rule*: If *inclusion_rule* is TRUE, the rules are added to the positive rule set for the Streams client. If *inclusion_rule* is FALSE, the rules are added to the negative rule set for the Streams client.

The following example will be used to illustrate the Apply creation process. The following SQL statement creates an Apply process named *ln1_apply* and defines rules for the table NY1.ALLINSURED1:

```
PROMPT ** Creating Apply Side Table rules at Destination(DNYOIP20)

BEGIN
DBMS_STREAMS_ADM.ADD_TABLE_RULES(
  table_name              => 'ny1.allinsured1',
  streams_type            => 'apply',
  streams_name            => 'ln1_apply',
  queue_name              => 'ln1_queue',
  include_dml             => true,
  include_ddl             => true,
  source_database         => 'DNYTST10.world',
  inclusion_rule          => true);
END;
/
```

In the above example:

- Since both the *include_dml* and *include_ddl* parameters have been specified to TRUE, both DML and DDL rules are created.

- Because the *inclusion_rule* parameter is set to TRUE, the rules are added to the positive rule set. The procedure creates positive rules set and associates them with the capture process.

Next the *add_subset_rules* procedure will be introduced as well as how to use it to create the Apply process.

Using *add_subset_rules* for Apply Creation

This method is a variation of the *add_table_rules* method where DML conditions can be added. For example, to a particular destination, the goal is to apply only a specific set of rows based on a WHERE clause type condition. Based on some attribute within a row, the DBA may chose to replicate only some subset of the data. This procedure helps specify the where clause type condition.

Figure 5.4 shows the signature and the arguments for the *add_subset_rules* procedure. The argument *dml_condition* specifies the where clause type condition which basically sets the filter condition.

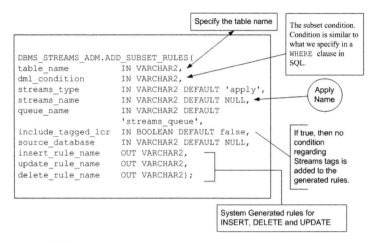

Figure 5.4 *add_subset_rules procedure parameters*

This will be illustrated by an example. The example begins with the table named ALLINSURED1 which is residing in schema NY3. The usual capture and propagation will be configured at the source database. At the destination database, the *add_subset_rules* procedure will be used and the DBA will specify the DML condition.

The configuration process follows the following steps.

1. Create the queue at the source database using *set_up_queue*

2. Create the Capture process at the source database using *add_table_rules*.

3. Create the queue at the destination database using *set_up_queue*

4. Create the Apply process using *add_subset_rules*.

5. Create the propagation process using *add_table_propagation_rules*.

6. Instantiate the table

7. Start the Apply process at the destination

8. Start the Capture process at the source

In the example, the following databases have been used:

- Source Database: DNYTST10

- Destination Database: DNYOIP20

The following SQL statements configure the replication flow:

```
sqlplus /nolog

prompt Connecting to Source DNYTST10 .....
connect strmadm/strmadm@dnytst10

prompt (1) Creating the Queue NY3_QUEUE at Source DNYTST10 .....
BEGIN
DBMS_STREAMS_ADM.SET_UP_QUEUE(
queue_table     => 'strmadm.ny3_queue_table',
queue_name      => 'strmadm.ny3_queue');
END;
/
PROMPT (2) Creating the Table Rules at Source DNYTST10
BEGIN
DBMS_STREAMS_ADM.ADD_TABLE_RULES(
table_name       => 'ny3.allinsured1',
streams_type     => 'capture',
streams_name     => 'ny3_capture',
queue_name       => 'ny3_queue',
include_dml      => true,
include_ddl      => true,
include_tagged_lcr => false,
source_database  => NULL,
inclusion_rule   => true);
END;
/
```

At the destination, the Apply Process will be created using the *add_subset_rules* procedure where the *dml_condition sales_id* > 100 has been set.

The following is a full example involving the Capture, the Propagation at the source database and a subset data apply at destination.

At destination database side, create the queue and Apply process:

```
connect strmadm/strmadm@dnyoip20

PROMPT (3) Creating Queue Table at Destination ..
BEGIN
DBMS_STREAMS_ADM.SET_UP_QUEUE(
queue_table     => 'strmadm.ln3_queue_table',
queue_name      => 'strmadm.ln3_queue');
END;
/
PROMPT (4) Add SUBSET Rules and create the APPLY Process
BEGIN
DBMS_STREAMS_ADM.ADD_SUBSET_RULES(
table_name           => 'ny3.allinsured1',
dml_condition        => ' SALES_ID > 100 ',
streams_type         => 'apply',
streams_name         => 'ln3_apply',
queue_name           => 'ln3_queue',
include_tagged_lcr   => false,
source_database      => 'DNYTST10.world' );
END;
/
```

At the Source database, create propagation rules and then instantiate the table manually:

```
Connect strmadm/strmadm@dnytst10

PROMPT (5) Create propagate rules for the table AllInsured1
BEGIN
DBMS_STREAMS_ADM.ADD_TABLE_PROPAGATION_RULES(
table_name                  => 'ny3.allinsured1',
streams_name                => 'ny3_propagate',
source_queue_name           => 'strmadm.ny3_queue',
destination_queue_name      => 'strmadm.ln3_queue@DNYOIP20.world',
include_dml             => true,
include_ddl             => true,
include_tagged_lcr      => false,
source_database         => 'DNYTST10.world',
inclusion_rule          => true);
END;
/
Prompt (6) Now instantiate SCN
set serveroutput on
DECLARE
  iscn  NUMBER;  -- Variable to hold instantiation SCN value
BEGIN
  iscn := DBMS_FLASHBACK.GET_SYSTEM_CHANGE_NUMBER();
    dbms_output.put_line ('Instantiation SCN : ' || iscn ) ;
  DBMS_APPLY_ADM.SET_TABLE_INSTANTIATION_SCN@DNYOIP20.world (
    source_object_name   => 'ny3.allinsured1',
    source_database_name => 'DNYTST10.world',
    instantiation_scn    => iscn
    );
END;
/
```

Start the Capture and Apply processes at the source and destination, respectively.

```
connect strmadm/strmadm@dnyoip20
PROMPT (7) Starting the Apply Prcoess at destination DNYOIP20
begin
dbms_apply_adm.start_apply (apply_name => 'ln3_apply' ) ;
end ;
/
connect strmadm/strmadm@dnytst10
PROMPT (8) Starting the Cature Prcoess at source`DNYTST10
begin
dbms_capture_adm.start_capture (capture_name => 'NY3_CAPTURE' ) ;
end ;
/
```

The next step is to load some rows into the table at the source database by running the *load_ny3_allinsured1.sql* script. A full listing of this script is provided in the code depot.

Prior to execution of the script, there are no rows either in the source or destination tables. The following SQL statement shows:

```
select  (select count(*) from ny3.allinsured1) at_source,
(select count(*) from ny3.allinsured1@dnyoip20) at_dest  from dual
/
gives output ..
```

```
AT_SOURCE    AT_DEST
----------   ----------
        0            0
```

Run the script to insert 60,000 records and commits for every 1000 records of insert. Therefore, there are 60 commits.

```
>@load_ny3_allinsured1.sql

Start Time =19-OCT-2004 22:30
Before Loading, the SCN : 13455161
Job ENDED.....Success
End Time =19-OCT-2004 22:30
Total Output Records = 60000
Total Commits        = 60
After Loading the SCN : 13466195

PL/SQL procedure successfully completed.
```

After applying all of the table inserts, query the *v$streams_apply_coordinator* view to see the transactions that have applied. The output shows that 60 transactions have been received and applied at destination database.

```
DNYOIP20 SQL>1
SELECT APPLY_NAME, TOTAL_RECEIVED, TOTAL_APPLIED, TOTAL_ERRORS,
(TOTAL_ASSIGNED - (TOTAL_ROLLBACKS +  TOTAL_APPLIED))  BEING_APPLIED,  TOTAL_IGNORED  FROM
V$STREAMS_APPLY_COORDINATOR
/
Output shows that the 60 transaction were applied:

                   Trans     Trans    Apply  Trans Being    Trans
Apply Process    Received   Applied  Errors     Applied    Ignored
-----------------  --------- -------- ------ ----------- ---------
LN3_APPLY             60        60       0           0          0
```

Even though 60,000 records have been loaded at the source destination and *v$streams_apply_coordinator* shows the number of transactions applied as 60, only 24,032 records have been added at the destination because of the DML condition that has been specified.

```
select  (select count(*) from ny3.allinsured1) at_source,
(select count(*) from ny3.allinsured1@dnyoip20) at_dest  from dual
/
gives output ..

AT_SOURCE    AT_DEST
----------   ----------
    60000       24032
```

To show all the relevant information in a single glance, the *show_apply_server.sql* script has been developed. A full listing of the script is in the code depot. It selects various columns from dictionary views such as:

- *v$streams_apply_server*

- *v$streams_apply_reader*

- *v$buffered_queues*

- *v$buffered_subscribers* and *dba_apply*

The output of the query is shown below:

```
DNYOIP20 SQL>@show_apply_server

FROM_STREAMS_APPLY_SERVER
-----------------------------------------------------------
SID (streams_aply_reader)     : 20
APPLY Name                    : LN3_APPLY
Current State                 : DEQUEUE MESSAGES
TOT MSGs Dequed               : 49120
Time last msg received        : 2004-10-19 22:46
Last DeQued MSG  NUM          : 13489274
CRT-Time at SRCDB of Last MSG :
SGA Used so far               : 584
Last browse SCN               : 0
Oldest SCN                    : 13489274

SID (streams_apply_server)    : 30
APPLY Name                    : LN3_APPLY
Current State                 : IDLE
Tot Trans Assgned             : 60
Tot Admin                     : 65
TOT MSGs APPLIED              : 49092
Time last msg applied         : 2004-10-19 22:46
Last APPLIED_MSG_NUM          : 13466194
CRTTime at SRC of LastAPPL_MSG: 2004-10-19 22:30
ELAPSED_DEQUEUE_TIME          : 364400
ELAPSED_APPLY_TIME            : 5191

Subscriber(Apply)             : LN3_APPLY
Que Schema.Name               : STRMADM.LN3_QUEUE
LAST_DEQUEUED_SEQ             : 49120
NUM_MSGS                      : 0
CURRENT_ENQ_SEQ               : 0
CNUM_MSGS                     : 49120
TOTAL_DEQUEUED_MSG            : 49120
```

Some interesting information can be verified from the *v$streams_capture* view. The following listing shows information such as full evaluations, time when most recent message captured, etc.:

```
SID of (v$streams_capture) ----> : 25
CAPTURE_NAME and State ..      : NY3_CAPTURE    CAPTURING CHANGES
TOTAL_MESSAGES_CREATED         : 458298
TOTAL_FULL_EVALUATIONS         : 60001
Tot Msg Enqueued from start    : 60210
Last Enqueued Messg #          : 13489274
Last redo SCN flushed to the log : 13496251
Most recently captured message : 13496246
Time when most recent msg captd : 23:28:30 10/19/2004
TOTAL_MSG_CAPT(from last start) : 338088
```

The next section provides details on the rules *add_subset_rules* procedure that was created for the Apply process presented previously which was created with *add_subset_rules*. The following SQL statement shows the rules and rule set name:

```
SELECT  RULE_NAME,  RULE_SET_NAME ,
  RULE_SET_TYPE,   STREAMS_RULE_TYPE,
  SCHEMA_NAME,   RULE_TYPE
```

```
      FROM DBA_STREAMS_RULES where streams_name = 'LN3_APPLY'
      /
                                            Streams
      Rule             Rule Set      Rule Set Rule     Schema       Rule
      Name             Name          Type     Level    Name         Type
      --------------   ------------  -------- -------  ----------   ----
      ALLINSURED168    RULESET$_69   POSITIVE TABLE    NY3          DML
      ALLINSURED166    RULESET$_69   POSITIVE TABLE    NY3          DML
      ALLINSURED167    RULESET$_69   POSITIVE TABLE    NY3          DML
```

From the results, it is apparent that there are three DML rules generated to
control, update, delete and insert. As an example, the following SQL gives
the rule condition for the ALLINSURED168 rule:

```
SELECT
dbms_lob.substr(rule_condition,dbms_lob.getlength(rule_condition),1) rule_condition
FROM dba_rules where rule_name = 'ALLINSURED168'
/

RULE_CONDITION
--------------------------------------------------
:dml.get_object_owner ()='NY3' AND :dml.get_object_
name()='ALLINSURED1' AND :dml.is_null_tag()='Y' AN
D :dml.get_source_database_name ()='DNYTST10.WORLD'
 AND :dml.get_command_type () IN ('UPDATE','DELETE'
) AND (:dml.get_value('OLD','"SALES_ID"') IS NOT N
ULL) AND (:dml.get_value('OLD','"SALES_ID"').Acces
sNumber()>100) AND (:dml.get_command_type ()='DELET
E' OR ((:dml.get_value('NEW','"SALES_ID"') IS NOT
NULL) AND NOT EXISTS (SELECT 1 FROM SYS.DUAL WHERE
 (:dml.get_value('NEW','"SALES_ID"').AccessNumber(
)>100))))
```

The following section presents information on another method that can be
used to configure the Capture process.

Using *add_schema_rules* to Create an Apply process

In this method, Apply rules are created at the schema level and the Apply
process, which acts on all of the objects of the schema, is created. The Apply
process applies captured LCRs to the destination database.

For example, to create positive rule set and associate with Apply process for
the schema NY2, use the following SQL statement. It creates a positive rule
set and associates it with the Apply process.

```
BEGIN
DBMS_STREAMS_ADM.ADD_SCHEMA_RULES(
schema_name       => 'ny2',
streams_type      => 'apply',
streams_name      => 'ln2_apply',
queue_name        => 'ln2_queue',
include_dml       => true,
include_ddl       => true,
include_tagged_lcr        => false,
source_database           => 'dnytst10.world',
```

```
inclusion_rule          => true);
END;
/
```

The above example creates the following rules and rule sets:

```
SELECT STREAMS_TYPE,
 RULE_NAME, RULE_SET_NAME ,
 RULE_SET_TYPE, STREAMS_RULE_TYPE,
 SCHEMA_NAME, RULE_TYPE
 FROM DBA_STREAMS_RULES where STREAMS_NAME='LN2_APPLY'
/
```

```
Streams Rule    Rule Set    Rule Set   Rule     Schema    Rule
Type    Name    Name        Type       Level    Name      Type
------- -----   --------    --------   -------   -------   ---
APPLY   NY270   RULESET$_72  POSITIVE   SCHEMA   NY2       DML
APPLY   NY271   RULESET$_72  POSITIVE   SCHEMA   NY2       DDL
```

The following SQL statements show the rule conditions for the above mentioned rules:

```
SELECT  dbms_lob.substr(rule_condition,dbms_lob.getlength(rule_condition),1)  rule_condition
FROM dba_rules where rule_name = 'NY270'
/
```

```
RULE_CONDITION
------------------------------------------------
((:dml.get_object_owner () = 'NY2') and :dml.is_nul
l_tag() = 'Y' and :dml.get_source_database_name ()
= 'DNYTST10.WORLD' )
```

```
SELECT
dbms_lob.substr(rule_condition,dbms_lob.getlength(rule_condition),1) rule_condition
FROM dba_rules where rule_name = 'NY271'
/
```

```
RULE_CONDITION
------------------------------------------------
((:ddl.get_object_owner () = 'NY2' or :ddl.get_base
_table_owner() = 'NY2') and :ddl.is_null_tag() = '
Y' and :ddl.get_source_database_name () = 'DNYTST10.WORLD' )
```

Next, the *create_apply* procedure that can be used to configure the Capture process will be introduced.

Using the *create_apply* Procedure to Create an Apply Process

This section will present another method by which an Apply process can be created. It allows the association of customized rules and rule sets that have already been created. For this, the *create_apply* procedure of the *dbms_apply_adm* package is used. When custom rule sets and rule conditions are designed, this method becomes the natural choice.

This method provides a flexible way to create a basic Apply process and then extend it to associate various apply handlers.

Figure 5.5 shows the parameters or arguments that can be passed on to execute the *create_apply* procedure.

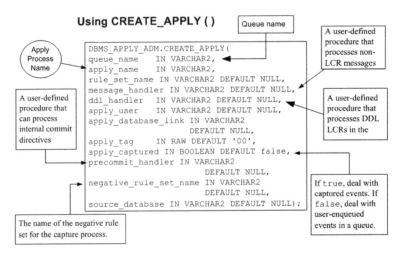

Figure 5.5 *create_apply procedure parameters*

The parameters from the procedure are explained as follows:

- *rule_set_name* This is the name of the positive rule set for the Apply process. The positive rule set contains the rules that instruct the Apply process to apply events. The rule set should exist.

- *message_handler* This is a user-defined procedure that processes non-LCR messages in the queue for the Apply process. An existing procedure must be specified.

- *ddl_handler* This is a user-defined procedure that processes DDL LCRs in the queue for the Apply process. An existing procedure must be specified.

- *apply_user:* This is the user who applies all DML and DDL changes that satisfy the Apply process rule sets and who runs user-defined Apply handlers.

- *apply_tag:* This is a binary tag that is added to redo entries generated by the specified Apply process.

Oracle Streams

- *include_dml:* If true, this parameter creates a DML rule for DML changes. If false, it does not create a DML rule. NULL is not permitted.

- *include_ddl:* If true, this parameter creates a DDL rule for DDL changes. If false, it does not create a DDL rule. NULL is not permitted.

- *apply_captured:* If true, the Apply process applies only the events in a queue that were captured by a Streams Capture process. If false, the Apply process applies only the user-enqueued events in a queue.

- *precommit_handler:* This is a user-defined procedure that can receive internal commit directives in the queue for the Apply process before they are processed by the Apply process.

- *negative_rule_set_name:* This is the name of the negative rule set for the Apply process. The negative rule set contains the rules that instruct the Apply process to discard events.

In this method, rules and rule sets are created prior to creating the Apply process. Rules are added to the rule set. Then, the rules are associated with the Steams client Apply process.

In the following example, the Capture process will be created using the *add_table_rules* procedure and the propagate process using the *add_table_propagation_rules* procedure. In case of the Apply Process, the *create_apply* procedure will be used.

Before the Apply process is created, the rule set will be created and a rule added to the rule set. It will have these three steps:

- For creating the rule, the *create_rule* procedure will be used.

- For creating the rule set, the *create_rule_set* procedure of *dbms_rule_adm* package can be used.

- The rule set will be specified as a parameter to the *create_apply* procedure.

Streams_config.sql, which is available in the code depot, lists SQL statements that display details of the configuration of the Streams clients:

The next step is to load records at the source database table by using the script *load_ny4_allinsured1.sql* which can be found in the code depot:

```
> load_ny4_allinsured1.sql

Start Time =20-OCT-004 12:29
Before Loading, the SCN : 13573483
Job ENDED.....Success
```

```
End Time =20-OCT-004 12:30
Total Output Records = 7000
Total Commits      = 7
After Loading the SCN : 13574547

PL/SQL procedure successfully completed.
```

At this point, the same number of records exists at both the source and the destination:

```
  1  select  (select count(*) from ny4.allinsured1) at_source,
  2* (select count(*) from ny4.allinsured1@dnyoip20) at_dest  from dual
DNYTST10 SQL>/

AT_SOURCE    AT_DEST
---------- ----------
     7000       7000
```

The above example showed the use of the *create_apply* procedure where the pre-created rules could be associated.

The next section will present information on topics related to the administration of the Apply process. It will focus on how to set up the extra attributes and how to handle the alteration of parameters, etc.

Managing the Apply Process

In this section, information will be presented on how to manage the Apply process.

Using the *dbms_apply_adm* Package

Oracle provides a package called *dbms_apply_adm* which has many useful procedures that help manage the Apply process. The list of procedures includes the following:

- *alter_apply* procedure alters an Apply process and sets certain parameters.

- *create_apply* procedure creates an Apply process

- *delete_all_errors* procedure deletes all the error transactions for the specified Apply process

- *delete_error* procedure deletes the specified error transaction

- *drop_apply* procedure drops an Apply process

- *execute_all_errors* procedure re-executes the error transactions for the specified Apply process

- *execute_error* procedure re-executes the specified error transaction

- *get_error_message* returns the message payload from the error queue for the specified message number and transaction identifier

- *set_dml_handler* procedure alters operation options for a specified object with a specified Apply process

- *set_enqueue_destination* sets the queue where an event that satisfies the specified rule is enqueued automatically by an Apply process

- *set_execute* procedure specifies whether an event that satisfies the specified rule is executed by an Apply process

- *set_parameter* procedure sets an Apply parameter to the specified value.

- *set_schema_instantiation_scn* records the specified instantiation SCN for the specified schema in the specified source database and, optionally, for the tables owned by the schema at the source database

- *set_table_instantiation_scn* records the specified instantiation SCN for the specified table in the specified source database

- *set_update_conflict_handler* adds, updates, or drops an update conflict handler for the specified object

- *start_apply* procedure instructs the Apply process to start applying events

- *stop_apply* procedure stops the Apply process from applying any events and rolls back any unfinished transactions being applied

Next, some of these procedures will be examined in more detail.

Setting the Apply Parameters

Once the Apply process is created, certain attributes of the process can be altered as needed. By altering the attributes suitably, the DBA will be allowed to change the behavior of the Apply process so as to suit it to the data needs. Many times, the default attributes for the Apply process may not suffice. This can be achieved by using the *set_parameter* procedure in the *dbms_apply_adm* package. The Apply process parameters control the way an Apply process operates. The following is a description of the parameters:

- *commit_serialization:* Specifies the order in which applied transactions are committed. If set to FULL, the Apply process commits applied transactions in the order in which they were committed at the source database. This is a desirable situation since the goal is to preserve the commit order and keep the dependencies properly maintained. If set to NONE, the Apply process may commit transactions in any order. Performance is good if the specified value is NONE.

- *disable_on_error:* If Y, the Apply process is disabled on the first unresolved error, even if the error is not fatal. If N, the Apply process continues regardless of unresolved errors. This is an important parameter. In a heavily active replication configuration, the DBA may want to consider keeping the value set to N so that the main Apply process continues, leaving the errors in the queue. Errors can be handled by the DBA in due course.

- *disable_on_limit:* If Y, the Apply process is disabled if the Apply process terminates because it reached a value specified by the *time_limit* parameter or *transaction_limit* parameter. If N, the Apply process is restarted immediately after stopping because it reached a limit.

- *maximum_scn:* The Apply process is disabled before applying a transaction with a commit SCN greater than or equal to the value specified.

- *parallelism:* This parameter specifies the number of transactions that may be concurrently applied. Altering the *parallelism* parameter automatically stops and restarts the Apply process when the currently executing transactions are applied. This may take some time depending on the size of the transactions. Setting the *parallelism* parameter to a number higher than the number of available parallel execution servers may disable the Apply process. Therefore after altering *parallelism*, always ensure that the Apply process is in an enabled state. If the Apply process parameter of *parallelism* is set to a value greater than 1, a conditional supplemental log group must be specified at the source database for all of the unique and foreign key columns in the tables for which an Apply process applies changes.

- *startup_seconds:* The maximum number of seconds to wait for another instantiation of the same Apply process to finish.

- *time_limit:* The Apply process stops as soon as possible after the specified number of seconds since it started.

- *trace_level:* Set this parameter only under the guidance of Oracle Support Services.

- *transaction_limit:* The Apply process stops after applying the specified number of transactions.

- *write_alert_log:* If Y, the Apply process writes a message to the alert log on exit.

The following is the syntax of the procedure that can be used to set parameters:

```
DBMS_APPLY_ADM.SET_PARAMETER(
 apply_name    IN VARCHAR2,
 parameter     IN VARCHAR2,
 value                 IN VARCHAR2);
```

For example, the following procedure sets the *parallelism* parameter for a capture process named NY1_CAPTURE to 3.

```
BEGIN
 DBMS_APPLY_ADM.SET_PARAMETER(
  apply_name => 'ln4_apply',
  parameter => 'parallelism',
  value => 3 );
END;
/
```

NOTE: The parameter value is always entered as a VARCHAR2 even if the parameter value is a number.

How can the DBA see what parameters are currently set for an Apply process? The *dba_apply_parameters* view can be used to list the parameters set for a particular Apply process.

The following SQL statement displays the current setting for each Apply process parameter:

```
col apply_name format a12
col PARAMETER format a25
col value format a20

SELECT APPLY_NAME,PARAMETER,VALUE, SET_BY_USER
FROM DBA_APPLY_PARAMETERS;
/

APPLY_NAME   PARAMETER                VALUE                SET
-----------  -----------------------  -------------------- ---
LN4_APPLY    PARALLELISM              3                    YES
LN4_APPLY    STARTUP_SECONDS          0                    NO
LN4_APPLY    TRACE_LEVEL              0                    NO
LN4_APPLY    TIME_LIMIT               INFINITE             NO
LN4_APPLY    TRANSACTION_LIMIT        INFINITE             NO
LN4_APPLY    MAXIMUM_SCN              INFINITE             NO
LN4_APPLY    WRITE_ALERT_LOG          Y                    NO
LN4_APPLY    DISABLE_ON_LIMIT         N                    NO
LN4_APPLY    DISABLE_ON_ERROR         Y                    NO
LN4_APPLY    COMMIT_SERIALIZATION     FULL                 NO

10 rows selected.
```

The following section presents information on another useful method that deals with apply handlers.

apply_alter Procedure

This is a procedure that is useful for setting or unsetting the Apply handlers. It can set or unset the positive or negative rule sets. When the DBA wishes to change or assign a new rule set, this procedure will be useful. Figure 5.6 shows the arguments.

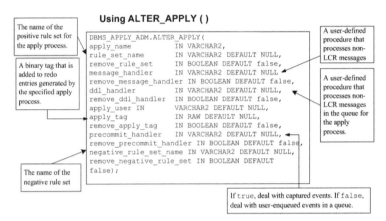

Figure 5.6 *alter_apply procedure parameters*

The parameters in the procedure are explained as below:

- *rule_set_name:* This is the name of the positive rule set for the Apply process. The positive rule set contains the rules that instruct the Apply process to apply events. When *remove_rule_set* is set to TRUE, it removes the positive rule set for the specified Apply process.

- *message_handler:* This is a user-defined procedure that processes non-LCR messages in the queue for the Apply process. When *remove_message_handler* is set to TRUE, it removes the *message_handler*

- *ddl_handler:* This is a user-defined procedure that processes DDL LCRs in the queue for the Apply process. When *remove_ddl_handler* is set to TRUE, it removes *ddl_handler.*

- *apply_user:* This is the user who applies all DML and DDL changes that satisfy the Apply process rule sets and who runs user-defined apply handlers.

- *apply_tag:* This is a binary tag that is added to redo entries generated by the specified Apply process. When *remove_apply_tag* is set to TRUE, it removes the *apply_tag.*

- *precommit_handler:* This is a user-defined procedure that can receive internal commit directives in the queue for the Apply process before they are processed by the Apply process. When *remove_precommit_handler* is set to TRUE, it removes the *precommit_handler.*

- *negative_rule_set_name:* This is the name of the negative rule set for the Apply process. The negative rule set contains the rules that instruct the Apply process to discard events.

Handlers are basically extensions of the apply process. By setting and using the code in the handlers, many apply issues will be able to be resolved.

Next, details will be presented on how the *alter_apply* procedure can be used to assign or unassign the handlers to an Apply process.

For example, the following SQL statement sets the message handler for an Apply process named LN4_APPLY to the *msg_handler* procedure:

```
BEGIN
DBMS_APPLY_ADM.ALTER_APPLY(
apply_name              => 'LN4_APPLY',
message_handler         => 'strmadm.msg_handler');
END;
/
```

If the goal is to remove the message handler, the *remove_message_handler* parameter will be used. An example is shown below:

```
BEGIN
DBMS_APPLY_ADM.ALTER_APPLY(
apply_name              => 'LN4_APPLY',
remove_message_handler  => TRUE );
END;
/
```

It is important to note that an Apply process is stopped and restarted automatically when the value of one or more of the following *alter_apply* procedure parameters is changed:

- *message_handler*

- *ddl_handler*

- *apply_user*

- *apply_tag*

- *precommit_handler*

To view the handlers, the *dba_apply* view can be queried:

```
Select apply_name, ddl_handler, precommit_handler,
message_handler from dba_apply
/
```

To view the DML handlers, which can number more than one for an Apply process, the *dba_apply_dml_handlers* view can be queried:

```
Select apply_name, user_procedure, operation_name,
Object_owner, object_name, error_handler
from dba_apply_dml_handlers
/
```

The next section introduces some of the procedures that help to handle the errors.

delete_error Procedure

The *delete_error* procedure deletes the specified error transaction. When the error transaction has been resolved by other means, the DBA may not be interested in using the error transaction. In this case, the error transaction can be dropped from the error queue. The following SQL block shows the usage of the *delete_error* proedure:

```
Syntax:
EXEC DBMS_APPLY_ADM.DELETE_ERROR( local_transaction_id IN VARCHAR2);
```

local_transaction_id is the identification number of the error transaction to delete.

delete_all_errors Procedure

The *delete_all_errors* procedure deletes all the error transactions for a given Apply process. When the error condition has been resolved by other means, the errors will have to be cleared from the queue. When there are a large number of error transactions to delete, this procedure will be useful. For example, the following SQL drops all the error transactions from the LN4_APPLY Apply process:

```
BEGIN
DBMS_APPLY_ADM.DELETE_ALL_ERRORs(
Apply_name => 'LN4_APPLY');
END;
/
```

It is important to note that if the *apply_name* is specified as NULL, error transactions of all the Apply Processes are dropped. Beware of this. Sometimes, this may not the intention. When that happens, the record of all errors is lost.

drop_apply Procedure

When a particular apply process is no longer needed, the *drop_apply* procedure helps to drop it.

```
Here is the syntax:
DBMS_APPLY_ADM.DROP_APPLY(
apply_name                  IN VARCHAR2,
drop_unused_rule_sets    IN BOOLEAN DEFAULT false);
```

When *drop_unused_rule_sets* is set to TRUE, it drops any rule sets; positive and negative, used by the specified Apply process provided these rule sets are not used by any other Streams client. Other Streams clients include Capture Processes, Propagations, Apply processes, and messaging clients. If this procedure drops a rule set, the procedure also drops any rules in the rule set that are not in another rule set. Any particular rule can be in multiple rules sets.

For example, to drop the Apply process named LN1_APPLY and remove all the rule sets and rules, the following statement can be used:

```
PROMPT dropping the Apply Process
BEGIN
DBMS_APPLY_ADM.DROP_APPLY(
 APPLY_NAME => 'LN_APPLY',
 drop_unused_rule_sets => true);
END;
/
```

The following section outlines how error transactions can be re-executed.

execute_all_errors Procedure

The *execute_all_errors* procedure re-executes the error transactions for the specified Apply process. The transactions are re-executed in commit SCN order. Error re-execution stops if an error is raised. In many situations, when the error condition arises, administrators analyze and rectify the problem. For example, rows are being inserted with a dependent foreign key. Since the row in the parent table is missing, there will be an integrity violation which results in errors. Once the row is made good in the parent table, the errors can be re-executed to insert the failed rows. The following is the syntax for the *execute_all_errors* procedure:

```
Syntax:
DBMS_APPLY_ADM.EXECUTE_ALL_ERRORS(
apply_name                IN VARCHAR2 DEFAULT NULL,
execute_as_user           IN BOOLEAN DEFAULT false);
```

When the *execute_as_user* parameter is set to TRUE, the transactions are executed in the security context of the current user.

The procedure presented in the next section is almost the same as the one presented above, but it acts on a specific error transaction.

execute_error Procedure

The *execute_error* procedure re-executes the specified error transaction.

```
Syntax:
DBMS_APPLY_ADM.EXECUTE_ERROR(
 local_transaction_id     IN VARCHAR2,
 execute_as_user                  IN BOOLEAN DEFAULT false);
```

The *local_transaction_id* is the identification number of the error transaction to execute. If the specified transaction does not exist in the error queue, an error is raised. When the parameter *execute_as_user* is set to TRUE, the procedure re-executes the transaction in the security context of the current user.

get_error_message Function

The *get_error_message* procedure is very useful. This function returns the message payload from the error queue for the specified message number and transaction identifier. The message is an event which may be a LCR or a non-LCR event. With the help of this procedure, the DBA will be able to find out the inner details such as the source database name, old and new values, etc. Once the details of the payload have been read, the reason for failure can be established.

```
Syntax:
DBMS_APPLY_ADM.GET_ERROR_MESSAGE(
message_number            IN NUMBER,
local_transaction_id      IN VARCHAR2,
destination_queue_name    OUT VARCHAR2,
execute                          OUT BOOLEAN)
RETURN SYS.AnyData;
```

message_number is the identification number of the message of the Apply process. This number identifies the position of the message in the transaction. This number can be obtained from the *dba_apply_error* data dictionary view. *local_transaction_id* is the identifier of the error transaction.

set_dml_handler Procedure

The *set_dml_handler* procedure sets a user procedure as a DML handler for a specified operation on a specified object. The user procedure, acting as the handler, actually alters the apply behavior for the specified operation on the specified object. Whenever the intention is to perform extra action on the transaction, the handlers are used.

```
Syntax
DBMS_APPLY_ADM.SET_DML_HANDLER(
 object_name            IN VARCHAR2,
 object_type            IN VARCHAR2,
 operation_name              IN VARCHAR2,
 error_handler          IN BOOLEAN DEFAULT false,
 user_procedure             IN VARCHAR2,
 apply_database_link    IN VARCHAR2 DEFAULT NULL,
 apply_name             IN VARCHAR2 DEFAULT NULL);
```

Object Name is the table where the DML is intended. *operation_name* values can be INSERT, UPDATE, DELETE and LOB_UPDATE.

When *error_handler* is set to TRUE, the specified user procedure is run when a row LCR involving the specified operation on the specified object raises an Apply process error.

user_procedure specifies the user-defined procedure that is invoked during the apply for the specified operation on the specified object.

set_enqueue_destination Procedure

The *set_enqueue_destination* procedure sets the queue such that an event that satisfies the specified rule is enqueued automatically by an Apply process.

```
Syntax
DBMS_APPLY_ADM.SET_ENQUEUE_DESTINATION(
rule_name        IN VARCHAR2,
destination_queue_name IN VARCHAR2);
```

set_execute Procedure

The *set_execute* procedure specifies whether an event that satisfies the specified rule is executed by an Apply process.

```
Syntax :
DBMS_APPLY_ADM.SET_EXECUTE(
 rule_name IN VARCHAR2,
 execute IN BOOLEAN);
```

set_update_conflict_handler Procedure

The *set_update_conflict_handler* procedure adds, modifies, or removes an update conflict handler for the specified object.

```
Syntax
DBMS_APPLY_ADM.SET_UPDATE_CONFLICT_HANDLER(
 object_name            IN VARCHAR2,
 method_name            IN VARCHAR2,
 resolution_column           IN VARCHAR2,
 column_list           IN DBMS_UTILITY.NAME_ARRAY,
 apply_database_link    IN VARCHAR2 DEFAULT NULL);
```

More details about this procedure are included in subsequent chapters. This procedure is the main function used to manage the update conflict handler. This handler helps to resolve the conflicts in the multi-way replication configuration.

set_key_columns Procedure

The *set_key_columns* procedure records the set of columns to be used as the substitute primary key for apply purposes and removes existing substitute primary key columns for the specified object if they exist. Unlike true primary keys, these columns may contain NULL values. This is one of the methods that is used to resolve the conflicts in a multi-way replication configuration

```
Syntax
DBMS_APPLY_ADM.SET_KEY_COLUMNS(
 object_name IN VARCHAR2,
 { column_list IN VARCHAR2, |
 column_table IN DBMS_UTILITY.NAME_ARRAY, }
 apply_database_link IN VARCHAR2 DEFAULT NULL);
```

start_apply Procedure

The *start_apply* procedure instructs the Apply process to start applying events. When the Apply process is stopped for any maintenance or disabled for some error situation, the Apply process will have to be started manually. The

---

start_apply procedure is used to achieve this result. The syntax for the procedure is shown below:

```
Syntax :
DBMS_APPLY_ADM.START_APPLY(
apply_name IN VARCHAR2);
```

For example, to start the Apply process named LN4_APPLY, the following SQL block can be used:

```
PROMPT Starting the Apply Process
begin
dbms_apply_adm.start_apply (apply_name => 'LN4_APPLY' ) ;
end ;
/
```

The next section will present information on how to stop the Apply process.

stop_apply Procedure

The *stop_apply* procedure stops the Apply process from applying events and rolls back any unfinished transactions being applied.

```
Syntax :
DBMS_APPLY_ADM.STOP_APPLY(
 apply_name IN VARCHAR2,
 force IN BOOLEAN DEFAULT false);
```

If the *force* parameter is set to TRUE, it stops the Apply process as soon as possible. If it is set to FALSE, it stops the Apply process after ensuring that there are no gaps in the set of applied transactions. The behavior of the Apply process depends on the setting specified for the *force* parameter and the setting specified for the *commit_serialization* Apply process parameter.

For example, to start the Apply process named LN4_APPLY, use the following SQL block:

```
PROMPT Starting the Apply Process
begin
dbms_apply_adm.stop_apply (apply_name => 'LN4_APPLY' ) ;
end ;
/
```

Conclusion

In this chapter, greater focus has been placed on how to create and manage the Apply process.

The main points of this chapter include:

- Apply process architecture has three main components. They are the reader server, coordinator server and apply server.

- Apply processes can be created by several different procedures. Apply processes can also be extended by setting up Apply handlers. Examples were included for how to use the *add_table_rules* procedure and the *add_subset_rules* procedure to create the Apply process.

- Oracle provides many useful procedures that can be used to alter the attributes of the Apply process and its behavior.

- To manage the Apply process, to stop and to start, and to handle the error transaction, there are many procedures. Information on these procedures has been included.

The next chapter will focus on information about setting up Apply handlers. Examples, as well as details on how apply handlers help control the replication process, are included.

Apply Handlers

Some administrators handle well

In this chapter, the extensions to the Apply process will be presented through the creation of suitable user-defined procedures called the Apply handlers. In earlier chapters, the fact that the Apply process is an optional Oracle background process was presented. The Apply process dequeues logical change records and user messages from a specific queue.

The following sections also cover some sample procedures that are used as the handler routines.

Apply Process and Apply Handlers

The Apply process dequeues the LCRs and user messages from a queue. When the Apply process dequeues, the events may be applied to database objects directly as transactions or may be passed on as the parameters to user-defined procedures. These procedures are the user-defined Apply handlers. The database changes may include the DML or DDL changes.

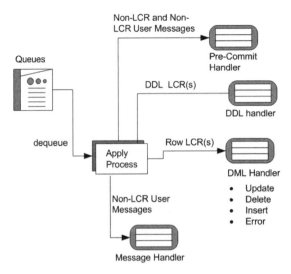

Figure 6.1 *Apply Process and Apply Handlers*

As shown in Figure 6.1, Apply handlers typically include a DML handler, a DDL handler, a Message handler and Pre-Commit handlers. The concept of handlers has been introduced in previous chapters.

Table 6.1 shows the summary of event processing options.

Apply Handler	Event Type	Default Apply Behavior	Scope
DML or Error Handler	Row LCR	Execute DML	One operation on one table
DDL Handler	DDL LCR	Execute DDL	Entire Apply process
Precommit Handler	Commit Directive (Row LCR and Non-LCR User message)	Commit transactions	Entire Apply process
Message Handler	Non-LCR User message	Creates error, if no handler is specified	Entire Apply process

Table 6.1 *Summary of event processing options*

DML and the Error Handler process row LCRs and execute the DML transactions. DML handlers act on a table and are specific to an SQL operation. If the SQL operation such as Delete, Update or Insert is not specified, the handler is applicable to all the operations on the table.

The DDL handler processes the DDL LCR events and executes the DDL operation. The scope of the DDL handler is for a given Apply process. Thus, there is only one DDL handler for an Apply process.

In case of a pre-commit handler, the commit directive for transactions which include the Row LCR(s) or non-LCR user messages is processed. The scope of the pre-commit handler is the entire Apply process.

The Message handler processes the non-LCR user messages and operates at the Apply process level.

Considerations for Apply Handlers

The following guidelines are applicable to the Apply handlers:

- DML handlers, DDL Handlers, and message handlers can execute an LCR by calling the LCR's EXECUTE member procedure.

- All applied DDL LCRs commit automatically. Therefore, if a DDL handler calls the EXECUTE member procedure of a DDL LCR, a commit is performed automatically.

- When needed, an Apply handler can set a Streams session tag.

- An Apply handler may call a Java stored procedure that is published or wrapped in a PL/SQL procedure.

- Ensure that the procedure that is specified as the handler is available and is valid. If an Apply process tries to invoke an Apply handler that does not exist or is invalid, the Apply process aborts.

- If an Apply handler invokes a procedure or function in an Oracle-supplied package, the user running the Apply handler must have direct EXECUTE privilege on the package. It is not sufficient to grant this privilege through a role.

In the next sections, more details about the handlers will be presented along with suitable examples.

DML Handlers

A user procedure that processes row LCRs resulting from DML statements is called a DML handler. An Apply process can have many DML handlers. Why

---

are these important? It is because these handlers provide a mechanism to use the LCR information and execute custom operations on the database tables. There are many ways in which LCR information can be utilized. One instance would be to make changes to the payload and insert them at the destination or develop some kind of audit trail.

The Error handler is also a DML handler. In case of the Error handler, the parameter *error_handler* is set to TRUE. In this case, the specified user procedure is run when a row LCR involving the specified operation on the specified object creates an Apply process error. The user procedure may try to resolve possible error conditions, or it may simply notify administrators of the error or it may log the error.

For each table associated with an Apply process, a separate DML handler can be set to process each of the following types of operations in row LCRs:

- INSERT
- UPDATE
- DELETE
- LOB_UPDATE

For example, the NY4.ALLINSURED1 table may have one DML handler to process INSERT operations, a different DML handler to process UPDATE operations, and yet another for DELETE operations.

Figure 6.2 shows the signature of the procedure used to set the DML handler.

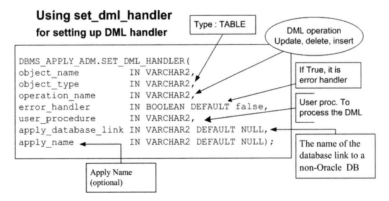

Figure 6.2 *Package Procedure to set the DML Handler*

The next section will present information on the DML handlers.

Update DML handler

The update handler is used to track the update transactions and to extend the Apply process functionality. It acts on the update transactions. In the following example, selected records will be updated on the source database table, and the propagation to destination database table will be shown. The Apply process that dequeues the transaction is set up with an Update DML Handler.

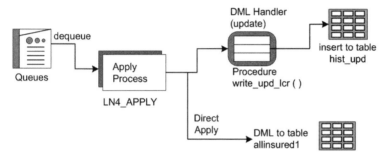

Figure 6.3 *Setting Up of Update Apply Handler*

Figure 6.3 shows all of the components involved in setting up a typical DML Update handler.

In the presentation of details of the DML handler setup methodology, the following assumptions should be made:

```
Source Table          : NY4.allinsured1 at DNYTST10 database
Source DB Capture Proc : NY4_CAPTURE
Destination Table      : NY4.allinsured1 at DNYOIP20 database
Source DB Apply Proc   : N4_APPLY
```

In order to show the use of the Update DML handler, a stored procedure called NY4.WRITE_UPD_LCRS has been created and the Update DML handler has been set up using this procedure. A new table named NY4.HIST_UPD has been created at DNYOIP20 where the DML handler writes the details about the update operation.

The following SQL statements show the creation and setting up of the Update DML handler:

```
-- Create a Table to record Update DML history (at DNYOIP20)
CREATE TABLE NY4.hist_upd (
  timestamp            DATE,
  source_database_name VARCHAR2(40),
  command_type         VARCHAR2(30),
  object_owner         VARCHAR2(32),
  object_name          VARCHAR2(32),
  tag                  RAW(10),
  transaction_id       VARCHAR2(10),
  scn                  NUMBER,
  commit_scn           NUMBER,
  username             varchar2(30),
  tx_name              varchar2(20),
  source_session#      number(6),
  old_values           SYS.LCR$_ROW_LIST,
  new_values           SYS.LCR$_ROW_LIST)
NESTED TABLE old_values STORE AS hist_upd_old_ntable
NESTED TABLE new_values STORE AS hist_upd_new_ntable
/
-- Now create a stored procedure (at DNYOIP20)
CREATE OR REPLACE PROCEDURE ny4.write_upd_lcrs(
in_any IN SYS.ANYDATA)
IS
 lcr SYS.LCR$_ROW_RECORD;
 rc PLS_INTEGER;
 blk_user        varchar2(30) ;
 blk_txname      varchar2(20) ;
 blk_sid         number(6) ;
 ext_attr        SYS.AnyData;
 res             NUMBER;
BEGIN
-- First Access the LCR ; Object is placed in LCR variable
rc       := in_any.GETOBJECT(lcr);
-- from LCR variable, Anydata is placed in ext_attr variablee
ext_attr := lcr.GET_EXTRA_ATTRIBUTE('username') ;
res      := ext_attr.GETVARCHAR2(blk_user);
ext_attr := lcr.GET_EXTRA_ATTRIBUTE('tx_name') ;
res      := ext_attr.GETVARCHAR2(blk_txname);
ext_attr := lcr.GET_EXTRA_ATTRIBUTE('session#') ;
res      := ext_attr.GETNUMBER(blk_sid);
-- Insert info about the LCR into the hist_upd table
INSERT INTO ny4.hist_upd VALUES
 (SYSDATE,
 lcr.GET_SOURCE_DATABASE_NAME(),
 lcr.GET_COMMAND_TYPE(),
 lcr.GET_OBJECT_OWNER(),
 lcr.GET_OBJECT_NAME(),
 lcr.GET_TAG(),
 lcr.GET_TRANSACTION_ID(),
 lcr.GET_SCN(),
 lcr.GET_COMMIT_SCN,
 blk_user,
 blk_txname,
 blk_sid,
 lcr.GET_VALUES('old'),
 lcr.GET_VALUES('new', 'n') );
-- Apply row LCR
lcr.EXECUTE(true);
END;
/
```

From the above procedure, it is apparent that the old and new values of updated columns besides the other details can be saved into the table, NY4.HIST_UPD. Every update transaction is recorded into the table. It also records some additional attributes such as username, transaction name, etc.

The next step is to set up the Update DML Handler using the following statement:

```
-- To set up the DML Handler
BEGIN
DBMS_APPLY_ADM.SET_DML_HANDLER(
 object_name        => 'ny4.allinsured1',
 object_type        => 'TABLE',
 operation_name     => 'UPDATE',
 error_handler      => false,
 user_procedure     => 'ny4.write_upd_lcrs',
 apply_database_link => NULL,
 apply_name => NULL);
END;
/
```

To verify the Apply handlers, execute the SQL below:

```
SELECT OBJECT_OWNER, OBJECT_NAME, OPERATION_NAME, USER_PROCEDURE
 FROM DBA_APPLY_DML_HANDLERS ORDER BY OBJECT_OWNER, OBJECT_NAME
/

Table
Owner     Table Name     Operation    Handler Procedure
-------   ----------     ---------    --------------------
NY4       ALLINSURED1    UPDATE       "NY4"."WRITE_UPD_LCRS"
NY4       ALLINSURED1    DELETE       "NY4"."WRITE_DEL_LCRS"
```

To unset the DML handler, set the *user_procedure* parameter to NULL. For example, use the following SQL Statement to unset the apply handler:

```
BEGIN
DBMS_APPLY_ADM.SET_DML_HANDLER(
 object_name        => 'ny4.allinsured1',
 object_type        => 'TABLE',
 operation_name     => 'UPDATE',
 error_handler      => false,
 user_procedure     => NULL ,
 apply_database_link => NULL,
 apply_name => NULL);
END;
/
```

At the source database, some extra attributes have been included in the Capture process called NY4_CAPTURE. Use the following SQL statements:

```
-- AT CAPTURE side, include some Extra Attributes

BEGIN
DBMS_CAPTURE_ADM.INCLUDE_EXTRA_ATTRIBUTE(
capture_name => 'NY4_CAPTURE', attribute_name => 'tx_name',
include => true);
END;
/
BEGIN
DBMS_CAPTURE_ADM.INCLUDE_EXTRA_ATTRIBUTE(
capture_name => 'NY4_CAPTURE', attribute_name => 'username',
include => true);
END;
/
BEGIN
DBMS_CAPTURE_ADM.INCLUDE_EXTRA_ATTRIBUTE(
```

```
capture_name => 'NY4_CAPTURE', attribute_name => 'session#',
include => true);
END;
/
```

To verify the extra attributes included, the following SQL can be used:

```
DNYTST10 SQL>@show_capture_extra_attrib

Capture Process      Attribute Name  Include Attrib in LCRs
-------------------  --------------  ----------------------
NY4_CAPTURE          THREAD#         NO
NY4_CAPTURE          ROW_ID          NO
NY4_CAPTURE          SESSION#        YES
NY4_CAPTURE          SERIAL#         NO
NY4_CAPTURE          USERNAME        YES
NY4_CAPTURE          TX_NAME         YES

6 rows selected.
```

Next, the transaction name at source database is set before an update operation is executed. In the following example, the transaction name is set to *my_txn10*:

```
DNYTST10 SQL>SET TRANSACTION NAME 'my_txn10' ;

Transaction set.
```

The next step is to run the following SQL statements to execute Update DML at the source database table:

```
-- connect strmadm/strmadm@dnytst10
DNYTST10 SQL>update ny4.allinsured1 set premium = 10
where pol_no = 15000 and SALES_ID = 174 ;

1 row updated.

DNYTST10 SQL>commit ;

Commit complete.
-- After update
DNYOIP20 SQL>select pol_no, sales_id, premium from ny4.allinsured1 where pol_no = 15000 ;

    POL_NO   SALES_ID    PREMIUM
---------- ---------- ----------
     15000        174         10
```

The transaction is then propagated and applied to the destination table by the procedure specified as the DML handler. The procedure, besides inserting into the *hist_upd* table, executes the LCR event (lcr.EXECUTE(true)).

The statement below shows the entry added to the *hist_upd* table at DNYOIP20 by way of the DML handler procedure NY4.WRITE_UPD_LCRS:

```
select TIMESTAMP, COMMAND_TYPE, OBJECT_NAME, TRANSACTION_ID, COMMIT_SCN, TX_NAME from
ny4.hist_upd
/
TIMESTAMP COMMAND_TYPE Table Name   TRANSACTIO COMMIT_SCN TX_NAME
--------- ------------ ------------ ---------- ---------- -------
30-OCT-04 UPDATE       ALLINSURED1  3.44.16636 14324527   MY_TXN10
```

The *hist_upd* table, which is written by the DML Handler procedure, provides a record of all the updates to the base table.

The next step is to examine the handlers for delete DML operations.

Delete DML Operation

There are some situations where deleting records may need to be controlled. Accidental deletes need to be avoided. If a deletion takes place, the DBA may not want to reflect the deletion at the destination and may want to record the details. This is where the Delete DML Handler would be very handy.

In this example, a Delete DML handler that manipulates the incoming LCR event will be created at the destination. Whenever a delete transaction arrives to the destination queue, the LCR is modified to write to an alternate table with an additional column. The Apply process that dequeues the transaction is set up with a Delete DML handler.

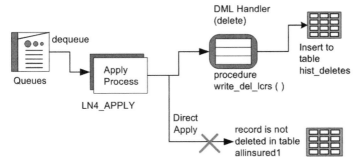

Figure 6.4 *Setting up of Delete DML Handler*

Figure 6.4 shows all of the components involved in setting up a typical Delete DML handler.

Next, information will be presented on the DML delete handler setup methodology. The following are the assumptions:

```
Source Table            : ny4.allinsured1 at DNYTST10 database
Source DB Capture Proc  : NY4_CAPTURE
Destination Table       : ny4.allinsured1 at DNYOIP20 database
Alternate Table         : ny4.hist_deletes at DNYOIP20 database
Destination Apply Proc  : LN4_APPLY
```

In order to show the use of Delete DML handler, a stored procedure named NY4.WRITE_DEL_LCRS has been created, and the Delete DML handler has been set up. A new table named NY4.HIST_DELETES has been created at DNYOIP20. This table is where the DML handler writes the details about the delete operation.

The following SQL statements show the creation and setting up of the Update DML handler:

```
--(1) First Create the Table to save the deleted.
create table ny4. hist_deletes
as select * from ny4.allinsured1 where 1=2
/

--(2)  Then added constraint
ALTER TABLE NY4. hist_deletes
ADD CONSTRAINT ALLINS1_DEL_PK4 PRIMARY KEY (POL_NO)
/

--(3) Then added a new column to the table which records sysdate
alter table NY4.hist_deletes add time_of_dml date
/
```

Next, the stored procedure named NY4.WRITE_DEL_LCRS must be created at the destination schema. The following procedure will be used for the delete DML Handler:

```
CREATE OR REPLACE PROCEDURE ny4.write_del_lcrs (
in_any IN SYS.AnyData) IS
  lcr           SYS.LCR$_ROW_RECORD;
  rc            PLS_INTEGER;
  command       VARCHAR2(10);
  old_values    SYS.LCR$_ROW_LIST;

BEGIN
  -- Access the LCR
  rc := in_any.GETOBJECT(lcr);

  -- Get the object command type
  command := lcr.GET_COMMAND_TYPE();

  -- Check for DELETE command on the ny4.allinsured1_del table
  IF command = 'DELETE' THEN
    -- Set the command_type in the row LCR to INSERT
    lcr.SET_COMMAND_TYPE('INSERT');
    -- Set the object_name in the row LCR to EMP_DEL
    lcr.SET_OBJECT_NAME('hist_deletes');
    -- Set the object_name in the row LCR to EMP_DEL
    lcr.SET_OBJECT_OWNER('NY4');
    -- Get the old values in the row LCR
    old_values := lcr.GET_VALUES('old');
    -- Set the old val of row LCR to new values of row LCR
    lcr.SET_VALUES('new', old_values);
    -- Set the old values in the row LCR to NULL
    lcr.SET_VALUES('old', NULL);
    -- Add a SYSDATE value for the timestamp column
    lcr.ADD_COLUMN('new', 'time_of_dml',
              SYS.AnyData.ConvertDate(SYSDATE));
    -- Apply row LCR as an INSERT into the NY4.hist_deletes table
    lcr.EXECUTE(true);
  END IF;
END;
```

In the above procedure, the LCR event has been altered as follows:

- the command type has been changed to INSERT
- the *object_name* has been changed to *hist_deletes*
- the command type has been changed to NY4
- a new column named TIME_OF_DML has been added and a value of SYSDATE has been assigned to it

The next step is the execution of the LCR event. This has the effect of the inserting to a new table called NY4.HIST_DELETES instead of the originally intended ALLINSURED1 table.

The procedure can be assigned as the DML Delete Handler by executing the following SQL statement:

```
-- To Assign Delete DML Handler, use the following SQL block
BEGIN
DBMS_APPLY_ADM.SET_DML_HANDLER(
 object_name        => 'ny4.allinsured1',
 object_type        => 'TABLE',
 operation_name     => 'DELETE',
 error_handler      => false,
 user_procedure     => 'ny4. write_del_lcrs',
 apply_database_link => NULL,
 apply_name => NULL);
END;
/
```

When the use of a typical delete DML handler is not needed, the DBA may want to disable or remove it from execution. To remove or unset the Delete DML Handler, use the following SQL block:

```
BEGIN
DBMS_APPLY_ADM.SET_DML_HANDLER(
 object_name               => 'ny4.allinsured1',
 object_type               => 'TABLE',
 operation_name            => 'DELETE',
 error_handler             => false,
 user_procedure            => NULL ,
 apply_database_link => NULL,
 apply_name => NULL);
END;
/
```

The next step is to execute an SQL statement to delete records at the source database table. Before execution of the delete, it might be useful to look at the rows in the source table.

```
DNYOIP20 SQL>select pol_no, SALES_ID, SUM_ASSURED, PREMIUM, plan_id from  ny4.hist_deletes
where sales_id = 460
/
```

```
   POL_NO   SALES_ID SUM_ASSURED    PREMIUM    PLAN_ID
---------- ---------- ----------- ---------- ----------
      1171        460       93810       2976         18
      1211        460       15090       4849        147
      1271        460       57720       4092         21
      2703        460       95790       2702        108
      2890        460       31270       2591        116
      3075        460       28510        856        110
      3364        460       58050        800         57
      3536        460       41250       4207         86
      4685        460       90760       4534         23
      5780        460       74310       2577         52

10 rows selected.
```

Now, a delete operation is executed at the source database.

```
DNYTST10 SQL>delete ny4.allinsured1 where SALES_ID = 460 ;

10 rows deleted.

DNYTST10 SQL>commit ;

Commit complete.
```

Once the transaction propagates to the destination queue named LN4_APPLY, the Apply handler modifies the row LCR event and executes the event which inserts rows into the alternate table named HIST_DELETES. It will also add an additional column value named TIME_OF_DML.

The following SQL shows the rows added to the NY4.HIST_DELETES table at the destination database.

```
select pol_no, SALES_ID, SUM_ASSURED, PREMIUM, plan_id, time_of_dml from  ny4.hist_deletes
/

   POL_NO   SALES_ID SUM_ASSURED    PREMIUM    PLAN_ID TIME_OF_D
---------- ---------- ----------- ---------- ---------- ---------
      1171        460       93810       2976         18 22-OCT-04
      1211        460       15090       4849        147 22-OCT-04
      1271        460       57720       4092         21 22-OCT-04
      2703        460       95790       2702        108 22-OCT-04
      2890        460       31270       2591        116 22-OCT-04
      3075        460       28510        856        110 22-OCT-04
      3364        460       58050        800         57 22-OCT-04
      3536        460       41250       4207         86 22-OCT-04
      4685        460       90760       4534         23 22-OCT-04
      5780        460       74310       2577         52 22-OCT-04

10 rows selected.
```

This is a classic example of diverting the delete statement into an insert operation, thus saving the target table rows. With the help of extra attributes captured at source, proper investigation of delete operations at the source database can be done.

The following section introduces information on the details of the error DML handler.

Error DML Handler

In a typical Streams replication, there will be errors. Errors occur due to a variety of reasons. At the target, a row may be missing for an update. A row foreign key may be missing in the parent table. The Error DML handler understands the error condition and attempts to resolve it on the fly. As part of the Apply process, it will try to use the pre-defined logic to resolve the error.

In the case of the Error DML handler, simply called Error handler much of the time, the DBA may want to build some kind of action routines. Such action procedures typically correct the error scenario and process the transactions without the intervention of the administrator or end user.

An Error handler may simply log the error record and notify the administrators or users so that corrective actions can be taken later.

Setting an Error Handler

An Error handler can process errors resulting from a row LCR dequeued by any Apply process that contains a specific operation on a specific table. Multiple Error handlers can be specified on the same table in order to handle Errors resulting from different operations on the table. An Error handler can either be set for a specific Apply process or as a general Error handler that is used by all Apply processes that apply the specified operation to the specified table.

An Error handler can be created by running the *set_dml_handler* procedure in the *dbms_apply_adm* package and setting the *error_handler* parameter to TRUE. If the *error_handler* parameter is not set to TRUE, it becomes a general DML handler.

An Error handler procedure should have the following signature:

```
PROCEDURE write_fk_lcr (
  Err_message          IN SYS.AnyData,
  err_stack_depth             IN NUMBER,
  err_numbers          IN DBMS_UTILITY.NUMBER_ARRAY,
  err_messages         IN emsg_array);
```

write_fk_lcr represents the name of the procedure in the example. Each parameter is required and must have the specified data type. However, the names of the parameters can be changed. The *emsg_array* parameter must be a user-defined array that is a PL/SQL table of type VARCHAR2 with at least 76 characters. Once the procedure *write_fk_lcr* is created at the destination database, it can be set as the DML handler. The procedure will have the logic to rectify the error condition.

For example, to set an Error handler for the Insert operation on the NY4.ALLINSURED1 table, use the following SQL statements:

```
BEGIN
DBMS_APPLY_ADM.SET_DML_HANDLER(
  object_name            => 'ny4.allinsured1',
  object_type            => 'TABLE',
  operation_name            => 'INSERT',
  error_handler          => true,
  user_procedure            => 'error_pkg.write_fk_lcr',
  apply_database_link    => NULL,
  apply_name             => 'LN4_APPLY');
END;
/
```

In this example, there is a foreign key constraint on the ALLINSURED1 table that references to *sales_id* of the SALESPERSON1 table. When a row is inserted into the ALLINSURED1 table and if there is no parent row with *sales_id* in SALESPERSON1 table, an integrity constraint violation would be raised. The Error handler procedure, *write_fk_lcr*, processes such an error by inserting a row into the table SALESPERSON1 and then re-executing the transaction.

In another example, to set an Error handler for the Update Operation on the table NY4.ALLINSURED1 table, use the following procedure:

```
BEGIN
DBMS_APPLY_ADM.SET_DML_HANDLER(
  object_name            => 'ny4.allinsured1',
  object_type            => 'TABLE',
  operation_name            => 'UPDATE',
  error_handler          => true,
  user_procedure            => 'error_pkg.write_nodata_lcr',
  apply_database_link    => NULL,
  apply_name             => 'LN4_APPLY');
END;
/
```

In this example, the *write_nodata_lcr* procedure processes an error condition which is caused by a *no data found* error at the destination database table for the update operation.

If the *apply_name* parameter is set to NULL, the Error handler becomes a general Error handler that will be used by all of the Apply processes in the database. Beware of this. Unless there is a generic error handler that is applicable to all of the Apply processes in the destination database, the Apply process name must be specified.

UnSetting an Error Handler

When the error handler is no longer needed, the error handler setting can be removed from the Apply process. To unset an Error handler, the *set_dml_handler* procedure in the *dbms_apply_adm* package can be used. The *user_procedure* parameter will have to be set to NULL for a specific operation on a specific table.

For example, the following procedure unsets the Error handler for INSERT operations on the NY4.ALLINSURED1 table:

```
BEGIN
DBMS_APPLY_ADM.SET_DML_HANDLER(
  object_name            => ' ny4.allinsured1',
  object_type            => 'TABLE',
  operation_name         => 'INSERT',
 user_procedure          => NULL,
 apply_name              => NULL);
END;
/
```

The *error_handler* parameter does not need to be specified since it has the default value of FALSE.

Next, an example of the above mentioned stored procedure, *write_fk_lcr*, will be presented.

Creating an Error Handler

Figure 6.5 shows all the components involved in this example.

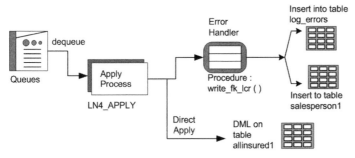

Figure 6.5 *Setting up an Error handler*

In this example, a stored procedure named *write_fk_lcr* will be created. This procedure creates a row in the SALESPERSON1 table and re-executes the transaction.

This example can be extended to some other situations like *no data found* or any other error condition. As noted in the example, ORA errors can be monitored.

In order to show the use of the Error DML handler, the stored procedure named *write_fk_lcr* has been created in the NY4 schema and the Error DML handler has been set up. A new table named NY4.LOG_ERRORS has been created at the DNYOIP20 database to record error transaction details.

Error_DML_Handler.sql, which is available in the code depot, creates and sets up an Error DML handler. First the table that will be used to store the error details will be set up:

```
Table Name    Operation  Handler Procedure                 Err.Hndl
-----------   ---------- --------------------------------- -------
ALLINSURED1   INSERT     "NY4"."ERRORS_PKG"."WRITE_FK_LCR"   Y
```

The *write_fk_lcr* package procedure detects foreign key violations, an error condition with the number 2091, and inserts a record into the SALESPERSON1 table with minimum values. By inserting a record into the SALESPERSON1 table, the integrity violation error was avoided. The main transaction of inserting into the table ALLINSURED1 is then re-executed.

The following statement can be used to set up the Error DML handler:

```
--to set

BEGIN
  DBMS_APPLY_ADM.SET_DML_HANDLER(
    object_name         => 'ny4.allinsured1' ,
    object_type         => 'TABLE',
    operation_name      => 'INSERT',
    error_handler       => TRUE,
    user_procedure      => 'ny4.errors_pkg.write_fk_lcr',
    apply_database_link => NULL,
    apply_name          => NULL);
END;
/

-- to unset the error handler

BEGIN
  DBMS_APPLY_ADM.SET_DML_HANDLER(
    object_name         => 'ny4.allinsured1' ,
    object_type         => 'TABLE',
    operation_name      => 'INSERT',
    user_procedure      => NULL ,
    apply_database_link => NULL,
    apply_name          => NULL);
END;
```

In the event that a row is present with the same primary key, a primary key violation Constraint Failure with error number 2290 or 1 will occur. In such a situation:

- This new record may be deleted and added again.

- This new record may be added with a new primary key value.

This sample example has been provided to show the capability of the error processing by using the error handler. Many of the well known solutions can be built-in into the error handlers. In this way, the replication process continues to move forward without waiting for an administrator's intervention.

The next section presents information on the role of the DDL and handler and how it can be configured.

DDL Handler

A user procedure that processes DDL LCRs resulting from DDL statements is called a DDL handler.

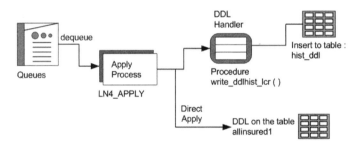

Figure 6.6 *Setting up of DDL Handler*

An Apply process may have many DML handlers but only one DDL handler, which processes all DDL LCRs dequeued by the Apply process.

A DDL handler can be used for the customized processing of DDL LCRs. For example, the handler may modify the LCR and execute it using the EXECUTE member procedure for the LCR. When a DDL LCR is executed in a DDL handler, the Apply process applies the LCR without calling the DDL handler again. A DDL handler may also be used to record the history of DDL changes. For example, a DDL handler may insert information about an LCR it processes into a table and then apply the LCR using the EXECUTE member procedure.

Setting the DDL Handler for an Apply Process

A DDL handler processes all DDL LCRs dequeued by an Apply process. The DDL handler for an Apply process can be set using the *ddl_handler* parameter in the *alter_apply* procedure in the *dbms_apply_adm* package.

For example, the following SQL block sets the DDL handler for an Apply process named LN4_APPLY to the NY4.WRITE_DDLHIST_LCR procedure:

```
-- Set DDL handler for apply proc. using the ddl_handler param.
BEGIN
DBMS_APPLY_ADM.ALTER_APPLY(
  apply_name  => 'LN4_APPLY',
  ddl_handler => 'ny4.write_ddlhist_lcr');
END;
/
```

The DDL handler for an Apply process can be removed by setting the *remove_ddl_handler* parameter to TRUE in the *alter_apply* procedure in the *dbms_apply_adm* package. For example, the following SQL block removes the DDL handler from an Apply process named LN4_APPLY:

```
-- Removing the DDL Handler for an Apply Process
BEGIN
  DBMS_APPLY_ADM.ALTER_APPLY(
  apply_name         => 'LN4_APPLY',
  remove_ddl_handler => true);
END;
/
```

DDL Handler User Procedure

The procedure that inserts the information about the DDL LCR into the HIST_DDL table and executes the DDL LCR will be created using the *DDL_LCR_Hist.sql* script from the code depot.

The following commands will show whether or not the changes have been effected:

```
DNYTST10 SQL>alter table ny4.allinsured1 add (test_col number(3) ) ;
Table altered.

DNYTST10 SQL>alter table ny4.allinsured1 drop column test_col;
Table altered.

DNYTST10 SQL>
```

The next section will present information on the pre-commit handler details. What is a pre-commit handler and how can it be set and used?

Pre-Commit Handler

The Pre-Commit handler is a user-defined PL/SQL procedure that can receive the commit information for a transaction and process the commit information in a customized way. It can deal with LCRs and messages. It helps to keep track of transactional history and helps in the audit process.

An internal commit directive is enqueued into a queue when a capture process captures the commit directive for a transaction that contains row LCRs. The same thing also happens when a user or application enqueues messages into a queue and then issues a COMMIT statement. For a captured row LCR, a commit directive contains the commit SCN of the transaction from the source database, but for a user-enqueued event, the commit SCN is generated by the Apply process.

An existing procedure can be specified to be the pre-commit handler. An error is returned if the specified procedure does not exist.

The user who invokes the *alter_apply* procedure must have EXECUTE privilege on a specified pre-commit handler. If the *schema_name* is not specified, the user who invokes the *alter_apply* procedure is the default.

The pre-commit handler procedure must conform to the following guidelines:

- Any work that commits must be an autonomous transaction.

- Any rollback must be to a named save point created in the procedure.

- There can be only one pre-commit handler for a given Apply process.

- If a pre-commit handler raises an exception, the entire apply transaction is rolled back, and all of the events in the transaction are moved to the error queue.

Figure 6.7 shows the typical components involved in setting up a pre-commit handler.

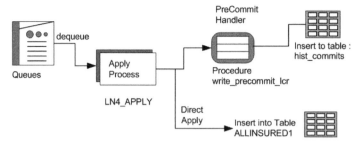

Figure 6.7 *Setting up of precommit handler*

Setting the Pre-Commit Handler for an Apply Process

Whenever commits and their information need to be tracked, the precommit handlers can be used to record into a table and analyze subsequently. An Apply process needs to be set up to obtain the commit information.

The pre-commit handler for an Apply process can be set two ways:

- Using the *precommit_handler* parameter in the *alter_apply* procedure in the *dbms_apply_adm* package.

- Specify a pre-commit handler when an Apply process is created using the *create_apply* procedure in the *dbms_apply_adm* package.

For example, the following procedure sets the pre-commit handler for an Apply process named LN_APPLY in the *record_precommit* procedure in the STRMADM schema:

```
BEGIN
DBMS_APPLY_ADM.ALTER_APPLY(
apply_name              => 'ln4_apply',
precommit_handler       => 'strmadm.record_precommit');
END;
/
```

The pre-commit handler for an Apply process can be removed by setting the *remove_precommit_handler* parameter to TRUE in the *alter_apply* procedure in the *dbms_apply_adm* package.

For example, the following procedure removes the pre-commit handler from an Apply process named LN4_APPLY:

```
BEGIN
DBMS_APPLY_ADM.ALTER_APPLY(
apply_name                      => 'ln4_apply',
remove_precommit_handler  => true);
END;
/
```

The following section includes detailed information about the message handler procedures.

Message Handler Procedure

The Message handler is a user-defined procedure that can process non-LCR user messages in a customized way. A Message handler can be specified for an Apply process using the *message_handler* parameter in the *create_apply* or *alter_apply* procedures in the *dbms_apply_adm* package.

For example, the following SQL block sets the Message handler for an Apply process named NY4_APPLY to the *msg_handler* procedure in the STRMADM schema. The user who runs the *alter_apply* procedure must have EXECUTE privilege on the specified Message handler.

```
BEGIN
DBMS_APPLY_ADM.ALTER_APPLY(
apply_name               => 'ny4_apply',
message_handler          => 'strmadm.msg_handler');
END;
/
```

The message handler for an Apply process can be removed by setting the *remove_message_handler* parameter to TRUE in the *alter_apply* procedure in the *dbms_apply_adm* package. For example, the following SQL block removes the Message handler from an Apply process named NY4_APPLY.

```
BEGIN
DBMS_APPLY_ADM.ALTER_APPLY(
apply_name                     => 'ny4_apply',
remove_message_handler    => true);
END;
/
```

Conclusion

In this chapter, detailed information has been presented on the Apply process and its extensions in the form of Apply handlers.

The main points in the chapter include:

- The Apply process can be greatly expanded by writing user defined procedures and setting them as the apply handlers.

- There are separate handlers for DDL operations and DML operations.

- DML handlers include Update DML handler, delete DML handler and error DML hander.

- Sample code has been included for the user procedures acting as the handlers. Information has been included on how to set them and subsequently unset them when they are not needed.

- There is another type of handler, called a pre-commit handler, which can keep track of the commits information

In the next chapter, the focus will shift to topics related to monitoring the Streams environment and troubleshooting the Streams data flow.

Monitoring and Troubleshooting Oracle Streams

Introduction

In this chapter, information on topics related to monitoring of the Streams process, Streams configuration and replicated data flow will be presented. Information on error conditions and how to troubleshoot them is also presented.

Because the Streams replication goes unattended all the time, good monitoring methods are needed so that it is possible to detect interruptions in the Streams process. Another important point to the monitoring process is to detect load issues on the source database and delays in the arrival of events to the destination.

The monitoring of error conditions deserves special mention. The Apply process can be configured to halt on an error. In that case, administrators need to get immediate notification so that the error can be examined and the situation rectified. Otherwise, there will be a large quantity of transactions in the queue waiting to be applied. For this reason, the DBA might choose to continue the Apply process in spite of error conditions, so the error condition can be dealt with at an appropriate time.

Monitoring

The monitoring of Streams event flow involves four main areas: monitoring for potential load problems; checking errors; looking for disabled Apply, Propagation and Capture processes; and setting up of the right configuration details for the various Streams client processes.

Oracle provides various static and dynamic views which help administrators understand the Streams configuration and track the performance details. In the next section, information will be presented on the related static and dynamic views.

Static and Dynamic Dictionary Views

The 10g release of the Oracle database has included many new and useful views and enhanced the existing views. Views can be categorized as static and dynamic. Static views serve mostly to store the configuration details. Dynamic views show real time information and statistics. Many of the dynamic views are populated when a particular process is in use. When the Streams clients are restarted, the counters in dynamic views are generally reset and new statistics would be present in the dynamic views.

The static and dynamic views can be categorized into five broad groups:

- Capture related

- Apply related

- Rule related

- Queue and Propagation related

- General/other useful views

The following section will examine the views and their usage details.

At the end of the section, some useful SQL statements have been included that can be used to query these views to provide Streams clients information.

Capture Related Views

Static dictionary views show the basic configuration details, and the dynamic dictionary views show Capture process statistics. Dynamic Dictionary views are normally populated when a particular process is running. They are generally related to performance statistics.

Figure 7.1 shows all of the views related to capture, both static and dynamic.

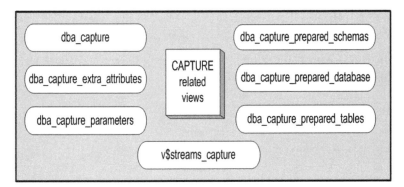

Figure 7.1 *Capture Related Static and Dynamic Performance Views*

The following section includes a description of each of these views:

v$streams_capture

This view displays information about each Capture process. This is an important view that provides many useful statistics about the progress and load of the Streams flow as well as the status of the Capture process. With the help of this view's contents, the load of the messages can be determined; the SCN values for the messages can be found and the load of the rule evaluations can be better understood.

Some of the more useful columns include:

- TOTAL_MESSAGES_CAPTURES shows total changes captured since the Capture process was last started.

- CAPTURE_TIME shows the time when the most recent message was captured. This helps the DBA see if the Capture process has discontinued scanning and the Capture process is lagging behind.

- CAPTURE_MESSAGE shows the SCN number of the most recently captured message. When this number is compared with current system SCN of *v$log* or of *v$database*, the lag of the Capture process is shown.

- AVAILABLE_MESSAGE_NUMBER is the last redo SCN flushed to the redo log files for the local capture. For downstream capture, it is the last SCN added to LogMiner via the archive logs.

- TOTAL_FULL_EVALUATIONS is the count associated with *elapsed_rule_time* in order to calculate rate

- TOTAL_MESSAGES_ENQUEUED shows the total LCR events enqueued since the Capture process was last started

To display this information for each Capture process in a database, the following SQL statement can be used:

```
COLUMN CAPTURE_NAME HEADING 'Capture|Name' FORMAT A10
COLUMN PROCESS_NAME HEADING 'Capture|Process|Number' FORMAT A7
COLUMN SID HEADING 'Session|ID' FORMAT 9999
COLUMN SERIAL# HEADING 'Session|Serial|Number' FORMAT 9999
COLUMN STATE HEADING 'State' FORMAT A27
COLUMN TOTAL_MESSAGES_CAPTURED HEADING 'Redo|Entries|Scanned'
FORMAT 9999999
COLUMN TOTAL_MESSAGES_ENQUEUED HEADING 'Total|LCRs|Enqueued'
FORMAT 999999

SELECT c.CAPTURE_NAME,
 SUBSTR(s.PROGRAM,INSTR(S.PROGRAM,'(')+1,4) PROCESS_NAME,
 c.SID, c.SERIAL#, c.STATE,
 c.TOTAL_MESSAGES_CAPTURED,
 c.TOTAL_MESSAGES_ENQUEUED
FROM V$STREAMS_CAPTURE c, V$SESSION s
WHERE c.SID = s.SID AND c.SERIAL# = s.SERIAL#
/
```

The output gives a glance at the scanning rates of the redo entries. The TOTAL_MESSAGES_ENQUEUED column is an important indicator showing the total LCR events enqueued to the source queue by Capture process. Redo entries produced by all DML and DDL statements are included into this statistic. In addition, the control statements such as commit and rollback are added to this value.

dba_capture

This view displays information about the Capture processes that enqueue the captured changes into queues. There is one row for each one Capture process configured. This is a view that shows comprehensive details about the Capture processes. This view is an important tool that can be used to help the user understand the basic configuration details.

Some important columns are shown below:

- RULE_SET_NAME shows the positive rule set assigned for the Capture process.

- The STATUS column shows the current position of the Capture process. The STATUS may be ENABLED, DISABLED or ABORTED.

- STARTED_SCN shows the System Change Number (SCN) from which the Capture process will start to capture changes.

- CAPTURED_SCN represents the SCN of the last redo log record scanned.

- APPLIED_SCN shows the SCN of the most recent message dequeued by the relevant Apply processes. All changes below this SCN have been dequeued by all Apply processes that apply changes captured by this Capture process. This is an important indicator to monitor the progress of dequeue by the Apply process.

- FIRST_SCN shows the SCN from which the Capture process can be restarted

- LOGMINER_ID shows the session ID of the LogMiner session associated with the Capture process. *v$session* provides more details about the SID.

- MAX_CHECKPOINT_SCN shows the SCN at which the last checkpoint was taken by the Capture process

- REQUIRED_CHECKPOINT_SCN represents the lowest checkpoint SCN for which the Capture process requires redo information. This helps to monitor the redo log file that is not needed.

- CAPTURE_TYPE shows the type of the Capture process: DOWNSTREAM or LOCAL

Some SQL statements that can be used to view the contents of the *dba_capture* view are shown below:

```
set     linesize 140
COLUMN capture_name   FORMAT A20
COLUMN queue_name     FORMAT A20
COLUMN rule_set_name  FORMAT A20
COLUMN status         FORMAT A10
COLUMN captured_scn   FORMAT 99999999999

SELECT capture_name, queue_name, rule_set_name,
status, CAPTURED_SCN, APPLIED_SCN FROM DBA_CAPTURE
/
```

To find the various SCN values of the Capture process, the following SQL statement can be used:

```
select  CAPTURE_NAME,START_SCN,  CAPTURED_SCN,  MAX_CHECKPOINT_SCN,  REQUIRED_CHECKPOINT_SCN
from                                                                              dba_capture
/
```

To display the APPLIED_SCN for all of the Capture processes in a database, the following SQL can be used:

```
COLUMN CAPTURE_NAME HEADING 'Capture Process Name' FORMAT A30
COLUMN APPLIED_SCN HEADING 'Applied SCN' FORMAT 99999999999

SELECT CAPTURE_NAME, APPLIED_SCN FROM DBA_CAPTURE
/
Capture Process Name                 Applied SCN
----------------------------         -----------
NY4_CAPTURE                          24872317
```

dba_capture_extra_attributes

This view displays information about the extra attributes for all the Capture processes in the database. The INCLUDE column indicates whether or not the extra attribute was added and the column ROW_ATTRIBUTE indicates if it is a row attribute or not. Information presented earlier indicated that extra attributes can be set in a Capture process that can affect the behavior of the Capture process

```
COLUMN CAPTURE_NAME HEADING 'Capture Process' FORMAT A20
COLUMN ATTRIBUTE_NAME HEADING 'Attribute Name'        FORMAT A15
COLUMN INCLUDE HEADING 'Include Attribute in LCRs?' FORMAT A30

SELECT CAPTURE_NAME, ATTRIBUTE_NAME, INCLUDE,
ROW_ATTRIBUTE, DDL_ATTRIBUTE
FROM DBA_CAPTURE_EXTRA_ATTRIBUTES
ORDER BY CAPTURE_NAME
/
```

dba_capture_parameters

This view displays information about the parameters for all the Capture processes in the database. The PARAMETER and VALUE column pair show the name and the value for that parameter. When any additional parameters are set to the Capture process, the capture behavior can be influenced.

```
COLUMN parameter FORMAT A20
COLUMN value FORMAT A20
COLUMN set_by_user FORMAT A20

SELECT CAPTURE_NAME, parameter,
value, set_by_user
FROM DBA_CAPTURE_PARAMETERS
/
```

dba_capture_prepared_database

This view displays information about when the local database was prepared for the instantiation. If the local database was not prepared for instantiation, this view contains no rows.

dba_capture_prepared_schemas

This view displays information about the schemas prepared for instantiation in the local database. Whenever a schema is not prepared for instantiation, it fails to capture and apply the database changes.

dba_capture_prepared_tables

This view displays information about the tables prepared for instantiation in the database. When the data system consists of a large number of tables, it is important to ensure that the desired tables are prepared for instantiation. This helps to troubleshoot the Capture process. Whenever a table is not prepared for instantiation, it fails to capture and apply the database changes. In turn, this has a negative impact on overall performance.

In the following section, some SQL statements will be presented that can be used to view the configuration of the Capture process and to monitor the Streams Capture process details.

Capture Related Useful SQL Queries

The *v$streams_capture* and *dba_capture* views provide useful details about the overall Capture process and its health. The following sections present some examples.

Determining Event Enqueuing Latency

The event enqueuing latency specifies the number of seconds between when an event was recorded in the redo log and when the event was enqueued by the Capture process. This is indicative of the lag in scanning the redo file and the preparing of LCR events by the Capture process. The lag may be caused by low buffers or the general load on the system. In this case, consideration should be given to adding *parallelism* to the Capture process. Consideration should also be given to adding to the Streams buffer pool. Sometimes shortage in the Streams pool may slow the capture activity since the events will have to be written to physical table instead of keeping them in the SGA buffers.

The associated values are the event creation time, which is the time when the DML or DDL change generated the redo information for the most recently enqueued event. The enqueue time shows when the Capture process enqueued the event into its queue. These values are for a specific message number. It is a representative in nature. This needs to be verified periodically to assess the latency. Monitoring the latency delays will help DBAs identify the need for and to take corrective action. Otherwise, messages may pile up and cause a big backlog for replication

The following SQL statements show the latency details:

```
COLUMN CAPTURE_NAME HEADING 'Capture|Process|Name' FORMAT A12
COLUMN LATENCY_SECONDS HEADING 'Latency|in|Seconds' FORMAT 999999
COLUMN CREATE_TIME HEADING 'Event Creation|Time' FORMAT A20
COLUMN ENQUEUE_TIME HEADING 'Enqueue Time' FORMAT A20
COLUMN ENQUEUE_MESSAGE_NUMBER HEAD 'Message|Number' FORMAT 999999999
SELECT CAPTURE_NAME,
 (ENQUEUE_TIME-ENQUEUE_MESSAGE_CREATE_TIME)*86400 LATENCY_SECONDS,
 TO_CHAR(ENQUEUE_MESSAGE_CREATE_TIME, 'HH24:MI:SS MM/DD/YY')
 CREATE_TIME,
 TO_CHAR(ENQUEUE_TIME, 'HH24:MI:SS MM/DD/YY') ENQUEUE_TIME,
 ENQUEUE_MESSAGE_NUMBER
FROM V$STREAMS_CAPTURE
/
```

Some more useful SQL statements are shown below:

```
SELECT CAPTURE_NAME, CAPTURE_MESSAGE_NUMBER ,
 TO_CHAR(CAPTURE_MESSAGE_CREATE_TIME, 'HH24:MI:SS MM/DD/YY')
 CAPT_MSG_CREATE_TIME, TOTAL_MESSAGES_CAPTURED,
 TOTAL_MESSAGES_ENQUEUED, ENQUEUE_MESSAGE_NUMBER,
 TO_CHAR(ENQUEUE_MESSAGE_CREATE_TIME, 'HH24:MI:SS MM/DD/YY') ENQ_MSG_CREATE_TIME, STATE
from  V$STREAMS_CAPTURE
/

COLUMN LATENCY_SECONDS  FORMAT 9999
COLUMN LAST_STAT_SECS   FORMAT 9999
COLUMN capture_time     FORMAT A18
COLUMN create_mesg_time FORMAT A18
SELECT
 capture_name,
 TO_CHAR(capture_message_create_time, 'HH24:MI:SS MM/DD/YY')
 CREATE_MESG_TIME,
 (SYSDATE - capture_message_create_time ) * 86400 LATENCY_SEC,
 TO_CHAR(capture_time, 'HH24:MI:SS MM/DD/YY') CAPTURE_TIME,
 (SYSDATE - capture_time)*86400 LAST_STAT_SECS,
 total_messages_captured tot_msg_captd,
 total_messages_enqueued tot_msg_enqd
FROM V$STREAMS_CAPTURE
/
```

SQL Statement Showing Information about Rule Evaluations

Many rule and evaluation statistics are available from the *v$streams_capture* view. These statistics help users understand the rules evaluation process. Some of the important fields are below:

- *total_full_evaluations* shows the number of full evaluations since the Capture process was last started. Full evaluations are generally expensive, so in relative terms, a lower number of evaluations is good for Capture process performance.

- *total_prefilter_discarded* shows the number of events discarded during prefiltering since the Capture process was last started. The Capture process determined that these events definitely did not satisfy the Capture process rule sets during pre-filtering.

- *total_prefilter_kept* shows the number of events kept during pre-filtering since the Capture process was last started. The Capture process determined that these events definitely satisfied the Capture process rule sets during pre-filtering. Such events are converted into LCRs and enqueued into the Capture process queue.

The following SQL statement shows the evaluation details:

```
COL CAPTURE_NAME HEADING 'Capture|Name' FORMAT A15
COL TOTAL_PREFILTER_DISCARDED HEAD 'Prefilter|Events|Discarded' FORMAT 9999999999
COL TOTAL_PREFILTER_KEPT HEAD 'Prefilter|Events|Kept' FORMAT 9999999
COL TOTAL_PREFILTER_EVALUATIONS HEAD 'Prefilter|Evaluations'
FORMAT 9999999999
COL UNDECIDED HEAD 'Undecided|After|Prefilter' FORMAT 9999999999
COL TOTAL_FULL_EVALUATIONS HEAD 'Full|Evaluations' FORMAT 9999999999

SELECT CAPTURE_NAME,
 TOTAL_PREFILTER_DISCARDED,
 TOTAL_PREFILTER_KEPT,
 TOTAL_PREFILTER_EVALUATIONS,
 (TOTAL_PREFILTER_EVALUATIONS -
 (TOTAL_PREFILTER_KEPT + TOTAL_PREFILTER_DISCARDED)) UNDECIDED,
 TOTAL_FULL_EVALUATIONS
FROM V$STREAMS_CAPTURE
/
```

Determining Redo Log Scanning Latency

The redo log scanning latency represents the number of seconds between the creation time of the most recent redo log event scanned by a Capture process and the current time. This number may be relatively large immediately after a Capture process is started; therefore, it should be ignored. At other times, the DBA should be concerned if the latency is high. It is at those times that the DBA should dig deeper. Is the load on the system is heavy? Is there a lot of contention?

The event creation time represents the time when the DML or DDL change generated the redo information for the most recently captured event.

The following SQL statement can be used to determine the redo scanning latency for each Capture process:

```
COL CAPTURE_NAME      HEAD 'Capture|Process|Name'      FORMAT A10
COL LATENCY_SECONDS HEAD 'Latency|in|Seconds'          FORMAT 999999
COL LAST_STATUS       HEAD 'Seconds Since|Last Stat' FORMAT 999999
COL CAPTURE_TIME      HEAD 'Current|Process|Time'
COL CREATE_TIME       HEAD 'Event|Creation Time'      FORMAT 999999

SELECT CAPTURE_NAME,
((SYSDATE - CAPTURE_MESSAGE_CREATE_TIME)*86400) LATENCY_SECONDS,
((SYSDATE - CAPTURE_TIME)*86400) LAST_STATUS,
TO_CHAR(CAPTURE_TIME, 'HH24:MI:SS MM/DD/YY') CAPTURE_TIME,
TO_CHAR(CAPTURE_MESSAGE_CREATE_TIME, 'HH24:MI:SS MM/DD/YY') CREATE_TIME
FROM V$STREAMS_CAPTURE
/
```

The *latency in seconds* returned by the above query is the difference between the current time, SYSDATE, and the event creation time. The *seconds since last status* is the difference between SYSDATE and the *current process time*.

Monitor the Elapsed Times

The view *v$capture_process* shows elapsed times for the various activities as shown below:

- *elapsed_capture_time* – The elapsed time, in hundredths of a second, scanning for changes in the redo log since the Capture process was last started.

- *elapsed_rule_time* – The elapsed time, in hundredths of a second, evaluating rules since the Capture process was last started.

- *elapsed_enqueue_time* – The elapsed time, in hundredths of a second, messages have been enqueuing since the Capture process was last started.

- *elapsed_lcr_time* - The elapsed time, in hundredths of a second, LCRs have been creating since the Capture process was last started.

- *elapsed_redo_wait_time* – The elapsed time, in hundredths of a second, spent by the Capture process in the WAITING FOR REDO state.

These times tell the DBA where the Capture process is spending most of its time. In this way, the problem area can be pinpointed as a way to tune the process.

The following SQL shows a sample query to verify the timings:

```
select sid, capture#, capture_name,
  ELAPSED_CAPTURE_TIME/100  capture_time ,
  ELAPSED_RULE_TIME/100  rule_time ,
  ELAPSED_ENQUEUE_TIME/100 enqueue_time ,
  ELAPSED_LCR_TIME/100 lcr_time ,
  ELAPSED_REDO_WAIT_TIME/100 redo_wait_time,
  ELAPSED_PAUSE_TIME/100  pause_time
from V$STREAMS_CAPTURE
/
```

In the next section, the Apply related views will be introduced.

Apply Related Views

Apply related static dictionary views show the basic configuration details and the dynamic dictionary views show Capture process statistics. Figure 7.2 shows all of the Apply related views, both dynamic and static.

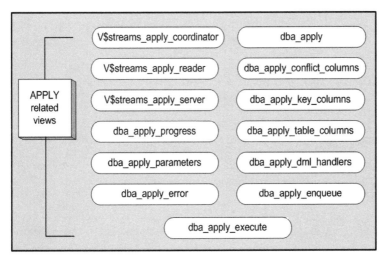

Figure 7.2 *Apply Process related static and dynamic views*

The Apply process is basically an Oracle process which performs DMLs on the destination database. Transactional activity on the target or destination is prone to all kinds of configuration issues. The Apply related views help users understand the issues and will aid in tuning. Next the views and their important fields and statistics will be examined.

v$streams_apply_coordinator

This view displays information about each Apply process coordinator. The coordinator for an Apply process gets transactions from the Apply process reader and passes them to Apply servers. Information presented earlier indicated that the apply coordinator is an important component in the overall apply mechanism. The coordinator process is an Oracle background process which gets the transactions from the reader server and passes them to apply servers.

Some of the useful fields include:

- *total_applied* – The total number of transactions applied by the Apply process since it was last started

- *total_admin* – The number of administrative jobs issued since the Apply process was last started

- *total_assigned* – The number of transactions assigned to Apply servers since the Apply process was last started

- *total_received* – The total number of transactions received by the coordinator process since the Apply process was last started.

- *hwm_message_number* – The number of the message corresponding to the high watermark. In other words, it shows the highest message number that has been applied.

- *hwm_message_create_time* – The creation time at the source database of the message corresponding to the high watermark.

- *startup_time* – The time when the Apply process was last started.

The following SQL statement shows the basic details of the coordinator process:

```
COLUMN APPLY_NAME HEADING 'Apply Process|Name' FORMAT A25
COLUMN PROCESS_NAME HEADING 'Coordinator|Process|Name' FORMAT A11
COLUMN SID HEADING 'Session|ID' FORMAT 9999
COLUMN SERIAL# HEADING 'Session|Serial|Number' FORMAT 999999
COLUMN STATE HEADING 'State' FORMAT A21

SELECT c.APPLY_NAME,
SUBSTR(s.PROGRAM, INSTR(S.PROGRAM,'(')+1,4) PROCESS_NAME,
c.SID, c.SERIAL#, c.STATE
FROM V$STREAMS_APPLY_COORDINATOR c, V$SESSION s
WHERE c.SID = s.SID AND
c.SERIAL# = s.SERIAL#
/
```

The following SQL statement shows the details about the transactions received, applied, and being applied by each Apply process:

```
COLUMN APPLY_NAME HEADING 'Apply Process Name' FORMAT A25
COLUMN TOTAL_RECEIVED HEADING 'Total|Trans|Received' FORMAT 99999999
COLUMN TOTAL_APPLIED HEADING 'Total|Trans|Applied' FORMAT 99999999
COLUMN TOTAL_ERRORS HEADING 'Total|Apply|Errors' FORMAT 9999
COLUMN BEING_APPLIED HEADING 'Total|Trans Being|Applied' FORMAT 99999999
COLUMN TOTAL_IGNORED HEADING 'Total|Trans|Ignored' FORMAT 99999999

SELECT APPLY_NAME, TOTAL_RECEIVED,
TOTAL_APPLIED, TOTAL_ERRORS,
(TOTAL_ASSIGNED - (TOTAL_ROLLBACKS + TOTAL_APPLIED)) BEING_APPLIED,
TOTAL_IGNORED
FROM V$STREAMS_APPLY_COORDINATOR
/
```

The above SQL statements help to monitor the overall apply activity.

v$streams_apply_reader

This view displays information about each Apply reader. The Apply reader for an Apply process is a process which dequeues messages from the queue, computes message dependencies, builds transactions, and passes the transactions on to the Apply process coordinator in commit order for assignment to the Apply servers.

The following SQL statement shows full details about the Apply server reader processes. This SQL outputs a multi line format display to improve the readability of the details.

```
COL FROM_STREAMS_APPLY_READER format a60

select 'Session SID         : ' || SID || chr(10) ||
'APPLY Name          : ' || APPLY_NAME|| chr(10) ||
'Current State       : ' || STATE || chr(10) ||
'TOT MSGs Dequed     : ' || TOTAL_MESSAGES_DEQUEUED || chr(10) ||
'Time last msg received: ' || to_char(DEQUEUE_TIME, 'YY-MM-DD HH24:MI')  || chr(10) ||
'Last DeQued MSG  NUM : ' || DEQUEUED_MESSAGE_NUMBER || chr(10) ||
'CRT-Time at SRCDB of Last MSG : ' ||
to_char(DEQUEUED_MESSAGE_CREATE_TIME, 'YY-MM-DD HH24:MI')||chr(10)||
'SGA Used so far      : ' || SGA_USED || chr(10) ||
'Last browse SCN      : ' || LAST_BROWSE_NUM || chr(10) ||
'Oldest SCN           : ' || OLDEST_SCN_NUM
FROM_STREAMS_APPLY_READER
from V$STREAMS_APPLY_READER
/
```

There are two columns that provide the elapsed time details. They are:

- ELAPSED_DEQUEUE_TIME – The time elapsed, in hundredths of a second, during the dequeuing of messages since the Apply process was last started.

- ELAPSED_SCHEDULE_TIME – The time elapsed, in hundredths of a second, during the scheduling of messages since the Apply process was last started. Scheduling includes computing dependencies between messages and assembling messages into transactions.

The following statement shows elapsed times:

```
select SID, APPLY_NAME, APPLY#, SGA_USED,
ELAPSED_DEQUEUE_TIME, ELAPSED_SCHEDULE_TIME
from V$STREAMS_APPLY_READER
/
```

A check of the elapsed times helps the administrators see the performance of reader component.

v$streams_apply_server

This view displays information about each Apply server and its activities. An Apply server receives events from the apply coordinator for an Apply process. For each event received, an Apply server either applies the event or sends the event to the appropriate Apply handler.

Some of the fields that are useful in the monitoring of the Apply activity are as follows:

- *server_id* – The parallel execution server number of the Apply server.

- *total_assigned* – The total number of transactions assigned to the Apply server since the Apply process was last started.

- *total_messages_applied* – The total number of messages applied by this Apply server since the Apply process was last started.

- *applied_message_number* – The number of the last message applied.

- *elapsed_dequeue_time* – The time elapsed, in hundredths of a second, during the dequeuing of messages since the Apply process was last started.

- *elapsed_apply_time* – The time elapsed, in hundredths of a second, during the applying of messages since the Apply process was last started.

The following SQL statement shows some useful statistics related to messages applied:

```
select          SID,           APPLY_NAME,          TOTAL_ASSIGNED,          TOTAL_ADMIN,
TOTAL_MESSAGES_APPLIED,ELAPSED_DEQUEUE_TIME ,
ELAPSED_APPLY_TIME from V$STREAMS_APPLY_SERVER
/
```

dba_apply

This view displays information about the Apply processes. This view shows basic configuration details including the status, rule set names and the apply handlers. This view helps the DBA examine and rectify any issues associated with configuration.

The following SQL statement shows details about Apply process. It gives a multi-line output for each Apply process.

```
select
'Apply Name          :  '  ||  APPLY_NAME  ||  chr(10)  ||
'QUEUE_NAME          ;  '  ||  QUEUE_NAME  ||  chr(10)  ||
'APPLY_CAPTURED      :  '  ||  APPLY_CAPTURED  ||  chr(10)  ||
'RULE_SET_NAME       :  '  ||  RULE_SET_NAME  ||  chr(10)  ||
'APPLY_USER          :  '  ||  APPLY_USER     ||  chr(10)  ||
'APPLY_DATABASE_LINK :  '  ||  APPLY_DATABASE_LINK  ||  chr(10)  ||
'DDL_HANDLER         :  '  ||  trim(DDL_HANDLER)  ||  chr(10)  ||
'PRECOMMIT_HANDLER   :  '  ||  PRECOMMIT_HANDLER  ||  chr(10)  ||
'MESSAGE_HANDLER     :  '  ||  MESSAGE_HANDLER   ||  chr(10)  ||
'STATUS              :  '  ||  STATUS  ||  chr(10)  ||
'MAX_APPLIED_MSG_NUM :  '  ||  MAX_APPLIED_Message_number  ||  chr(10)  ||
'ERROR_NUMBER        :  '  ||  ERROR_NUMBER  ||  chr(10)  ||
'ERROR_MESSAGE       :  '  ||  ERROR_MESSAGE  ||  chr(10)  ||
'------------------------------------------------'
apply_profile
from DBA_APPLY
/
```

dba_apply_conflict_columns

The *dba_apply_conflict_columns* view displays information about conflict handlers on all tables in the database: The important fields of the view are:

- *method_name* shows the name of the update handler used to resolve conflicts.

- *resolution_column* shows the name of the column used to resolve conflicts.

- *column_name* shows the name of a column in the column list for the update conflict handler.

The following SQL statement shows details of conflict columns:

```
select object_owner, object_name, method_name,
resolution_column, column_name
from dba_apply_conflict_columns
/
```

dba_apply_dml_handlers

This view displays information about the DML handlers on all tables in the database. The column USER_PROCEDURE shows the PL/SQL procedure assigned to function as the DML handler. OPERATION_NAME shows the type command such as Delete, Update, Insert. When ERROR_HANDLER is specified as TRUE, the DML handler becomes an Error Handler.

The following SQL statement shows details of DML Handlers on the apply side:

```
COLUMN OBJECT_OWNER HEADING 'Table|Owner' FORMAT A8
COLUMN OBJECT_NAME HEADING 'Table Name' FORMAT A16
COLUMN OPERATION_NAME HEADING 'Operation' FORMAT A10
COLUMN USER_PROCEDURE HEADING 'Handler Procedure' FORMAT A40
COLUMN APPLY_NAME HEADING 'Apply Proc|Name' FORMAT A15
COLUMN ERROR_HANDLER HEADING 'Error|Hndlr' FORMAT A5

SELECT OBJECT_OWNER, OBJECT_NAME, OPERATION_NAME, USER_PROCEDURE,
APPLY_NAME, ERROR_HANDLER FROM DBA_APPLY_DML_HANDLERS
ORDER BY OBJECT_OWNER, OBJECT_NAME
/
```

While querying the same view, to display the details of the pre-commit handlers, use the following SQL statement:

```
COLUMN APPLY_NAME HEADING 'Apply Process Name' FORMAT A20
COLUMN PRECOMMIT_HANDLER HEADING 'Precommit Handler' FORMAT A30
COLUMN APPLY_CAPTURED HEADING 'Type of|Events|Applied' FORMAT A15

SELECT APPLY_NAME, PRECOMMIT_HANDLER,
DECODE(APPLY_CAPTURED, 'YES', 'Captured', 'NO', 'User-Enqueued') APPLY_CAPTURED
FROM DBA_APPLY
WHERE PRECOMMIT_HANDLER IS NOT NULL
/
```

dba_apply_enqueue

This view displays information about the Apply enqueue actions for all the rules in the database.

dba_apply_error

This view displays information about error transactions generated by the Apply processes in the database. This is a very useful view to keep track of the errors generated by the Apply process. This view should be queried as often as possible to see if there are any errors. In case error rows show up in this view, the DBA should immediately begin further investigation of the errors and rectify them.

Some useful columns include:

- LOCAL_TRANSACTION_ID shows the local transaction ID for the error transaction whereas the SOURCE_TRANSACTION_ID shows original transaction ID at the source database.

- MESSAGE_COUNT is useful as it shows the total number of events inside the error transaction.

- SOURCE_COMMIT_SCN displays the original commit SCN for the transaction at the source database.

As an example, the following SQL statement shows details of Apply Error Transactions:

```
COLUMN APPLY_NAME HEADING 'Apply|Process'            FORMAT A15
COLUMN SOURCE_DATABASE HEADING 'Source|Database' FORMAT A16
COLUMN SOURCE_COMMIT_SCN HEAD 'Source|CommitSCN' FORMAT 9999999999
COLUMN LOCAL_TRANSACTION_ID HEADING 'Local|Trans ID' FORMAT A12
COLUMN ERROR_NUMBER HEADING 'Error |Number'   FORMAT 9999999
COLUMN ERROR_MESSAGE HEADING 'Error Message'  FORMAT A40
COLUMN MESSAGE_COUNT HEADING 'Events in|ErrTrans' FORMAT 999999

SELECT APPLY_NAME, SOURCE_COMMIT_SCN ,
MESSAGE_NUMBER   , SOURCE_DATABASE,
LOCAL_TRANSACTION_ID, ERROR_NUMBER,
ERROR_MESSAGE, MESSAGE_COUNT
FROM DBA_APPLY_ERROR
order by SOURCE_COMMIT_SCN
/
```

In the latter part of this chapter, an example has been included on how to display the full details of the error transaction. The full details obtained will help to show the problems involved.

dba_apply_execute

This view displays information about Apply execute actions for the rules in the database.

dba_apply_key_columns

This view displays information about substitute key columns for all the tables in the database. Substitute key columns are set using the *set_key_columns* procedure in the *dbms_apply_adm*

The following SQL statement shows the key columns:

```
select OBJECT_OWNER, OBJECT_NAME, COLUMN_NAME
from DBA_APPLY_KEY_COLUMNS
/
```

dba_apply_parameters

This view displays information about the parameters for the Apply processes in the database. It keeps track of the Apply parameters that have been set. The combination of parameter name and its value can be displayed by the following SQL statement:

```
COLUMN parameter        FORMAT A20
COLUMN value            FORMAT A20
COLUMN set_by_user      FORMAT A20

SELECT apply_name, parameter, value, set_by_user
FROM DBA_APPLY_PARAMETERS
order by apply_name, parameter
/
```

dba_apply_progress

This view displays information about the progress made by the Apply processes that dequeues events from queues that are accessible to the current user. This view only contains information about captured events. It does not contain information about user-enqueued events. This is an important view which keeps track of the applied messages.

Some useful columns include:

- APPLIED_MESSAGE_NUMBER shows the message number up to which all transactions have definitely been applied. This represents the low watermark for the Apply process. It means the messages with a commit message number less than or equal to this message number have definitely been applied.

- OLDEST_MESSAGE_NUMBER shows the earliest message number of the transactions currently being dequeued and applied. The difference between the *apply_time* and *applied_message_create_time* is the latency time.

The following SQL statement shows details of the Apply progress:

```
COLUMN APPLY_NAME HEADING 'Apply Process|Name'        FORMAT A16
COLUMN 'Latency in Seconds'                            FORMAT 999999999
COLUMN 'Event Creation'                               FORMAT A18
COLUMN 'Apply Time'                                    FORMAT A18
COLUMN APPLIED_MESSAGE_NUMBER HEADING 'Applied|Message|Number' FORMAT 99999999

SELECT APPLY_NAME,
(APPLY_TIME - APPLIED_MESSAGE_CREATE_TIME)*86400 "Latency in Seconds",
TO_CHAR(APPLIED_MESSAGE_CREATE_TIME,'HH24:MI:SS MM/DD/YY')
"Event Creation",
TO_CHAR(APPLY_TIME,'HH24:MI:SS MM/DD/YY') "Apply Time",
APPLIED_MESSAGE_NUMBER
FROM DBA_APPLY_PROGRESS
/
```

dba_apply_table_columns

This view displays information about the destination table object columns for all tables in the database.

Some useful columns include:

- The COMPARE_OLD_ON_DELETE column indicates whether to compare the old value of the column on deletes for YES or not for NO

- The COMPARE_OLD_ON_UPDATE column indicates whether to compare the old value of the column on updates for YES or not for NO.

This view is populated when conflict resolution methods are configured. A query of this view helps to understand the conflict resolution defined.

Apply-related useful queries

Capture to Dequeue Latency for an Event

To find out the latency for the last dequeued event, some of the fields in the dynamic *v$streams_apply_reader* view can be used. For the captured events, the latency is the amount of time between when the event was created at a source database and when the event was dequeued by the Apply process. In the case of user-enqueued events, the latency represents the amount of time between when the event enqueued at the local database and when the event was dequeued by the Apply process. The goal should be to reduce the latency. Reduced latency indicates that transactional activity is progressing well at the destination database.

The following SQL statement shows the dequeue latency. In order to assess the latency pattern, this SQL should be run repeatedly when an Apply process is actively dequeuing messages.

```
COLUMN APPLY_NAME HEADING 'Apply Process|Name' FORMAT A17
COLUMN LATENCY HEADING 'Latency|in|Seconds' FORMAT 9999
COLUMN CREATION HEADING 'Event Creation' FORMAT A17
COLUMN LAST_DEQUEUE HEADING 'Last Dequeue Time' FORMAT A20
COLUMN DEQUEUED_MESSAGE_NUMBER HEADING 'Dequeued|Message Number' FORMAT 999999

SELECT       APPLY_NAME,(DEQUEUE_TIME-DEQUEUED_MESSAGE_CREATE_TIME)*86400       LATENCY,
TO_CHAR(DEQUEUED_MESSAGE_CREATE_TIME,'HH24:MI:SS       MM/DD/YY')       CREATION,
TO_CHAR(DEQUEUE_TIME,'HH24:MI:SS MM/DD/YY') LAST_DEQUEUE,
DEQUEUED_MESSAGE_NUMBER
FROM V$STREAMS_APPLY_READER
/
```

Latency can also be found in the *dba_apply_progress* view. The difference between *apply_time* and *applied_message_create_time* determine the latency in seconds as shown below:

```
SELECT APPLY_NAME, (APPLY_TIME-APPLIED_MESSAGE_CREATE_TIME) * 86400 "Latency in Seconds",
APPLIED_MESSAGE_NUMBER
FROM DBA_APPLY_PROGRESS
/
```

Even though the above specified views are both dependable, the following differences between these two queries exist:

- The Apply process should be enabled when the query is run on the *v$streams_apply_coordinator* view. The Apply process can be either enabled or disabled when the query is run on the *dba_apply_progress* view.

- The query on the *v$streams_apply_coordinator* view may show the latency for a more recent transaction than the query on the *dba_apply_progress* view.

Display Error Transaction Details

Even though a query of the *dba_apply_error* view provides the list of Apply errors, the event itself needs to be queried in order to fully understand the details of the event and error details. Without the full details, it may not possible to pinpoint the problem.

This section contains the PL/SQL code for three procedures that help inquire about the event details. These procedures are not mutually exclusive. They compliment each other in the search for event details.

The procedures are:

- *lcr_print_errors_all* – This procedure is used to display all of the error transaction details.

- *lcr_print_error* – This procedure is used to display a specific error transaction detail.

- *lcr_print_values* – This procedure is called by both of the above two procedures. It actually displays the event details.

Using the code shown below the stored procedure named *lcr_print_errors_all* will be created:

```
-- ****************************************************
-- Copyright © 2005 by Rampant TechPress
-- This script is free for non-commercial purposes
-- with no warranties.  Use at your own risk.
--
-- To license this script for a commercial purpose,
-- contact info@rampant.cc
-- ****************************************************

-- To print all errors as obtained from the dba_apply_error
CREATE OR REPLACE PROCEDURE lcr_print_errors_all
IS
CURSOR C IS
SELECT LOCAL_TRANSACTION_ID,
 SOURCE_DATABASE, MESSAGE_NUMBER,
 MESSAGE_COUNT, ERROR_NUMBER,
 ERROR_MESSAGE FROM DBA_APPLY_ERROR
ORDER BY SOURCE_DATABASE, SOURCE_COMMIT_SCN;
--
i      NUMBER;
txnid  VARCHAR2(30);
source VARCHAR2(128);
msgno  NUMBER;
msgcnt NUMBER;
errnum NUMBER := 0;
errno  NUMBER;
errmsg VARCHAR2(255);
lcr    SYS.AnyData;
R      NUMBER;

BEGIN
FOR R IN C LOOP
  errnum        := errnum + 1;
  msgcnt        := r.MESSAGE_COUNT;
  txnid         := r.LOCAL_TRANSACTION_ID;
  source        := r.SOURCE_DATABASE;
  msgno         := r.MESSAGE_NUMBER;
  errno         := r.ERROR_NUMBER;
  errmsg        := r.ERROR_MESSAGE;
  DBMS_OUTPUT.PUT_LINE('****************************************');
  DBMS_OUTPUT.PUT_LINE('-- ERROR #' || errnum);
  DBMS_OUTPUT.PUT_LINE('-- Local Trans ID: ' || txnid);
  DBMS_OUTPUT.PUT_LINE('-- Source DB: ' || source);
  -- DBMS_OUTPUT.PUT_LINE('-- Error in Message: '|| msgno);
  DBMS_OUTPUT.PUT_LINE('-- Error Number: '||errno);
  DBMS_OUTPUT.PUT_LINE('-- Message Text: '|| substr(errmsg,1,60)  );

FOR i IN 1..msgcnt LOOP
  DBMS_OUTPUT.PUT_LINE('In record Loop Msg: ' || i);
  lcr := DBMS_APPLY_ADM.GET_ERROR_MESSAGE(i, txnid);
  lcr_print_values (lcr);
  END LOOP;
END LOOP;
END lcr_print_errors_all;
/
```

This procedure calls another procedure, *lcr_print_values*, which extracts the values from the SYS.AnyData type event and displays. The *lcr_print_values* code listing is located in the code depot.

To display information about a specified transaction, the *lcr_print_error* procedure will be used. The code listing is in the code depot and the *transaction id* will be passed as a parameter.

This first part of a typical output listing is shown below. Please refer to the code depot for the complete listing.

```
DNYOIP20 SQL>set serveroutput on size 200000
DNYOIP20 SQL>exec LCR_PRINT_ERRORS_ALL ;
****************************************************
-- ERROR #1
-- Local Trans ID: 3.8.2321
-- Source DB: DNYTST10.WORLD
-- Error Number: 1403
-- Message Text: ORA-01403: no data found
ORA-01403: no data found
ORA-06512:
In record Loop Msg: 1
Type Name : SYS.LCR$_ROW_RECORD
Source db  : DNYTST10.WORLD
Owner      : NY4  Object : ALLINSURED1
CMD Type   : UPDATE   Is tag null : Y
*Old(1): POL_NO => 2995
*Old(2): SUM_ASSURED => 98260
New(1): SUM_ASSURED => 50000
****************************************************
.
.
.
In record Loop Msg: 1
Type Name : SYS.LCR$_ROW_RECORD
Source db  : DNYTST10.WORLD
Owner      : NY4  Object : ALLINSURED1
CMD Type   : UPDATE   Is tag null : Y
*Old(1): POL_NO => 20042004
*Old(2): SUM_ASSURED => 2000
*Old(3): PREMIUM =>
*Old(4): NAME =>
New(1): SUM_ASSURED => 9999
New(2): PREMIUM => 8888
New(3): NAME => MADHU
session#: 11
transaction name:
username: STRMADM

PL/SQL procedure successfully completed.
```

As shown in the above output, error#1 and error#2 are the result of update failures because the corresponding rows were not found at destination table on the Apply side. The error message is *no data found*. Error#3 is the result of inserting a duplicate row which resulted in unique key constraint violation. Error#4 is the result of foreign key constraint violation at destination table.

General Streams Related Views

Figure 7.3 shows the general Streams related views in a single glance.

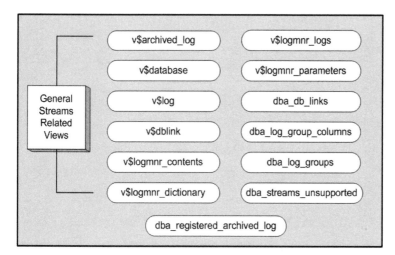

Figure 7.3 *General Streams Related static and dynamic views*

The description of each of the view follows:

v$archived_log

This view shows the archived log file details. It shows the names of the log files, and the start and end SCN values. Whenever a Capture process halted for any valid reason, on resumption it still must go back to archive log files to scan the redo entries. It is important to keep track of the archive log files location and monitor the removal of the archived log files from the file system. If the archived logs are removed before the Capture process has completed its scan, the Capture process will abort. Failing to have right archive log will abort the Capture process.

Some important and useful columns are shown below:

- RECID: This is the archived log record ID.

- STAMP: This is the archived log record stamp.

- NAME: This is the archived log file name. If set to NULL, the log file was cleared before it was archived.

- STATUS: This is the status of the archived log. It can have the following values: A – Available; D – Deleted; U – Unavailable; and X – Expired.

- COMPLETION_TIME_DATE: This is the time when the archiving for this log is completed

- DICTIONARY_BEING: This indicates whether the log contains the start of a LogMiner dictionary or not .

- DICTIONARY_END: This indicates whether the log contains the end of a LogMiner dictionary or not.

- FIRST_CHANGE#: This is the first change# in the archived log.

- FIRST_TIME DATE: This is the timestamp of the first change.

- NEXT_CHANGE#: This is the first change in the next log.

- NEXT_TIME DATE: This is the timestamp of the next change.

- BLOCKS: This is the size of the archived log, in blocks.

- BLOCK_SIZE: This is the redo log block size. This is the logical block size of the archived log, which is the same as the logical block size of the online log from which the archived log was copied. The online log logical block size is a platform-specific value that is not adjustable by the user.

dba_registered_archived_log

This view displays information about the registered archived logfiles in the database for the Capture processes which are the consumers of the log files.

The following SQL statement shows the details:

```
COLUMN CONSUMER_NAME HEADING 'Capture|Process|Name' FORMAT A15
COLUMN NAME HEADING 'Archived Redo Log|File Name' FORMAT A35
COLUMN FIRST_SCN HEADING 'First SCN' FORMAT 99999999999
COLUMN NEXT_SCN HEADING 'Next SCN' FORMAT 99999999999

SELECT r.CONSUMER_NAME, r.NAME,
 r.FIRST_SCN, r.NEXT_SCN
FROM DBA_REGISTERED_ARCHIVED_LOG r, DBA_CAPTURE c
WHERE r.CONSUMER_NAME = c.CAPTURE_NAME;
```

v$database

This view displays information about the database from the control file. Information such as the last SCN checkpointed, the number assigned to the database instantiation, and the highest NEXT_CHANGE# for an archive log is useful.

The following SQL statement shows information about the current state and current SCN values:

```
Select 'Database Name        : ' || a.NAME || chr(10) ||
'Log Mode                     : ' || a.LOG_MODE || chr(10)    ||
'Last SCN Archived            : ' || a.ARCHIVE_CHANGE# || chr(10)    ||
'Last SCN CheckPointed        : ' || a.CHECKPOINT_CHANGE# || chr(10)    ||
'Current SCN                  : ' || DBMS_FLASHBACK.GET_SYSTEM_CHANGE_NUMBER() || chr(10)    ||
'Control File Type            : ' || a.CONTROLFILE_TYPE    || chr(10)  ||
'Control File Sequence        : ' || a.CONTROLFILE_SEQUENCE#    || chr(10) ||
'CTLFL Chg#                   : ' || a.CONTROLFILE_CHANGE# || chr(10) ||
'Switch Status                : ' || a.SWITCHOVER_STATUS || chr(10)    ||
'Open Mode                    : ' || a.OPEN_MODE || chr(10)  ||
'Force Logging                : ' || a.force_logging    || chr(10)    ||
'Instance Name                : ' || b.INSTANCE_NAME    || chr(10) ||
'Host Name                    : ' || b.HOST_NAME        || chr(10) ||
'VERSION                      : ' || b.VERSION          || chr(10) ||
'Insatnce Start Up Time       : ' || to_char(STARTUP_TIME, 'MON-DD HH24:MI') || chr(10)  ||
'Instance Status              : ' || b.STATUS           || chr(10)  ||
'Database Status              : ' || b.DATABASE_STATUS || chr(10)    ||
'Logins                       : ' || LOGINS
Database_and_Instance_Details
from v$database a, v$instance b
/
```

A typical output from the above statement looks like this:

```
DATABASE_AND_INSTANCE_DETAILS
-----------------------------------------------
Database Name           : DNYTST10
Log Mode                : ARCHIVELOG
Last SCN Archived       : 15537780
Last SCN CheckPointed   : 15552965
Current SCN             : 15554208
Control File Type       : CURRENT
Control File Sequence   : 33733100
CTLFL Chg#              : 15553316
Switch Status           : SESSIONS ACTIVE
Open Mode               : READ WRITE
Force Logging           : NO
Instance Name           : DNYTST10
Host Name               : njs61d-5101b
VERSION                 : 10.1.0.2.0
Insatnce Start Up Time  : OCT-19 16:17
Instance Status         : OPEN
Database Status         : ACTIVE
Logins                  : ALLOWED
```

v$dblink

This view describes all of the database links with *in_transaction* = YES that have been opened by the session issuing the query on *v$dblink*. These database links must be committed or rolled back before being closed. The database links are main channels for the propagation of messages. Replication completely depends on the database links.

v$log

This view displays log file information from the control file. The FIRST_CHANGE# column shows the lowest SCN in the log, and the FIRST_TIME shows the time of the first SCN in the log.

v$logmnr_contents

This view contains log history information. When a SELECT statement is executed against the *v$logmnr_contents* view, the archive redo log files are read sequentially. Translated records from the redo log files are returned as rows in the *v$logmnr_contents* view. This continues until either the filter criteria, such as EndTime or endSCN, specified at startup is met or the end of the archive log file is reached.

v$logmnr_dictionary

This view contains log history information. This view shows the following useful information:

- *db_txn_scn* – This is the SCN at which the dictionary was created.

- *dictionary_scn* – This is the database checkpoint SCN at which the dictionary was created.

dba_db_links

This view describes the database links. This view does not display the PASSWORD column.

dba_log_groups

This view describes the log group definitions on the tables in the database. The following statement can be used to list the supplemental log groups:

```
set linesize 140
COLUMN  log_group_name FORMAT A30
COLUMN  owner          FORMAT A24
COLUMN  table_name     FORMAT A30
COLUMN  always HEADING 'Type of Log Group' FORMAT A30

SELECT  log_group_name, owner, table_name,
DECODE(always, 'ALWAYS', 'Unconditional',
               NULL, 'Conditional') ALWAYS
FROM DBA_LOG_GROUPS
/
```

The contents of this view show the supplemental logging configured. This information helps to troubleshoot apply issues.

dba_log_group_columns

This view describes all columns in the database that are specified in log groups. For example, to query the columns in the group ALLINS1_LOG_GRP1, use the following SQL statement:

```
col OWNER for a8
col LOG_GROUP_NAME for a20
col TABLE_NAME for a20
col COLUMN_NAME for a12

select * from dba_log_group_columns
where LOG_GROUP_NAME = 'ALLINS1_LOG_GRP1'
/
```

dba_streams_unsupported

This view displays information about the tables in the database that are not supported by Streams in this release of the Oracle Database. Especially before schema level replication is used, ensure that there are not any tables that have unsupported features for Streams. The contents of this view will indicate why a particular table is an unsupported one.

```
select * from DBA_STREAMS_UNSUPPORTED where owner like 'NY%'
/

OWNER     TABLE_NAME           REASON                          AUT
--------  -------------------- ------------------------------- ---
NY4       HIST_UPD             column with user-defined type   NO
NY4       HIST_UPD_NEW_NTABLE  column with user-defined type   NO
NY4       HIST_UPD_OLD_NTABLE  column with user-defined type   NO
NY4       LIST_ROW_LCRS        column with user-defined type   NO
NY4       LOG_ERRORS           column with user-defined type   NO
NY4       NEW_VALUES_NTAB      column with user-defined type   NO
NY4       OLD_VALUES_NTAB      column with user-defined type   NO

7 rows selected.
```

dba_streams_newly_supported

This view displays information about the tables in the database that are newly supported by Streams.

dba_type_attrs

This view describes the attributes of the object types defined in the database. The following SQL statement shows details from *dba_type_attrs*.

```
select OWNER, ATTR_TYPE_NAME , TYPE_NAME, ATTR_NAME from dba_type_attrs
where TYPE_NAME like 'LCR%'
```

dba_type_methods

This view describes the methods of the object types accessible in the database.

dba_types

This view describes the object types accessible in the database.

Queue and Propagation Related Views

There are many dynamic and static views that help to look at the queue and propagation processes. Figure 7.4 shows such views.

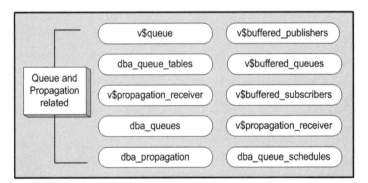

Figure 7.4 *Queue and Propagation Related static and dynamic views*

v$buffered_publishers

This view displays information about all buffered publishers in the instance. There is one row per queue per sender. The values are reset to zero when the database, or instance in a RAC environment, restarts. Therefore, the statistics should be used carefully as they may not give a total picture.

```
COL SENDER_NAME HEADING 'Capture|Process' FORMAT A20
COL SENDER_ADDRESS HEADING 'Sender Queue' FORMAT A25
COL QUEUE_NAME HEADING 'Queue Name' FORMAT A15
COL CNUM_MSGS HEADING 'Number|of LCRs|Enqueued' FORMAT 99999999
COL LAST_ENQUEUED_MSG HEADING 'Last|Enqueued|LCR' FORMAT 99999999

SELECT SENDER_NAME,
       SENDER_ADDRESS,
       QUEUE_NAME,
       CNUM_MSGS,
       LAST_ENQUEUED_MSG
  FROM V$BUFFERED_PUBLISHERS
/
```

In the above statement, *sender_name* shows the Capture Process and the
sender_address shows source database

v$buffered_queues

This view displays information about all buffered queues in the instance.
There is one row per queue. It shows statistics such as LCR in memory and
spilled LCRs. The user's goal should be to control spilled LCRs. Spilled LCR
events are written in a physical table where they may have performance
impact on Streams processing

```
COLUMN QUEUE_SCHEMA HEADING 'Queue Owner' FORMAT A15
COLUMN QUEUE_NAME HEADING 'Queue Name' FORMAT A15
COLUMN MEM_MSG HEADING 'LCRs in Memory' FORMAT 99999999
COLUMN SPILL_MSGS HEADING 'Spilled LCRs' FORMAT 99999999
COLUMN NUM_MSGS HEADING 'Total Captured LCRs|in Buffered Queue' FORMAT 99999999

SELECT QUEUE_SCHEMA,
       QUEUE_NAME,
       (NUM_MSGS - SPILL_MSGS) MEM_MSG,
       SPILL_MSGS,
       NUM_MSGS
  FROM V$BUFFERED_QUEUES
/
```

v$buffered_subscribers

This view displays information about the subscribers for all buffered queues
in the instance. There is one row per subscriber per queue. If any object is
replicated to more than one destination, there will be multiple subscribers to
the same queue.

The following query shows the details of the subscribers:

```
select
'QUEUE_NAME          : ' || QUEUE_NAME         || chr(10) ||
'SUBSCRIBER_NAME     : ' || SUBSCRIBER_NAME    || chr(10) ||
'SUBSCRIBER_ADDRESS  : ' || SUBSCRIBER_ADDRESS || chr(10) ||
'SUBSCRIBER_TYPE     : ' || SUBSCRIBER_TYPE    || chr(10) ||
'STARTUP_TIME        : ' || STARTUP_TIME       || chr(10) ||
'LAST_BROWSED_SEQ    : ' || LAST_BROWSED_SEQ   || chr(10) ||
```

```
'LAST_BROWSED_NUM    : ' || LAST_BROWSED_NUM  || chr(10) ||
'LAST_DEQUEUED_SEQ   : ' || LAST_DEQUEUED_SEQ|| chr(10) ||
'LAST_DEQUEUED_NUM   : ' || LAST_DEQUEUED_NUM || chr(10) ||
'CURRENT_ENQ_SEQ     : ' || CURRENT_ENQ_SEQ   || chr(10) ||
'NUM_MSGS            : ' || NUM_MSGS          || chr(10) ||
'CNUM_MSGS           : ' || CNUM_MSGS         || chr(10) ||
'TOTAL_DEQUEUED_MSG  : ' || TOTAL_DEQUEUED_MSG|| chr(10) ||
'TOTAL_SPILLED_MSG   : ' || TOTAL_SPILLED_MSG subscribers_details
from V$BUFFERED_SUBSCRIBERS
where QUEUE_SCHEMA = 'STRMADM'
/
```

When the above statement is executed at Apply side, *subscriber_name* shows the name of the Apply process.

A typical output is displayed below:

```
SUBSCRIBERS_DETAILS
---------------------------
QUEUE_NAME          : LN4_QUEUE
SUBSCRIBER_NAME     : LN4_APPLY
SUBSCRIBER_ADDRESS  :
SUBSCRIBER_TYPE     : SUBSCRIBER
STARTUP_TIME        : 20-OCT-04
LAST_BROWSED_SEQ    : 9308
LAST_BROWSED_NUM    : 9308
LAST_DEQUEUED_SEQ   : 9308
LAST_DEQUEUED_NUM   : 9308
CURRENT_ENQ_SEQ     : 0
NUM_MSGS            : 0
CNUM_MSGS           : 9308
TOTAL_DEQUEUED_MSG  : 9308
TOTAL_SPILLED_MSG   : 31
```

v$propagation_receiver

This view displays information about buffer queue propagation schedules on the receiving side. The columns SRC_QUEUE_NAME and SRC_DBNAME show the Capture process name and source database name, respectively.

The following SQL query shows details:

```
select SRC_QUEUE_NAME, SRC_DBNAME ,
HIGH_WATER_MARK, ACKNOWLEDGEMENT,
ELAPSED_ENQUEUE_TIME from v$propagation_receiver
/
```

v$propagation_sender

This view displays information about buffer queue propagation schedules on the sending side. At the source side, execute this SQL to show details:

```
select   QUEUE_NAME,   SCHEDULE_STATUS,   HIGH_WATER_MARK,   TOTAL_BYTES,   TOTAL_MSGS   from
v$propagation_sender ;
```

v$queue

This view contains information on the shared server message queues. It shows the number of items in the queue and how many waited, etc.

dba_propagation

This view displays information about the Streams propagations in the database. The source queue and destination queue for each of the propagations can be determined by querying this view as shown in the SQL statement below:

```
COLUMN 'Source Queue' FORMAT A35
COLUMN 'Destination Queue' FORMAT A35

SELECT p.SOURCE_QUEUE_OWNER ||'.'||
p.SOURCE_QUEUE_NAME ||'@'||
g.GLOBAL_NAME "Source Queue",
p.DESTINATION_QUEUE_OWNER ||'.'||
p.DESTINATION_QUEUE_NAME ||'@'||
p.DESTINATION_DBLINK "Destination Queue"
FROM DBA_PROPAGATION p, GLOBAL_NAME g;
```

All propagation jobs from a source queue that share the same database link have a single propagation schedule. The query in this section displays the following information for each propagation:

- The name of the propagation

- The total time spent by the system executing the propagation schedule

- The total number of events propagated by the propagation schedule

- The total number of bytes propagated by the propagation schedule

The following SQL query can be used to display the above information for each propagation:

```
set linesize 140
COLUMN propagation_name FORMAT A26
COLUMN start_date              FORMAT a20
COLUMN propagation_window      FORMAT 99999
COLUMN next_time HEADING 'Next Window' FORMAT A12
COLUMN latency                 FORMAT 99999
COLUMN schedule_disabled HEADING 'Disabl' FORMAT A6
COLUMN process_name HEADING PROC FORMAT A8
COLUMN failures                FORMAT 999
COLUMN total_num               FORMAT 99999999

SELECT p.propagation_name propagation_name,
TO_CHAR(s.start_date, 'HH24:MI:SS MM/DD/YY') START_DATE,
s.propagation_window DURATION, s.latency, s.schedule_disabled,
TO_CHAR(s.next_run_date, 'HH24:MI:SS MM/DD/YY') NEXT_TIME,
process_name, total_number, failures
FROM dba_queue_schedules S , dba_propagation P
WHERE p.propagation_name in (select propagation_name from DBA_PROPAGATION)
/
```

This information shows just how busy the Propagation process is.

dba_queues

This view describes all queues in the database system.

To display all of the SYS.AnyData queues in a database, the following SQL query can be used:

```
COLUMN OWNER HEADING 'Owner' FORMAT A10
COLUMN NAME HEADING 'Queue Name' FORMAT A28
COLUMN QUEUE_TABLE HEADING 'Queue Table' FORMAT A22
COLUMN USER_COMMENT HEADING 'Comment' FORMAT A15
SELECT q.OWNER, q.NAME, t.QUEUE_TABLE, q.USER_COMMENT
FROM DBA_QUEUES q, DBA_QUEUE_TABLES t
WHERE t.OBJECT_TYPE = 'SYS.ANYDATA' AND
q.QUEUE_TABLE = t.QUEUE_TABLE AND
q.OWNER = t.OWNER;
```

In Streams, the majority of queues are sys.anydata queues.

dba_queue_tables

This view describes the queues in the queue tables in the database. It shows some useful information such as the primary and secondary affinity specifications and recipient details.

dba_queue_schedules

This view describes the current schedules for propagating messages. It shows the QNAME, which is source queue name, and DESTINATION, which is the destination name. This is currently limited to being a DBLINK name.

In the next section, information will be presented on the rule related views.

Rule and Rule Set Related Views

Figure 7.5 shows the rule and rule related views in a single glance. Rules are the key components that control the flow of the data and the filtering logic. The description of each of the view follows in the text of this section.

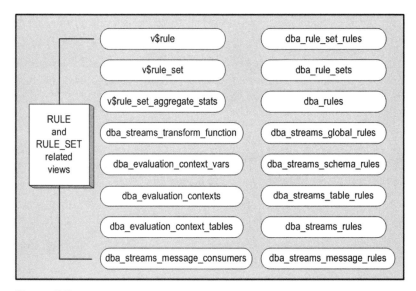

Figure 7.5 *Rule and Rule Set related views*

v$rule

This view displays rule statistics. This view has a row for every rule loaded into shared memory.

Important statistics that can be obtained from the *v$rule* view are:

- *true_hits* – This is the number of times the rule evaluated to TRUE.

- *maybe_hits* – This is the number of times the rule evaluated to MAYBE.

- *sql_evaluations* – This is the number of evaluations of the rule that were performed by issuing SQL.

v$rule_set

This view displays rule set statistics. This view has a row for every rule set loaded into shared memory. This view can be queried to display general information about rule set evaluations that have occurred since the database instance last started.

This view is particularly useful in finding the following information:

- The total number of evaluations of the rule set since the database instance last started.

- The total number of times SQL was executed to evaluate rules since the database instance last started. Generally, issuing SQL to evaluate rules is more expensive than evaluating rules without issuing SQL.

- The total number of evaluations on the rule set that did not issue SQL to evaluate rules since the database instance last started.

- The total number of TRUE rules returned to the rules engine clients using the rule set since the database instance last started.

- The total number of MAYBE rules returned to the rules engine clients using the rule set since the database instance last started

The following query can be used to display this information for each rule set in the database:

```
COLUMN OWNER               HEADING 'Rule Set|Owner' FORMAT A9
COLUMN NAME                HEADING 'Rule Set|Name' FORMAT A11
COLUMN EVALUATIONS         HEADING 'Total|Evaluations' FORMAT 999999
COLUMN SQL_EXECUTIONS      HEADING 'SQL|Executions' FORMAT 999999
COLUMN SQL_FREE_EVALUATIONS HEAD 'SQL Free|Eval' FORMAT 999999
COLUMN TRUE_RULES          HEADING 'True|Rules' FORMAT 999999
COLUMN MAYBE_RULES         HEADING 'Maybe|Rules' FORMAT 999999

SELECT OWNER, NAME, EVALUATIONS, SQL_EXECUTIONS,
SQL_FREE_EVALUATIONS, TRUE_RULES, MAYBE_RULES
FROM V$RULE_SET
/
```

The SQL statement shown below has the following **information about each rule set in a database:**

- The total number of seconds of CPU time used to evaluate the rule set since the database instance last started.

- The total number of seconds used to evaluate the rule set since the database instance last started.

- The total number of shared memory bytes used to evaluate the rule set since the database instance last started.

```
COLUMN OWNER               HEAD 'Rule Set|Owner' FORMAT A15
COLUMN NAME                HEAD 'Rule Set Name' FORMAT A15
COLUMN CPU_SECONDS         HEAD 'Seconds|of CPU|Time' FORMAT 999999.999
COLUMN ELAPSED_SECONDS HEAD 'Seconds of|Eval|Time' FORMAT 999999.999
COLUMN SHARABLE_MEM HEADING 'Bytes|of Shared|Memory' FORMAT 999999999

SELECT OWNER,NAME,
       (CPU_TIME/100) CPU_SECONDS,
       (ELAPSED_TIME/100) ELAPSED_SECONDS,
       SHARABLE_MEM
  FROM V$RULE_SET
/
```

The CPU and memory byte stats help the DBA understand the rule processing activity.

v$rule_set_aggregate_stats

This view displays statistics aggregated over all evaluations on all rule sets. This view has a row for each type of statistic.

```
COLUMN NAME HEADING 'Name of Statistic' FORMAT A55
COLUMN VALUE HEADING 'Value' FORMAT 999999999

SELECT NAME, VALUE FROM V$RULE_SET_AGGREGATE_STATS
/

Name of Statistic                                         Value
------------------------------------------------------- ----------
rule set evaluations (all)                                204181
rule set evaluations (first_hit)                          204181
rule set evaluations (simple_rules_only)                    2907
rule set evaluations (SQL free)                             4478
rule set evaluation time (CPU)                            269203
rule set evaluation time (elapsed)                        282559
rule set SQL executions                                   199703
rule set conditions processed                             206341
rule set true rules                                       179511
rule set maybe rules                                        2848
rule set user function calls (variable value function)    199711
rule set user function calls (variable method function) 1014025
rule set user function calls (evaluation function)        202612

13 rows selected.
```

The names of the statistics are as follows:

- rule set evaluations (*first_hit*) – This is the total number of evaluations on rule sets with *stop_on_first_hit* set to TRUE.

- rule set evaluations (*simple_rules_only*) – This is the total number of evaluations on rule sets with *simple_rules_only* set to TRUE.

- rule set evaluations (SQL free) – This is the total number of evaluations on rule sets which did not internally issue SQL to evaluate rules.

- rule set evaluation time (CPU) – This is the total CPU time, in hundredths of a second, spent in evaluations on rule sets.

- rule set evaluation time (elapsed) – This is the total elapsed time, in hundredths of a second, spent in evaluations on rule sets.

- rule set SQL executions – This is the total number of SQL statements executed during evaluations on rule sets.

- rule set conditions processed – This is the total number of fast indexed conditions processed during evaluations on rule sets.

- rule set true rules – This is the total number of TRUE rules returned during evaluations on rule sets.

- rule set maybe rules – This is the total number of MAYBE rules returned during evaluations on rule sets.

- rule set user function calls (variable value function) – This is the total number of calls made to user-defined functions to retrieve variable values, specified by the *variable_value_function* field in *re$variable_type*, made during evaluations on rule sets.

- rule set user function calls (variable method function) – This is the total number of calls made to user-defined functions to retrieve variable method values, specified by the *variable_method_function* field in *re$variable_type*, made during evaluations on rule sets.

- rule set user function calls (evaluation function) –This is the total number of calls made to user-defined evaluation functions, specified as the *evaluation_function* argument to the *create_evaluation_context* procedure, made during evaluations on rule sets.

dba_evaluation_context_tables

This view describes the tables in the rule evaluation contexts.

dba_evaluation_context_vars

This view describes the variables in the rule evaluation contexts.

dba_evaluation_contexts

This view describes the rule evaluation contexts in the database.

dba_rule_set_rules

This view describes the rules in the rule sets.

dba_rule_sets

This view describes all the rule sets in the database. The following SQL query displays the *rule_set* names and the default evaluation context for each rule set in a database:

```
COLUMN RULE_SET_OWNER HEADING 'Rule Set|Owner' FORMAT A10
COLUMN RULE_SET_NAME HEADING 'Rule Set Name' FORMAT A20
COLUMN RULE_SET_EVAL_CONTEXT_OWNER HEADING 'Eval Context|Owner' FORMAT A12
COLUMN RULE_SET_EVAL_CONTEXT_NAME HEADING 'Eval Context Name' FORMAT A30

SELECT RULE_SET_OWNER,
       RULE_SET_NAME,
       RULE_SET_EVAL_CONTEXT_OWNER,
       RULE_SET_EVAL_CONTEXT_NAME
  FROM DBA_RULE_SETS
/
```

dba_rules

This view describes the rules for all Streams clients in the database.

The RULE_CONDITION column shows the actual rule in a readable form. The data type of this column is CLOB. It has the expressions and conditions that make up the rule.

To list each rule in a database that contains a specified pattern in its condition, the *dba_rules* data dictionary view can be queried and the *dbma_lob.instr* function used to search for the pattern in the rule conditions. For example, the following query lists each rule that contains the pattern ALLINSURED1 in its condition:

```
COLUMN RULE_OWNER HEADING 'Rule Owner' FORMAT A30
COLUMN RULE_NAME HEADING 'Rule Name' FORMAT A30

SELECT RULE_OWNER, RULE_NAME FROM DBA_RULES
WHERE DBMS_LOB.INSTR(RULE_CONDITION, 'ALLINSURED1', 1, 1) > 0
/
```

In order to understand the current rule condition or to make any changes, this view would be a useful tool.

dba_streams_global_rules

This view displays information about the global rules.

This view only contains information about rules created using the *add_global_propagation* or *add_global_rules* procedures in the *dbms_streams_adm* package. It does not contain information about rules created using the *dbms_rule_adm* package.

dba_streams_message_consumer

This view displays information about the Streams messaging clients in the database.

dba_streams_message_rules

This view displays information about the Streams messaging rules in the database.

dba_streams_rules

This view displays information about the rules used by all the Streams processes in the database. This has more columns and comprehensive details than the *dba_rules* view. The following SQL query shows all the rules and rules sets for all the Streams clients:

```
COLUMN STREAMS_NAME       HEAD 'Streams|Name' FORMAT A14
COLUMN STREAMS_TYPE       HEAD 'Streams|Type' FORMAT A11
COLUMN RULE_NAME          HEAD 'Rule|Name' FORMAT A12
COLUMN RULE_SET_TYPE   HEAD 'Rule Set|Type' FORMAT A8
COLUMN STREAMS_RULE_TYPE HEAD 'Streams|Rule|Level' FORMAT A7
COLUMN SCHEMA_NAME        HEAD 'Schema|Name' FORMAT A6
COLUMN OBJECT_NAME        HEAD 'Object|Name' FORMAT A11
COLUMN RULE_TYPE          HEAD 'Rule|Type' FORMAT A4

SELECT STREAMS_NAME, STREAMS_TYPE, RULE_NAME,
RULE_SET_TYPE, TREAMS_RULE_TYPE,
SCHEMA_NAME, BJECT_NAME, RULE_TYPE
FROM DBA_STREAMS_RULES
/
```

The STREAMS_RULE_TYPE column shows the level at which the rule operates. The values include schema, global and table. The *object_name* is shown if the rule is for the table level. *streams_type* shows the type of client such as Capture or Apply. *rule_set_type* shows if the rule is positive or negative. The *rule_type* column shows if it is a DML type or DDL type.

The actual rule is shown by the *rule_condition* column. The following SQL statement shows the actual rule condition:

```
SET LONG 10000
SELECT RULE_NAME, RULE_CONDITION "Current Rule Condition"
FROM DBA_STREAMS_RULES
/
RULE_NAME        Current Rule Condition
---------------  -----------------------------------
RULE$_7          :"VAR$_6".JOB_NAME IS NOT NULL
RULE$_11         :"VAR$_10".JOB_NAME IS NOT NULL
RULE$_3          :"VAR$_2".GET_FLAGS() IS NOT NULL
LN4_RULE1_DML    :dml.get_object_owner () = 'NY4' AND
                 :dml.is_null_tag() = 'Y'
```

Another interesting piece of information that can be obtained is any modification made to the rule condition. The following query displays the rule name, the original rule condition, and the current rule condition for each Streams rule whose condition has been modified:

```
COLUMN RULE_NAME HEADING 'Rule Name' FORMAT A12
COLUMN ORIGINAL_RULE_CONDITION HEAD 'Original Rule Condi' FORMAT A35
COLUMN RULE_CONDITION HEADING 'Current Rule Condition' FORMAT A33

SET LONG 10000
SELECT RULE_NAME, ORIGINAL_RULE_CONDITION, RULE_CONDITION
FROM DBA_STREAMS_RULES
WHERE SAME_RULE_CONDITION = 'NO'
/
```

Note: The query in this section applies only to Streams rules. It does not apply to rules created using the *dbms_rule_adm* package because these rules always show NULL for the ORIGINAL_RULE_CONDITION column and NULL for the SAME_RULE_CONDITION column.

---

dba_streams_schema_rules

This view displays information about the schema rules. Schema rules are created for the Streams Capture processes that enqueue the captured changes into queues.

This view contains only information about rules created using the *add_schema_propagation_rules* or *add_schema_rules* procedures in the *dbms_streams_adm* package. It does not contain information about rules created using the *dbms_rule_adm* package.

dba_streams_table_rules

This view displays information about the table rules. Table rules are created for the Streams Capture processes that enqueue the captured changes into queues.

This view only contains information about rules created using the *add_table_rules, add_table_propagation_rules*, or *add_subset_rules* procedures in the *dbms_streams_adm* package. It does not contain information about rules created using the *dbms_rule_adm* package.

---

dba_streams_transform_function

This view displays information about the rule-based transformation functions in the database. A rule-based transformation is a modification to an event that results when a rule in a positive rule set evaluates to TRUE. A PL/SQL function that performs the modification can be specified. Query this view to help understand what kind of transformation is configured.

The following SQL statement shows the rule-based transformations specified in a database:

```
COLUMN RULE_OWNER HEADING 'Rule Owner'                    FORMAT A20
COLUMN RULE_NAME HEADING 'Rule Name'                      FORMAT A20
COLUMN TRANSFORM_FUNCTION_NAME HEAD 'Transform.Function'  FORMAT A30

SELECT RULE_OWNER, RULE_NAME, TRANSFORM_FUNCTION_NAME
FROM DBA_STREAMS_TRANSFORM_FUNCTION
/
```

So far, various static and dynamic views have been presented that help DBAs to understand details about the configuration and also about the run-time statistics. The next step is to address troubleshooting.

Troubleshooting

In this section, some of the useful methods that can be used to handle the error conditions, how to evaluate them and resolve them will be examined.

Capture Related

At times, the Capture process simply stops capturing the database changes. This section will present some scenarios which can affect the Capture process functionality.

Is the Redo File Missing?

Removing required redo log files before they are scanned by a Capture process causes the Capture process to abort and results in the following error in a Capture process trace file:

```
ORA-01291: missing logfile
```

A missing redo is possible when a logfile is dropped for any administrative reasons.

The *v$logmnr_logs* dynamic performance view can also be checked to determine the missing SCN range and add the relevant redo log files.

A Capture process needs the redo log file that includes the required checkpoint SCN and all subsequent redo log files. The REQUIRED_CHECKPOINT_SCN column in the *dba_capture* data dictionary view can be queried to determine the required checkpoint SCN for a Capture process.

At times, the archive log file required for a Capture process may have been compressed by the housekeeping job or removed by the backup job. In such cases, the Capture process writes an error message to a trace file. The trace file will have entries like those shown below:

```
*** SERVICE NAME:(SYS$USERS) 2004-09-10 21:51:16.935
*** SESSION ID:(34.139) 2004-09-10 21:51:16.935
error 308 in STREAMS process
ORA-00308: cannot open archived log
'/app/oracle/DNYTST10/flash_recovery_area/archivelog/2004_08_28/o1_mf_1_320_0m05kq4w_.arc'
ORA-27037: unable to obtain file status
SVR4 Error: 2: No such file or directory
Additional information: 3
ORA-06512: at "SYS.DBMS_CAPTURE_ADM_INTERNAL", line 630
ORA-06512: at "SYS.DBMS_CAPTURE_PROCESS", line 390
ORA-06512: at line 1
OPIRIP: Uncaught error 447. Error stack:
ORA-00447: fatal error in background process
ORA-00308: cannot open archived log
'/app/oracle/DNYTST10/flash_recovery_area/archivelog/2004_08_28/o1_mf_1_320_0m05kq4w_.arc'
ORA-27037: unable to obtain file status
SVR4 Error: 2: No such file or directory
Additional information: 3
ORA-06512: at "SYS.DBMS_CAPTURE_ADM_INTERNAL", line 630
ORA-06512: at "SYS.DBMS_CAPTURE_PROCESS", line 390
ORA-06512: at line 1
```

The solution is to restore the archive file required and restart the Capture process.

The need for restoration is the reason that the archive log files should be left on disk until the Capture process is finished with the logs. To determine the archive log that contains the required checkpoint SCN, the following query can be used. In this example, xxxx is the checkpoint SCN that is needed.

```
SELECT          name FROM          v$archived_log
where xxxx BETWEEN first_change# AND next_change#;
```

There may come a time when the need to re-adjust the SCN value for the Capture process will arise. For example, the following procedure sets the start and first SCN values for the Capture process so that it will skip the missing log file:

```
exec  DBMS_CAPTURE_ADM.ALTER_CAPTURE(capture_name  =>  'NYDATA1_CAPTURE',  start_scn  =>
9794905, first_scn =>9794905);
```

Is the Capture process current?

In review, the redo scanning latency can be determined by reading the *v$streams_capture* view. How far behind the *capture_message_create_time* is with respect to current system date can be verified. This helps to understand the lag the system is experiencing.

Also, the difference between *enqueue_time* and *enqueue_message_create_time* of the *v$streams_capture* view can be used to determine the event queue latency for the Capture process.

Verify that the Capture Process is Enabled

A Capture process captures changes only when it is ENABLED. The DBA can check whether a Capture process is ENABLED, DISABLED, or ABORTED by querying the *dba_capture* data dictionary view.

Does Not Capture - Check Rules

The Capture process is up and running, but it fails to create any LCR events for propagation to destination. First, verify that the rules are properly defined. Rule Condition in *dba_rules* provides the full text of the rule. Ensure that the rule condition is valid. *dba_streams_rules* can also be queried to find out the rule condition and context.

The next issues to be examined are the related to Propagation.

Propagation Issues

Separate Queue in Case of Bi-directional Replication

When configuring bi-directional replication between two sites, use two queues at each site. To help minimize the spill over to disk, configure two queues at each site. Each site will have:

- One queue for the changes from the local Capture process.

- One queue to receive the changes from other sites.

This helps to achieve better performance for the Streams client processes.

Propagation Schedule Stuck in Pending State

When there are issues with configuration, the DBA may want to stop the Streams process, including the propagation schedule.

A queueing propagation schedule can be unscheduled by executing the *dbma_awadm.unschedule_propagation* procedure. Here is an example. The system appeared to hang or take a long time when an abort is initiated by a <CTRL-C>. When unschedule is reattempted, the following statement is returned: ORA-24080:UNSCHEDULED PROPOGATION PENDING <QUEUE NAME>. The SCHEDULE_DISABLED column of the view has a value of P for this schedule. P shows it is in pending state.

For example:

```
DNYTST10 SQL>EXEC DBMS_STREAMS_ADM.REMOVE_STREAMS_CONFIGURATION();
BEGIN DBMS_STREAMS_ADM.REMOVE_STREAMS_CONFIGURATION(); END;

*
ERROR at line 1:
ORA-24080:  unschedule_propagation  pending  for  QUEUE  STRMADM.NY3_QUEUE  and  DESTINATION
DNYOIP20.WORLD
ORA-06512: at "SYS.DBMS_STREAMS_ADM", line 1644
ORA-06512: at line 1

BEGIN
DBMS_PROPAGATION_ADM.DROP_PROPAGATION(
propagation_name => 'ny3_propagate',
drop_unused_rule_sets => true);
END;
/
BEGIN
*
ERROR at line 1:
ORA-24080:  unschedule_propagation  pending  for  QUEUE  STRMADM.NY3_QUEUE  and  DESTINATION
DNYOIP20.WORLD
ORA-06512: at "SYS.DBMS_LOGREP_UTIL", line 1186
ORA-06512: at "SYS.DBMS_LOGREP_UTIL", line 1074
ORA-06512: at "SYS.DBMS_PROPAGATION_ADM", line 110
ORA-06512: at line 2

Resolution: First make queue processes zero, then find the OID value from aq$_queues table.

SQL> alter system set job_queue_processes = 0 ;

System altered.

SQL> select oid, name from system.aq$_queues where name = 'NY3_QUEUE' ;

OID                             NAME
------------------------------- -------------------------------
E6D2893064F308B7E0340003BA68067D NY3_QUEUE
```

Then update the PENDING status to N as shown below:

```
SQL> update aq$_schedules set DISABLED = 'N'
 where oid = 'E6D2893064F308B7E0340003BA68067D' and
 DESTINATION = 'DNYOIP20.WORLD' ;

1 row updated.

SQL> commit ;

Commit complete.

SQL> alter system set job_queue_processes = 6;

System altered.


-- Then remove the Configuration,  it works...

DNYTST10 SQL>EXEC DBMS_STREAMS_ADM.REMOVE_STREAMS_CONFIGURATION();

PL/SQL procedure successfully completed.
```

The next issues to be examined are the apply related issues as well as their possible solutions.

Apply Issues

Is the Apply Process Encountering Contention?

The Apply process has multiple Apply servers. Apply servers apply DML and DDL changes to database objects at a destination database. The *parallelism* Apply process parameter specifies the number of Apply servers that may concurrently apply transactions. For example, if *parallelism* is set to four, an Apply process uses a total of four Apply servers.

An Apply server can encounter contention when it must wait for a resource that is being used by another session. Contention may result from logical dependencies. For example, when an Apply server tries to apply a change to a row that a user has locked, the Apply server must wait for the user. Contention also may result from physical dependencies. For example, an Interested Transaction List (ITL) contention results when two transactions that are being applied, which may not be logically dependent, are trying to lock the same block on disk. This kind of contention can be monitored by looking at the waiting states it generates. When there is a wait, Apply process writes to the alert log file and an Apply process file. This information helps to pinpoint the exact problem area.

Waiting for an Event That is Not Related to Another Session

An example of an event that is not related to another session is a log file sync event. This is when redo information must be flushed because of a commit or rollback.

In these cases, nothing is written to the log initially because such waits are common and are usually transient. If the Apply server is waiting for the same event after a certain interval of time, the Apply server writes a message to the alert log and Apply process trace file. For example, apply server A001 may write a message similar to the following:

```
A001: warning -- apply server 1, sid 26 waiting for event:
A001: [log file sync] ...
```

This is a contention issue. The DBA will have to examine the root cause of the log file sync wait. The messages written to alert the log are informational.

Waiting for an Event that is Related to a Non Apply Server Session

The Apply server writes a message to the alert log and the Apply process trace file immediately. For example, apply server A001 may write a message similar to the following:

```
A001: warning -- apply server 1, sid 10 waiting on user sid 36 for event:
A001: [enq: TM - contention] name|mode=544d0003, object #=a078,
      table/partition=0
```

Again, this is a contention issue.

Waiting for Another Apply Server Session

This state may be caused by ITL contention, but it also may be caused by situations such as an Apply handler that obtains conflicting locks. In this case, the Apply server that is blocked by another Apply server writes only once to the alert log and the trace file for the Apply process. The blocked Apply server issues a rollback to the blocking Apply server. When the blocking Apply server rolls back, another message indicating that the Apply server has been rolled back is printed to the log files, and the rolled back transaction is reassigned by the coordinator process for the Apply process.

For example, if Apply server 1 of Apply process A001 is blocked by Apply server 2 of the same Apply process, the Apply process writes the following messages to the log files:

```
A001: apply server 1 blocked on server 2
A001: [enq: TX - row lock contention] name|mode=54580006, usn<<16 |
    slot=1000e, sequence=1853
A001: apply server 2 rolled back
```

Is an Apply Server Performing Poorly for Certain Transactions?

Sometimes one or more Apply servers used by the Apply process may be taking large amounts of time to apply certain transactions. The following SQL query shows information about the transactions being applied by each Apply server:

```
COLUMN SERVER_ID HEADING 'Apply Server ID' FORMAT 99999999
COLUMN STATE HEADING 'Apply Server State' FORMAT A20
COLUMN APPLIED_MESSAGE_NUMBER HEADING 'Applied Message|Number' FORMAT 99999999
COLUMN MESSAGE_SEQUENCE HEADING 'Message Sequence|Number' FORMAT 99999999

SELECT SERVER_ID, STATE, APPLIED_MESSAGE_NUMBER, MESSAGE_SEQUENCE
  FROM V$STREAMS_APPLY_SERVER
  ORDER BY SERVER_ID;
```

If this query is run repeatedly, the Apply server state, applied message number, and message sequence number should continue to change for each Apply server as it applies transactions. If these values do not change for one or more Apply servers, the Apply server may not be performing well. For each table to which the Apply process applies changes, every key column must have an index.

When there are a large number of tables, it may be necessary to determine the specific table and DML or DDL operation that is causing an Apply server to perform poorly. To do so, run the following SQL query when an Apply server is taking an inordinately long time to apply a transaction. In this example, assume that the name of the Apply process is LN4_APPLY and that Apply server number two is performing poorly:

```
COLUMN OPERATION HEADING 'Operation' FORMAT A20
COLUMN OPTIONS HEADING 'Options' FORMAT A20
COLUMN OBJECT_OWNER HEADING 'Object|Owner' FORMAT A10
COLUMN OBJECT_NAME HEADING 'Object|Name' FORMAT A10
COLUMN COST HEADING 'Cost' FORMAT 99999999

SELECT p.OPERATION, p.OPTIONS, p.OBJECT_OWNER, p.OBJECT_NAME, p.COST
  FROM V$SQL_PLAN p, V$SESSION s, V$STREAMS_APPLY_SERVER a
  WHERE a.APPLY_NAME = 'LN4_APPLY' AND a.SERVER_ID = 2
    AND s.SID = a.SID
    AND p.HASH_VALUE = s.SQL_HASH_VALUE;
```

This query shows the SQL operation that is currently being performed by the specified Apply server. The query also returns the owner and name of the table on which the operation is being performed and the cost of the operation. If the results show FULL for the COST column, the operation is causing full table scans, and indexing the table's key columns may solve the problem.

In addition, the following SQL query can be run to determine the specific DML or DDL SQL statement that is causing an Apply server to perform poorly. Assume that the name of the Apply process is LN4_APPLY and that Apply server number two is performing poorly:

```
SELECT t.SQL_TEXT
  FROM V$SESSION s, V$SQLTEXT t, V$STREAMS_APPLY_SERVER a
  WHERE a.APPLY_NAME = 'LN4_APPLY' AND a.SERVER_ID = 2
    AND s.SID = a.SID
    AND s.SQL_ADDRESS = t.ADDRESS
    AND s.SQL_HASH_VALUE = t.HASH_VALUE
    ORDER BY PIECE;
```

This query returns the SQL statement that is currently being run by the specified Apply server. The SQL statement shows the table on which the transaction is being applied.

Is the Apply Process Waiting for a Dependent Transaction?

When the *parallelism* parameter for an Apply process is set to a value higher than 1 and the *commit_serialization* parameter of the Apply process is set to FULL, the Apply process may detect ITL contention if there is a transaction that is dependent on another transaction with a higher SCN. ITL contention occurs because some other session has a lock on the rows in the contested block and there are no free ITL slots.

When does this usually happen? One probable scenario is the case of a shared bitmap index fragment. The very nature of a bitmap index could cause this. A bitmap index fragment usually covers many rows in the table. When a particular session intends to update the rows, but the some other rows are controlled by the same bitmap index fragment, the other session has to wait until the lock is lifted. This kind of situation has a performance impact.

What can be done to reduce this kind of contention? Increasing the *inittrans* setting for the table helps to reduce the contention. Another solution is to set *commit_serialization* to NONE for the Apply process, but this may not desirable because the idea is to adhere to commit serialization. Another method is to use the higher parallelism very selectively.

Apply Error handling

The Apply process is quite sensitive to errors that may result on account of a variety of situations. The following common types of Apply process errors may be encountered for LCR events:

```
ORA-01031 Insufficient Privileges
ORA-01403 No Data Found
ORA-23605 Invalid Value for Streams Parameter*
ORA-23607 Invalid Column*
ORA-24031 Invalid Value, parameter_name should be Non-NULL*
ORA-26687 Instantiation SCN Not Set
ORA-26688 Missing Key in LCR*
ORA-26689 Column Type Mismatch*
```

ORA-01031 Insufficient Privileges

This message is generated when the user designed as the Apply user does not have sufficient privileges to perform DDL or DML activities. The Apply user needs to be given the following privileges:

- For table level DML changes, the INSERT, UPDATE, DELETE, and SELECT privileges must be granted.

- For table level DDL changes, the ALTER TABLE privilege must be granted.

- For schema level changes, the CREATE ANY TABLE, CREATE ANY INDEX, CREATE ANY PROCEDURE, ALTER ANY TABLE, and ALTER ANY PROCEDURE privileges must be granted.

- For global level changes, ALL PRIVILEGES must be granted to the Apply user.

To determine what privileges are missing or are provided, login as the user "apply user" and query the *session_privs* data dictionary view.

ORA-01403 No Data Found

An ORA-01403 error message is generated when an Apply process tries to update an existing row and the *old_values* in the row LCR do not match the current values at this destination database object.

This situation could arise on account of any of the situations below:

- Supplemental logging is not specified for columns that require supplemental logging at the source database. In this case, LCRs from the source database may not contain values for key columns.

- There may be a problem with primary key in the destination table. If no primary key exists for the table or if the target table has a different primary key than the source table, substitute key columns can be specified using the *set_key_columns* procedure in the *dbms_apply_adm* package. Error ORA-23416 may be encountered if a table being applied does not have a primary key.

- There is a data mismatch between a row LCR and the table for which the LCR is applying a change. In this case, the destination has to be updated to match the data values before the error transaction can be executed again.

ORA-23605 Invalid Value for Streams Parameter

This error occurs if an incorrect value is used for a Streams parameter or if a row LCR does not contain the correct old and new values.

ORA-23607 Invalid Column

This error is caused by an invalid column specified in the column list of a row LCR. The column names in the row LCR need to be verified. This error message usually is generated if an Apply handler or rule-based transformation attempts one of the following actions:

- Delete a column from a row LCR that does not exist in the row LCR.

- Rename a column that does not exist in the row LCR.

ORA-24031 Invalid Value, *parameter_name,* Should Be Non-NULL

This error may occur when an Apply handler or a rule-based transformation passes a NULL value to an LCR member subprogram instead of a SYS.AnyData value that contains a NULL.

For example, the following call to the *add_column* member procedure for row LCRs may result in the specified error:

```
new_lcr.ADD_COLUMN('OLD','SALES_ID',NULL);
```

The following SQL shows the correct way to call the *add_column* member procedure for row LCRs:

```
new_lcr.ADD_COLUMN('OLD','SALES_ID',SYS.AnyData.ConvertVarchar2(NULL));
```

ORA-26687 Instantiation SCN Not Set

This error occurs because the instantiation SCN is not set on an object for which an Apply process is attempting to apply changes. The *dba_apply_instantiated_objects* data dictionary view can be queried to list the objects that have an instantiation SCN.

ORA-26688 Missing Key in LCR

Generally speaking, this error occurs because of one of the following conditions:

- The object for which an LCR is applying a change does not exist in the destination database. In this case, it is necessary to ensure that the object exists. Make sure that the correct character case is used in rule conditions, Apply handlers, and rule-based transformations.

- Supplemental logging is not specified for columns that require supplemental logging at the source database. In this case, LCRs from the source database may not contain values for key columns.

- There may be problem with the primary key in the destination table. If no primary key exists for the table or if the target table has a different primary key than the source table, substitute key columns can be specified using the *set_key_columns* procedure in the *dbms_apply_adm* package.

ORA-26689 Column Type Mismatch

This error message is returned because one or more columns at a table in the source database do not match the corresponding columns at the destination database.

The LCRs from the source database may contain more columns than the table at the destination database, or there may be a type mismatch for one or more columns. The Streams process assumes the same exact set of columns at the both source and destination end. If the columns differ at the databases, rule-based transformations can be used to modify and avoid the errors.

If an apply handler or a rule-based transformation is used, any SYS.AnyData conversion functions must match the data type in the LCR that is being converted. For example, if the column is specified as VARCHAR2, the SYS.AnyData.CONVERTVARCHAR2 function should be used to convert the data from type ANY to VARCHAR2.

Conclusion

In this chapter, information has been presented on various dynamic and static views that help the DBA understand the configuration details and the statistics of the Streams processes.

The main points of this chapter include:

- With the help of the dictionary views provided, a variety of useful reports can be developed using SQL statements. These reports show the progress and performance load of the Streams processes.

- Many useful queries have been included along with sample results.

- As part of the troubleshooting methods, many error conditions which can abort or slow down the Streams processes were included.

In the next chapter, details about Down Streams capture configuration will be examined.

Down Streams Capture

"I know LCR, HS, SCN and three other Streams acronyms"

In this chapter, information will be presented on the details about Down Streams capture. The nature of the configuration will be covered as well as details on the set up and the pros and cons of this capture method.

Down Streams Capture

Down Streams Capture involves the execution of the Capture process on a database other than the source database. The archive log files from the source database are copied to the remote database. The Capture process running on this remote database scans and processes the archived log files for the database changes and enqueues the Logical Change Record (LCR) into the queue. Down Streams capture is used when the goal is to shift the capture activity to another database, thereby enhancing the performance of the Capture process as well as freeing up resources at the source database.

This remote database is also known as the Down Streams database. The queue also resides on the Down Streams database. The archive log files are copied from the source database, where the transactions are taking place, to the intermediate or Down Streams database. This is accomplished by using the log transport services, a file transfer protocol (FTP), or by using the package *dbms_ftp_transfer* mechanism.

A typical scenario of Streams data flow involving Down Streams Capture is shown in Figure 8.1.

Features and Advantages

A Down Streams database can receive redo log files from multiple source databases where the transactional activity occurs and propagate the LCR events to the desired destination database. In addition, a single database may have one or more Capture processes that capture local changes and other Capture processes that capture changes from the redo log files of a remote source database. In this way, a single database can be configured to perform both local capture and Down Streams capture.

The first time a Down Streams capture process is started at the Down Stream database, Oracle uses data dictionary information in the redo log to create a LogMiner data dictionary at the Down Streams database. The *dbms_capture_adm*.build procedure is executed at the source database to extract the source data dictionary information to the redo log at the source database.

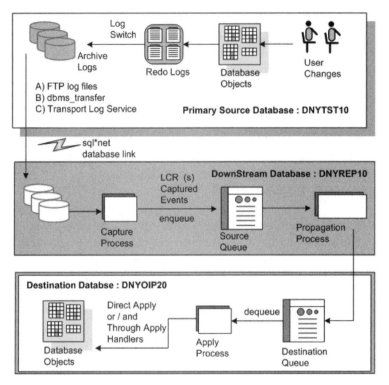

Figure 8.1 *Down Streams Capture and the Data Flow*

Supplemental logging at the source database places additional information in the redo log that may be needed for the Apply process. The configuration of supplemental logging has to be specified at the source database. Scanning the redo logs and capture rule evaluation is performed at the Down Streams database.

The Capture process enqueues changes that meet the rules in its rule set to the SYS.AnyData queue. If the captured changes are shared with one or more other databases, one or more propagations propagate these changes from the Down Streams database to the other databases.

In a Down Streams capture environment, the source database can be a single instance database or a multi-instance Real Application Clusters (RAC) database. The Down Streams database can be a single instance database or a multi-instance RAC database, regardless of whether the source database is single instance or multi-instance.

Advantages of the Down Streams process include:

- It uses fewer resources on the source database.

- When there is a scenario where multiple source database changes are to be processed, one Down Streams database can act as the central location for hosting the Capture process which obtains database changes from multiple sources.

- At the same time, from one source database, multiple targets can be serviced.

- Copying redo log files to one or more Down Streams databases provides improved protection against data loss. For example, the redo log files at the Down Streams database may be used for recovery of the source database in some situations.

Disadvantages

Because the Down Streams Capture process needs to wait for log switching of the redo log file and then subsequent copy of archive log files from the source database to the Down Steams database, there will be an unavoidable delay in capturing the database changes. This delay may not be acceptable for some situations.

The Down Streams capture configuration also requires an intermediate host as well as the database system, which is an additional expense that must be considered.

Using the Database Link

When a Down Streams Capture process uses a database link connecting to the source database, it performs certain administrative functions at the source database. They are as follows:

- When a Capture process is created, it automatically runs the *dbms_capture_adm.build* procedure at the source database in order to extract the data dictionary at the source database to the redo log.

- It prepares source database objects for instantiation. It obtains the *first_scn* for the Down Streams Capture process if the *first_scn* is not specified during Capture process creation. The *first_scn* is needed to create a Capture process.

- If a Down Streams Capture process does not use a database link, the above actions need to be carried out manually.

Requirements

The Oracle10g release is required for configuring Down Streams capture. In addition, 10g is required on both the source and destination sides. This is because the Down Streams feature is available only in the 10g version.

The operating system on the source and Down Streams capture sites must be the same, but the operating system releases need not be the same. In addition, the Down Streams sites can use a different directory structure from the source site.

Another requirement is that the hardware architecture on the source and Down Streams capture sites need to be the same but in a limited way. For example, a Down Streams capture configuration with a source database on a 32-bit Solaris must have a Down Streams database that is configured on a 32-bit Solaris system. The other hardware components like the number of CPUs, memory size, and storage configuration, can be different between the source and Down Streams sites.

Down Streams Capture Configuration

The configuration of Down Streams capture can be achieved with either of two broadly defined methods. These methods are Implicit Log Assignment capture and Explicit Log Assignment capture. The Implicit method is the more common method because the explicit method involves more manual tasks. Log assignment by SQL command is a cumbersome procedure.

As shown in Figure 8.2, one method is where log files are assigned implicitly to the Capture process running at Down Streams database, and the second one is to assign the redo log files explicitly by using the command ALTER DATABASE REGISTER LOGICAL LOGFILE. In the implicit method, the log transport service must be configured to transfer the archived log files to the Down Streams database. The explicit method involves the transfer of the archived redo log files using the FTP method or any other copy method.

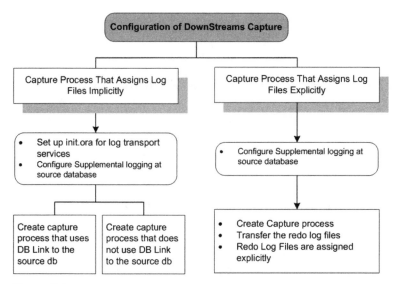

Figure 8.2 *Methods of Down Streams Capture Configuration*

In the case of the implicit method, the Down Streams database may or may not use the database link to the source. Depending on whether or not the database link is used, certain additional steps may be required. These steps include manual instantiation and running *dbms_capture_adm*.build procedure at the source database in order to extract the data dictionary at the source database to the redo log.

Creating a database link from the Down Streams capture database to the source database is optional. However, creating the database link to source database simplifies the configuration and management of the Down Streams database.

At times, it may not be feasible or desirable to configure a database link between the source and Down Streams databases. It is because:

- The Down Streams database is outside a firewall

- The DBA does not want an in-bound database link to the source database

If the database link does not exist from the Down Streams database to the source database, the following tasks must be completed manually at the source site when configuring Down Streams capture:

- Dictionary dump and obtain the *first_scn* value

- Instantiate replicated database objects

Steps in Case of Implicit Assignment of Logs

The implicit assignment means that the Down Streams Capture process automatically scans all redo log files added by log transport services from the source database to the Down Streams database. This method follows the steps shown below:

Step 1: Setup up Source Database Environment

At the source database, ensure that the required *init.ora* parameters used to configure log transport services are present in order to copy the redo log files from the source database to the Down Streams database. For example, the *log_archive_dest_2* parameter sets the log transport service at source database, DNYTST10.

```
LOG_ARCHIVE_DEST_2='SERVICE=DNYOIP20.world    ARCH    OPTIONAL    NOREGISTER    REOPEN=60
TEMPLATE=/db_dumps/oracle/archive/TST1_arc_%t_%s_%r.log'
```

The NOREGISTER attribute needs to be set to indicate that the location of the archived redo log should not be recorded at the corresponding destination. If this attribute is not specified, the following error may be returned:

```
ORA-16009: remote archive log destination must be a STANDBY database
```

The TEMPLATE attribute should be set to the directory specification and format template for archived redo logs at the Down Streams database. This parameter overrides the *standby_archive_dest* and *log_archive_format* initialization parameter settings at the remote destination. When specifying a directory within the template attribute value, it is important to make sure that the directory exists, or the following error may be returned:

```
ORA-00270: error creating archive log
```

The *log_archive_format* specification has %s, %t and %r. The %s corresponds to the sequence number and %r corresponds to the resetlogs ID that ensures unique names are constructed for the archived redo logs across multiple incarnations of the database. The %t, which is required for RAC configurations, corresponds to the thread.

Enable the archive destination by using the *log_archive_dest_state_2* parameter:

```
LOG_ARCHIVE_DEST_STATE_2=enable
```

At both the source database and the Down Streams database, the *remote_archive_enable* initialization parameter should be set to TRUE.

Step 2: Setup Up Supplemental Logging at Source Database

At the source database, specify primary key supplemental logging for the table desired. For example, to specify logging information for the table ALLINSURED1, the following SQL statement can be run:

```
ALTER TABLE NY1.allinsured1
ADD SUPPLEMENTAL LOG DATA (PRIMARY KEY) COLUMNS;
```

Step 3: Create Queue and Capture process

The next step is to create the queue and the Capture process at the Down Streams database. There are two methods that can be used to create the Capture process. One is to create the Capture process where the database link to source database is specified, and the other method is to not use the database link.

For example, by using the following SQL block a Capture process will be created where database link to source database is specified:

```
BEGIN
DBMS_CAPTURE_ADM.CREATE_CAPTURE(
queue_name              => 'LN1_queue',
capture_name            => 'LN1_capture',
rule_set_name                => NULL,
start_scn               => NULL,
source_database              => 'DNYTST10.world',
use_database_link       => TRUE,
first_scn               => NULL,
logfile_assignment      => 'implicit');
END;
```

In the above example, *use_database_link* => TRUE. This implies that the Capture process uses a database link with the same name as the source database global name to perform administrative actions at the source database.

The parameter *logfile_assignment* is set to IMPLICIT. It specifies that the Capture process accepts new redo log files implicitly from DNYTST10.world. Therefore, the Capture process scans any new log files copied from DNYTST10.

Step 4: Rules for Capture Process

Create the positive rule set for the Capture process and add a rule to it. Typically, the *add_table_rules* procedure of the *dbms_streams_adm* package is used for this process.

Step 5: Propagation and Apply

Now Propagation, Apply, or both can be configured for the LCRs captured by the LN1_CAPTURE Capture process. The *instantiation_scn* for the table ALLINSURED1 at DNYOIP20.world should be set by running the *set_table_instantiation_scn* procedure of the *dbms_apply_adm* package at the destination database

Not Using the Database Link

In Step 3 above, while creating the Capture process by using the *create_capture* procedure, there are some additional steps needed if the *use_database_link* is to be set to FALSE. A build of the source database data dictionary needs to be performed in the redo log. Since there is no database link, any configuration at a Down Streams database can not perform or execute database operations at the source database. Therefore, manual intervention is warranted.

For example, use the following SQL block to perform the data dictionary build:

```
SET SERVEROUTPUT ON
DECLARE
 scn NUMBER;
BEGIN
 DBMS_CAPTURE_ADM.BUILD( first_scn => scn);
 DBMS_OUTPUT.PUT_LINE('First SCN Value = ' || scn);
END;
```

This procedure displays the valid *first_scn* value, 155781561, for the Capture process that will be created at the Down Streams database. Jot down the SCN value from above step. This value will be used when creating the Capture process at the Down Streams database.

Next, prepare the required table for instantiation. For example run the following SQL block to instantiate the table ALLINSURED1:

```
BEGIN
DBMS_CAPTURE_ADM.PREPARE_TABLE_INSTANTIATION(
table_name      => 'NY1.allinsured1');
END;
/
```

The Capture process where *use_database_link* is set to FALSE can be created as shown below.

```
BEGIN
DBMS_CAPTURE_ADM.CREATE_CAPTURE(
queue_name              => 'ln1_queue',
capture_name            => 'ln1_capture',
rule_set_name           => NULL,
start_scn               => NULL,
source_database         => 'dbs1.net',
use_database_link       => false,
first_scn               => 155781561, -- Use value from build proc
logfile_assignment      => 'implicit');
END;
/
```

The *first_scn* for the Capture process has been specified. This value was obtained earlier at the source database. The *first_scn* is the lowest SCN for which a Capture process can capture changes.

Note: Since a *first_scn* is specified, the Capture process creates a new LogMiner data dictionary when it is first started, regardless of whether there are existing LogMiner data dictionaries for the same source database.

Explicit assignment of logs

In this method, the steps are pretty much the same those presented in the implicit section. The major difference is setting the *logfile_assignment* parameter to EXPLICIT for the procedure *create_capture* of *dbms_capture_adm* while creating the Capture process at Down Streams database.

An example of capture creation with explicit assignment is shown below:

```
BEGIN
DBMS_CAPTURE_ADM.CREATE_CAPTURE(
queue_name              => 'ln1_queue',
capture_name    => 'ln1_capture',
rule_set_name   => NULL,
start_scn               => NULL,
source_database         => 'dbs1.net',
use_database_link       => false,
first_scn               => 155781561, -- Use value from build proc
logfile_assignment      => 'explicit');
END;
/
```

In this method, the log files are assigned to the Capture process explicitly by a command. The required redo log files need to be transferred to the Down Streams database location by FTP or another copy method.

After a redo log file has been transferred to the host running the Down Streams database, the log file needs to be assigned to the Capture process explicitly using the following DDL statement at the Down Streams database:

```
Format:
ALTER DATABASE REGISTER LOGICAL LOGFILE file_name
FOR capture_process;
```

In the above format, the *file_name* is the name of the redo log file and *capture_process* is the name of the Capture process that will use the redo log file at the Down Streams database. Thus, the redo log files need to be added manually if the *logfile_assignment* parameter is set to EXPLICIT.

The following is an example. Following the SQL statement explicitly assigns the log file to the LN1_CAPTURE process.

```
ALTER DATABASE REGISTER LOGICAL LOGFILE
'/db_dumps/logs_from_tst10/1_14_1476.arc' FOR LN1_capture;
```

The explicit type of configuration is useful for controlling the capture flow. It allows the DBA to assign only the necessary logs. This kind of situation may be useful to create a lab type of replication environment that could be used to do investigations of transactions, etc.

Conclusion

In this chapter, details of some of the advanced Streams configuration details involving the Down Streams capture process were presented.

The main points of the chapter include:

- The Down Streams Capture methodology allows the use of a secondary database as the site of the Capture process.

- Once the logs are moved to the Down Streams Capture process, the scanning and constructing of LCR events is done at this secondary database.

- Enqueuing occurs at the secondary database. This method effectively moves the Capture process to another database.

- There are two methods of Down Streams capture: Implicit Log assignment capture and Explicit Log assignment capture. The Implicit method depends on the automatic feed of logs with help of log transport services. The Explicit method depends on manual SQL commands to assign the logs.

In the next chapter, information on the Streams configuration in a Real Application Cluster environment will be presented.

Streams and Real Application Cluster

The magic of Streams is in understanding its environment.

Introduction

In this chapter, the implementation of Streams in a typical Real Application Clusters (RAC) environment will be presented. With many businesses adopting RAC database technology for their data needs, the topic of Streams in a RAC environment will be of high importance. The differences in the Streams configuration in a RAC environment will be highlighted. Information will be included on the extra things that need to be considered on account of the database environment being a RAC.

Streams in a RAC Environment

A RAC is a single database with multiple instances. Each instance in the RAC database environment has its own set of redo log files. Each instance thread produces its own set of archived log files; however, those redo log files and archived log files are accessible to all of the instances. Redo and archived log files reside on shared storage. Shared storage is configured either as an approved cluster file system or through Oracle's Automatic Storage Management (ASM).

As shown in Figure 9.1, each of the RAC database instances consists of the following: Instance-1 has redo groups from 1 to 3; Instance-2 has redo groups 4 to 6; and Instance-3 has redo groups 7 to 9. The Streams Capture process extracts all the database changes recorded in all of the redo log files.

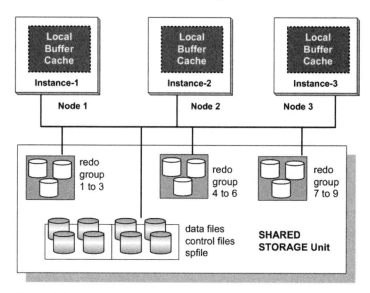

Figure 9.1 *Typical RAC database environment*

The Oracle10g Database release has brought in two important enhancements:

- In order to improve the performance of Streams for RAC databases, a Capture process can now capture changes from the archived redo logs or from the online redo. This feature allows changes to be captured closer to the time they were executed, thereby reducing the capture latency. In other words, the moment database changes are effected and committed the transactions are available for the Capture process to extract.

- When the owner instance for a queue table containing a queue used by a Capture process or Apply process fails, queue ownership is transferred automatically to another instance in the cluster. Then the Capture process or Apply process is restarted automatically, if it had been running. In previous releases, the Capture process or Apply process used to be ABORTED under these circumstances which would warrant a manual restart. This is an important improvement from the administrative point of view. Without the intervention of the DBA, the Streams process will be restarted.

Capture and Apply Processes in a RAC Instance

Since there are multiple instances in a RAC database, the database changes can occur at any instance. Such database changes are recorded in the respective instance's redo logs and corresponding archive log files. A Capture process configured within any instance of the RAC database can scan and extract the transactional activity from the all the participating instance's redo log files and convert them into LCR events. In this way, even though the Capture process is only running on one instance, it is aware of all the redo logs of all the RAC instances and does not miss any transactions.

Each Capture process is started on the owner instance for its SYS.AnyData queue, even if the start capture is executed on a different instance. The *dba_queue_tables* data dictionary view contains information about the owner instance for a queue table. Any parallel execution servers used by a single Capture process run on a single instance in a RAC environment.

Whenever an instance in an Oracle RAC cluster fails, the instance is recovered immediately by another instance in the cluster. The following actions occur that affect the Streams environment:

- Each queue owned by the failed instance is assigned to a new instance.

- The Capture process is restarted automatically on the instance that now owns the queue. If the failed instance is brought back online later, the Capture process does not move back to the original instance. Even though the failed instance was running the Capture process at the time of failure, it is no longer the owner of the queue used by the Capture process. This is the normal behavior unless it is altered by the *alter_queue_table* procedure, which is explained in a later section.

- All propagation jobs are automatically migrated to the new instance from the failed instance.

The SYS.AnyData queues can be configured on any instances within the RAC database. Only the owner instance may have a buffer for a queue, but different instances may have buffers for different queues. A buffered queue is

System Global Area (SGA) memory associated with a SYS.AnyData queue that contains only captured events.

Figure 9.2 shows that instance DNYDBA2A has the SYS.AnyData and the associated buffers.

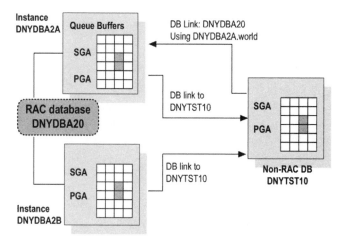

Figure 9.2 *Streams in a RAC environment*

Only the instance that has the queue, and therefore the buffers, can propagate and receive the LCR events. Each of the propagations that propagate captured events to a RAC destination database must use an instance-specific database link that refers to the owner instance of the destination queue. If the propagation connects to any other instance, the propagation will raise an error.

That is the reason that when the Non-RAC instance, DNYTST10, receives or propagates the captured events, it needs to use the instance specific database link to DNYDBA2A.

Whenever the owner instance for a queue table containing a destination queue becomes unavailable, the queue ownership is transferred automatically to another instance in the cluster.

Since the queue is migrated to a new instance, the database link will need to be recreated. For the propagations that were configured with the failed instance as the destination, the database link should be dropped and then recreated using the same global name. During recreation, the link will be pointed to the new instance that now owns the queue. Scripts that drop and re-create all necessary database links can be created and then run at the sites that are attempting to propagate to the failed instance. The propagation details do not need to be modified since the name of the database link is not being changed.

Next, the failover process with in the RAC environment will be illustrated with an example. Information on the effect of the failover process on the Streams related components will be presented.

As seen in Figure 9.2, the DNYTST10 database propagates and receives replication changes from the RAC database, DNYDBA20. The RAC database has two instances: DNYDBA2A and DNYDBA2B.

The DNYTST10 instance will have a database link to the RAC database named DNYDBA20, which corresponds to the database name. Assuming that the initial queue is on the DNYDBA2A instance, it will use the TNS entry that points to DNYDBA2A instance as shown below:

```
--Link Name matches the RAC DB name, but use the TNS entry that
--  points to the Instance : DNYDBA2A

CREATE DATABASE LINK DNYDBA20.world CONNECT TO strmadm IDENTIFIED BY strmadm USING '
DNYDBA2A.world'
/
```

When the DNYDBA2A fails, the queue moves over to the DNYDBA2B instance automatically. In that case, at the DNYTST10 site, the DNYDBA20.world link should be dropped and recreated with the same name but with the TNS entry that points to the DNYDBA2B instance. Recreate the database link as shown below:

```
CREATE DATABASE LINK DNYDBA20.world CONNECT TO strmadm IDENTIFIED BY strmadm USING
'DNYDBA2B.world'
/
```

Since the database link name is not changed, the propagation process attributes, if any at the DNYTST10 site, remain the same.

At the same time, for the RAC database DNYDBA20 to propagate to the DNYTST10, there is no need for any change in the configuration. Once the queue moves over to the DNYDBA2B instance, the propagation also moves over and resumes the replication to the destination of DNYTST10.

The following output shows the failover of queue buffers. It shows that the RAC database has two instances and the NY1_QUEUE_TABLE is currently on Instance-1, which is DNYDNA2A.

Use the following SQL queries to view the instance details and buffers details at the DNYDBA2A instance:

```
SQL> select * from v$active_instances ;

INST_NUMBER INST_NAME
----------- -----------------------------------------------
          1 nytms-a:DNYDBA2A
          2 nytms-b:DNYDBA2B

SQL> select instance_name, instance_number from v$instance ;

INSTANCE_NAME    INSTANCE_NUMBER
---------------- ---------------
DNYDBA2A                       1

SQL>  select   QUEUE_TABLE,   TYPE,   OBJECT_TYPE,   PRIMARY_INSTANCE,   SECONDARY_INSTANCE,
OWNER_INSTANCE from  DBA_QUEUE_TABLES where OWNER = 'STRMADM'
/
                                          Primry   Secndry  Owner
QUEUE_TABLE          TYPE    OBJECT_TYPE   Insta    Insta    Insta
------------------ ------- ------------ -------- --------- ------
NY1_QUEUE_TABLE      OBJECT  SYS.ANYDATA      0        0        1

SQL> show user
USER is "SYS"
SQL> shutdown immediate
Database closed.
Database dismounted.
ORACLE instance shut down.
SQL>
```

After the DNYDBA2A is shutdown, the queue buffers move over to instance DNYDBA2B automatically. Now, connect to the DNYDBA2B instance and query the owner instance for the NY1_QUEUE_TABLE queue.

```
SQL> select instance_name, instance_number from v$instance ;

INSTANCE_NAME    INSTANCE_NUMBER
---------------- ---------------
DNYDBA2B                       2

SQL>  select   QUEUE_TABLE,   TYPE,   OBJECT_TYPE,   PRIMARY_INSTANCE,   SECONDARY_INSTANCE,
OWNER_INSTANCE from  DBA_QUEUE_TABLES where OWNER = 'STRMADM'
/
                                          Primry   Secndry  Owner
QUEUE_TABLE          TYPE    OBJECT_TYPE   Insta    Insta    Insta
------------------ ------- ------------ -------- --------- ------
NY1_QUEUE_TABLE      OBJECT  SYS.ANYDATA      0        0        2
```

The owner instance is shown as 2, referring to DNYDBA2B.

In the above output, the primary and secondary instances are showing Zero, which indicates that instance affinity was not specified.

Queue Table Affinity for Primary and Secondary Instance

Streams processes and jobs support primary instance and secondary instance specifications for queue tables. When these specifications are used, the secondary instance assumes ownership of a queue table when the primary instance becomes unavailable, and ownership is transferred back to the primary instance when it becomes available again. This specification is useful when there are many instances within a RAC database so as to pre-determine the secondary instance which takes over the functionality. In a multi-node RAC configuration, one node may be designed for the Capture process while others may be designed for usual transaction processing. The affinity concept preserves the priorities.

The primary and secondary instance specifications can be set using the *alter_queue_table* procedure in the *dbms_aqadm* package.

The syntax for the procedure is:

```
DBMS_AQADM.ALTER_QUEUE_TABLE (
queue_table              IN VARCHAR2,
comment                         IN VARCHAR2 DEFAULT NULL,
primary_instance         IN BINARY_INTEGER DEFAULT NULL,
secondary_instance       IN BINARY_INTEGER DEFAULT NULL);
```

The *primary_instance* argument shows the primary instance owner of the queue table. Queue monitor scheduling and propagation for the queues in the queue table will be done in this instance.

The *secondary_instance* argument shows the instance to which the ownership of queue table fails over if the primary instance is not available.

In the following example, the instance called "1" will be set as the primary:

```
BEGIN
DBMS_AQADM.ALTER_QUEUE_TABLE (
queue_table              => 'NY1_QUEUE_TABLE',
primary_instance         => 1,
secondary_instance       => 2) ;
end;
/
```

The following SQL statement shows the queue table, owner instance, and the primary and secondary instances, etc.:

```
select QUEUE_TABLE, TYPE, OBJECT_TYPE, PRIMARY_INSTANCE, SECONDARY_INSTANCE, OWNER_INSTANCE
from  DBA_QUEUE_TABLES where OWNER = 'STRMADM'
/
```

```
                              Primry  Secndry  Owner
QUEUE_TABLE        TYPE    OBJECT_TYPE  Insta    Insta  Inst
------------------ ------- ------------ ------- -------- -------
NY1_QUEUE_TABLE    OBJECT  SYS.ANYDATA       1        2       1
```

Once instance 1, DNYDBA2A, is shutdown or fails for any reason, the
DNYDBA2B becomes the owner instance as show in the following output:

```
                              Primry  Secndry  Owner
QUEUE_TABLE        TYPE    OBJECT_TYPE  Insta    Insta  Inst
------------------ ------- ------------ ------- -------- -------
NY1_QUEUE_TABLE    OBJECT  SYS.ANYDATA       1        2       2
```

Since instance 1 has been associated as the primary instance, it becomes the
owner instance again when DNYDBA2A comes back online.

Queue Buffer Contents

The following SQL query shows buffer details. The *inst_id* field of the
gv$_buffered_queues view indicates the active instance where the buffers are
located. Knowing the details about the buffer's location helps to develop a
suitable monitoring method.

```
COLUMN QUEUE_NAME HEADING 'Queue| Name' FORMAT A18
COLUMN MEM_MSG HEADING 'LCRs in|Memory' FORMAT 999999
COLUMN SPILL_MSGS HEADING 'Spilled|LCRs' FORMAT 99999
COLUMN NUM_MSGS HEADING 'Captured LCRs|in Buff.Queue' FORMAT 9999999
COLUMN INST_ID HEADING 'Inst|ID' format 9999

SELECT INST_ID, QUEUE_NAME,
       (NUM_MSGS - SPILL_MSGS) MEM_MSG,
       SPILL_MSGS,
       NUM_MSGS
FROM GV$BUFFERED_QUEUES where QUEUE_SCHEMA = 'STRMADM'
/

Inst Queue              LCRs in Spilled Captured LCRs
  ID Name               Memory    LCRs  in Buff.Queue
----- ------------------ ------- ------- -------------
   2 NY4_QUEUE                0       0             0
   2 NY1_QUEUE                0       1             1
   1 NY2_QUEUE                8       0             8
```

Conclusion

In this chapter, the Streams configuration details involving the multiple
instances in a RAC database environment have been examined.

The main points of this chapter include:

- In a RAC environment, only one instance has the queue buffers.
  Therefore, the capture or apply is confined to that instance.

- Queue affinity can be controlled by setting up the specification of primary and secondary instance. Based on this affinity, queue buffers always move to the primary instance.

- When RAC is acting as the destination database for Streams replication, the source database should have the database link to the instance having the queue buffers.

- Information on the enhancements that were introduced in Oracle10g was presented. These enhancements were examined in terms of automatic failure of the Capture process to a surviving node in case of the instance failure where the Capture process is running and the hot mining of the redo logs by the Capture process.

In the next chapter, Streams replication to heterogeneous databases such as Sybase and SQL Server will be presented.

Streams for Heterogeneous Replication

Heterogeneous replication can be ugly if performed incorrectly.

In this chapter, topics related to heterogeneous Streams replication between Oracle and non-Oracle databases will be presented. The use of a user application enqueue mechanisms to replicate changes from non-Oracle to Oracle is also included.

Heterogeneous Streams Replication

In addition to information sharing between Oracle databases, Streams supports data flow and information sharing between Oracle databases and non-Oracle databases. The capability of heterogeneous Streams replication is important because many business enterprises have, besides Oracle, other RDMS systems supporting business operations. Often the data needs to be replicated from non-Oracle to Oracle systems and vice-versa

---

Oracle to Non-Oracle Data Flow

When the Oracle database is the source and a non-Oracle database is the destination, the non-Oracle database does not have the Oracle Streams mechanism running on the destination because Streams is a unique feature of the Oracle database.

Non-Oracle Database systems lack the following:

- A SYS.AnyData queue to receive the Logical Change Record (LCR) events.

- An Apply process to dequeue and apply the database changes.

In order to overcome this architectural difference and share DML changes between an Oracle source database and a non-Oracle destination database, the Oracle database functions as a proxy and carries out some of the steps that would normally be done at the destination database. The events intended for the non-Oracle destination database are dequeued in the Oracle database itself, and an Apply process at the Oracle database uses heterogeneous service to apply the events to the non-Oracle database. The application of transactions to the non-Oracle database uses the Oracle Transparent Gateway.

Figure 10.1 shows the graphical representation of an Oracle database sending database changes to a non-Oracle database destination.

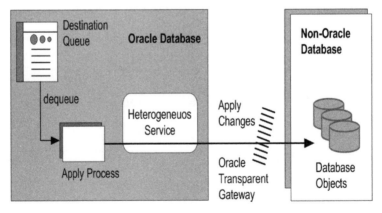

Figure 10.1 *Oracle to Non-Oracle database heterogeneous data flow*

In the following example, information will be presented on the replication changes that are to be sent to a Sybase database. The Sybase database is defined as DNYSYB01 and the transfer is from the Oracle source database, DNYTST10.

Assume the following:

```
Source database : DNYTST10
Object/Table name : NY4.allinsured1
Intermediate database hosting the Apply process: DNYOIP20
Destination non-Oracle database eg. Sybase): DNYSYB01
```

The next step is to configure the heterogeneous service.

In this case, the DNYOIP20.world database acts as a gateway to DNYSYB01.world; therefore, the Apply process for DNYSYB01.world must be configured at DNYOIP20.world. The Apply process cannot apply DDL changes to non-Oracle databases. Therefore, the *include_ddl* parameter is set to FALSE when the *add_table_rules* procedure is run. The *apply_database_link* parameter is set to DNYSYB01.world, which is the defined Sybase database in this example.

To create a basic Apply process, use the following SQL block at the DNYOIP20 database:

```
BEGIN
  DBMS_APPLY_ADM.CREATE_APPLY(
    queue_name          => 'strmadm.ln4_queue',
    apply_name          => 'ln4_apply',
    apply_database_link => 'DNYSYB01.world',
    apply_captured      => true);
END;
/
```

To add the rule for the table that is being replicated, use the following SQL statement at DNYOIP20. The source database is DNYTST10.world.

```
BEGIN
  DBMS_STREAMS_ADM.ADD_TABLE_RULES(
    table_name      => 'ny4.allinsured1',
    streams_type    => 'apply',
    streams_name    => 'ln4_apply', -- at OIP20 database
    queue_name      => 'strmadm.ln4_queue',
    include_dml     => true,
    include_ddl     => false,
    source_database => 'DNYTST10.world',
    inclusion_rule  => true);
END;
/
```

The implementation of these steps will enable the transfer of data in a heterogeous system.

Configuring the Heterogeneous Service

In the previous example, a sample Streams configuration was included. In that example, DNYSYB01.world was used as the apply database link. In fact, it is for a Sybase database. When a database link to Sybase from Oracle is set up, the Oracle Transparent Gateway (OTG) is used to support the link.

The steps involved in configuring Oracle Transparent Gateway will be used as an example.

At $ORACLE_HOME/tg4sybs/admin on the Oracle Database host, create the *initDNYSYB01.ora* file with the following entries:

```
# This is a sample agent init file that contains the HS
# parameters that are needed for the Transparent Gateway
# for Sybase

# HS init parameters
#
HS_FDS_CONNECT_INFO=DNYSYB01.PvsuRisk
HS_FDS_TRACE_LEVEL=OFF
HS_FDS_RECOVERY_ACCOUNT=RECOVER
HS_FDS_RECOVERY_PWD=RECOVER
#
# Environment variables required for Sybase
#
set SYBASE=/app/dbatools/open_client
```

Test Sybase connectivity from the host where the Oracle database is located.

```
$ nytms-c:/var/opt/oracle >export SYBASE=/app/dbatools/open_client
$ nytms-c:/var/opt/oracle >
$ nytms-c:/var/opt/oracle >export PATH=$PATH:$SYBASE/bin
$ nytms-c:/var/opt/oracle >isql -U otg_interface -S DNYSYB01 -w140
Password:
1> exit
```

Add the TNS entry for DNYSYB01.WORLD into the *tnsnames.ora* on the Oracle database host.

```
# Below is added for T.Gateway to Sybase

DNYSYB01.world =
   (DESCRIPTION=
      (ADDRESS=
         (PROTOCOL=TCP)
         (HOST=syb01-001)
         (PORT=1521)
      )
      (CONNECT_DATA=
         (SID= DNYSYB01))
      (HS=OK)
   )
```

Add the following entry into the LISTENER, and restart the LISTENER.

274

```
(SID_DESC=
  (SID_NAME=TLNCIFBI07)
  (ORACLE_HOME=/app/oracle/product/dbms/DNYOIP20)
  (PROGRAM=tg4sybs)
)
```

Create a database link to the Sybase server. Keep the login ID and password
in the correct case.

```
1   CREATE DATABASE LINK DNYSYB01.WORLD
2       CONNECT TO "otg_interface"
3       IDENTIFIED BY "otg_interface"
4*      USING 'DNYSYB01.WORLD'
SQL> /

Database link created.
```

The database link created above using the OTG is used by the Apply process.
This is how the Apply process communicates to the Sybase server to make a
DML change on the Sybase system

Overview of Non-Oracle to Oracle Data Sharing

To capture and propagate changes from a non-Oracle database to an Oracle
database, a custom written user application is required. This application
obtains changes made to the non-Oracle database by reading from
transaction logs, using triggers, or some other method. The application must
assemble and order the transactions and then convert each change into an
LCR event. The user application then has to enqueue the LCRs into a queue
in an Oracle database by using the PL/SQL interface, where they can be
processed by an Apply process. The Apply process applies changes to the
Oracle database object.

Figure 10.2 shows a sample involving data flow from non-Oracle database to
an Oracle database. The user application typically uses the
dbms_streams_messaging package or the *dmbs_aq* package to enqueue the LCRs
into a queue in an Oracle database. The application needs to commit after
enqueuing all LCRs in each transaction.

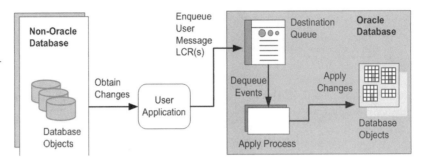

Figure 10.2 *Non-Oracle to Oracle database heterogeneous data flow*

In next section, an example on how to construct a DML LCR and enqueue into a queue will be presented.

User Application Enqueue

User applications can enqueue events into a queue explicitly. The user applications can format these user-enqueued events as LCRs or user messages. Once the events are enqueued explicitly into a queue, they can be propagated to another queue or explicitly dequeued from the same queue.

In order to create a row LCR that contains a change to a row that resulted from a Data Manipulation Language (DML) statement, the SYS.LCR$_ROW_RECORD constructor will have to be used. In order to create a DDL LCR that contains a data definition language changes, the SYS.LCR$_DDL_RECORD constructor can be used.

In the following section, information will be presented on how to explicitly enqueue some events by using the PL/SQL interface. As an example, a queue will be created at DNYTST10 where LCR events will be enqueued. An Apply process will be created at the same site to dequeue LCR events into a table.

The following example shows the Oracle side implementation. Once the transactions are read from the non-Oracle system's database, they have to be formatted to enqueue into Oracle's queue. This example is a simple PL/SQL based interface that is used to input transactions into the queue. This is to demonstrate the data flow into Oracle's queue. This can be very well done by using a C++ or Java program, too.

First, a table called MKT_PRICE will be created in a schema called TEST1:

```
CONNECT strmadm/strmadm@dnytst10

PROMPT Connected to DNYTST10

create user TEST1  identified by TEST1
default tablespace TB1
temporary tablespace TEMP
/
grant resource, connect to TEST1
/
create table TEST1.MKTPRICE (
 ticker     varchar2(6),
 open_px    number,
 close_px   number,
 px_date    date)
/
```

Then, create a queue called TEST1_QUEUE:

```
PROMPT Creating the Queue called test1_queue at TST10 ..
BEGIN
DBMS_STREAMS_ADM.SET_UP_QUEUE(
 queue_table            => 'test1_qtable',
 storage_clause              => NULL,
 queue_name             => 'test1_queue');
END;
/
```

Create the Apply process called TEST1_APPLY using the *create_apply* procedure and add the table rules. Do this in the same database.

```
PROMPT Creating the Apply called test1_apply at DNYTST10 ..

BEGIN
DBMS_APPLY_ADM.CREATE_APPLY(
queue_name      => 'test1_queue',
apply_name      => 'test1_apply',
apply_captured  => false,
apply_user      => 'test1');
END;
/
```

Create a positive rule set for the Apply process and add a rule that applies DML changes to the TEST1.MKTPRICE table

```
PROMPT Adding test1.mktprice table rules for Apply process  ..

BEGIN
DBMS_STREAMS_ADM.ADD_TABLE_RULES(
table_name               => 'test1.mktprice',
streams_type             => 'apply',
streams_name             => 'test1_apply',
queue_name               => 'test1_queue',
include_dml              => true,
include_ddl              => false,
include_tagged_lcr       => false,
source_database          => 'DNYTST10.world',
inclusion_rule           => true);
END;
/
PROMPT Starting the Apply process ..

EXEC DBMS_APPLY_ADM.START_APPLY('test1_apply');
```

The next step is to create a stored procedure that actually constructs the LCR record and enqueues the event. This procedure uses the *dbms_streams_messaging_enqueue* procedure provided by Oracle.

The following SQL block creates a procedure called LCR_ROW_ON_MKTPRICE:

```
CREATE OR REPLACE PROCEDURE lcr_row_on_mktprice (
  source_dbname   VARCHAR2,
  cmd_type        VARCHAR2,
  obj_owner       VARCHAR2,
  obj_name        VARCHAR2,
  old_vals        SYS.LCR$_ROW_LIST,
  new_vals        SYS.LCR$_ROW_LIST)
AS
row_lcr              SYS.LCR$_ROW_RECORD;
BEGIN

--Construct the LCR based on information passed to procedure

row_lcr := SYS.LCR$_ROW_RECORD.CONSTRUCT(
  source_database_name   => source_dbname,
  command_type           => cmd_type,
  object_owner           => obj_owner,
  object_name            => obj_name,
  old_values             => old_vals,
  new_values             => new_vals);

-- Enqueue the created row LCR

DBMS_STREAMS_MESSAGING.ENQUEUE(
  queue_name      => 'test1_queue',
  payload                 => SYS.AnyData.ConvertObject(row_lcr) );
END lcr_row_on_mktprice;
/
```

The above mentioned procedure will be used to perform some DML changes to the table named MKTPRICE:

To insert a row, use the following SQL block. This SQL block inserts a row with a ticker value of AMZN.

```
DECLARE
  newunit1        SYS.LCR$_ROW_UNIT;
  newunit2        SYS.LCR$_ROW_UNIT;
  newunit3        SYS.LCR$_ROW_UNIT;
  newunit4        SYS.LCR$_ROW_UNIT;
  newvals         SYS.LCR$_ROW_LIST;

BEGIN
newunit1 := SYS.LCR$_ROW_UNIT( 'TICKER',
  SYS.AnyData.ConvertVarchar2('AMZN'),
  DBMS_LCR.NOT_A_LOB, NULL, NULL);

newunit2 := SYS.LCR$_ROW_UNIT( 'OPEN_PX',  SYS.AnyData.ConvertNumber(40.45),
DBMS_LCR.NOT_A_LOB, NULL, NULL);

newunit3 := SYS.LCR$_ROW_UNIT( 'CLOSE_PX', SYS.AnyData.ConvertNumber(40.90),
DBMS_LCR.NOT_A_LOB, NULL, NULL);

newunit4 := SYS.LCR$_ROW_UNIT( 'PX_DATE',  SYS.AnyData.Convertdate(sysdate),
DBMS_LCR.NOT_A_LOB, NULL, NULL);
```

```
newvals := SYS.LCR$_ROW_LIST(newunit1, newunit2, newunit3, newunit4);

-- Now execute Store Proc to enqueue an INSERT DML lcr_row_on_mktprice(
 source_dbname  => 'dnytst10.world',
 cmd_type       => 'INSERT',
 obj_owner      => 'TEST1',
 obj_name       => 'MKTPRICE',
 old_vals       => NULL,
 new_vals       => newvals);
--
END;
/
```

To update a row and change the ticker AMZN to QCOM and also change the other columns' values, use the following SQL block:

```
DECLARE
  newunit1        SYS.LCR$_ROW_UNIT;
  newunit2        SYS.LCR$_ROW_UNIT;
  newunit3        SYS.LCR$_ROW_UNIT;
  newunit4        SYS.LCR$_ROW_UNIT;
  new_vals        SYS.LCR$_ROW_LIST;
  old_vals        SYS.LCR$_ROW_LIST;

BEGIN
newunit1 := SYS.LCR$_ROW_UNIT( 'TICKER',
  SYS.AnyData.ConvertVarchar2('AMZN'),
  DBMS_LCR.NOT_A_LOB, NULL, NULL);

newunit2   :=    SYS.LCR$_ROW_UNIT(   'OPEN_PX',    SYS.AnyData.ConvertNumber(40.45),
DBMS_LCR.NOT_A_LOB, NULL, NULL);

newunit3   :=    SYS.LCR$_ROW_UNIT(   'CLOSE_PX',   SYS.AnyData.ConvertNumber(40.90),
DBMS_LCR.NOT_A_LOB, NULL, NULL);

newunit4 :=  SYS.LCR$_ROW_UNIT( 'PX_DATE',   SYS.AnyData.Convertdate( trunc(sysdate) ),
DBMS_LCR.NOT_A_LOB, NULL, NULL);

old_vals := SYS.LCR$_ROW_LIST(newunit1, newunit2, newunit3, newunit4);

newunit1 := SYS.LCR$_ROW_UNIT( 'TICKER',
  SYS.AnyData.ConvertVarchar2('QCOM'),
  DBMS_LCR.NOT_A_LOB, NULL, NULL);

newunit2   :=    SYS.LCR$_ROW_UNIT(   'OPEN_PX',    SYS.AnyData.ConvertNumber(38.40),
DBMS_LCR.NOT_A_LOB, NULL, NULL);

newunit3   :=    SYS.LCR$_ROW_UNIT(   'CLOSE_PX',   SYS.AnyData.ConvertNumber(38.95),
DBMS_LCR.NOT_A_LOB, NULL, NULL);

newunit4   :=    SYS.LCR$_ROW_UNIT(   'PX_DATE',    SYS.AnyData.Convertdate(sysdate+1),
DBMS_LCR.NOT_A_LOB, NULL, NULL);

new_vals := SYS.LCR$_ROW_LIST(newunit1, newunit2,
           newunit3, newunit4);

-- Now execute Store Proc to enqueue an Update DML
lcr_row_on_mktprice(
 source_dbname => 'dnytst10.world',
 cmd_type       => 'UPDATE',
 obj_owner      => 'TEST1',
 obj_name       => 'MKTPRICE',
 old_vals       => old_vals,
 new_vals       => new_vals);
--
END;
/
```

This example shows a methodology that can be used to construct the LCR events and perform DML changes on the Oracle database table. This example can be embedded in a program that reads the changes at non-Oracle database tables. The changes in non-Oracle database tables can thus be input to an Oracle database table in the form of LCR events.

Conclusion

In this chapter, Streams configuration involving replication to a non-Oracle database was presented.

The main points of the chapter include:

- While replicating to the non-Oracle databases such as Sybase, Oracle database acts as the proxy and takes over the functionality of the Apply process and with the help of a heterogeneous service.

- Through the Oracle transparent gateway, the Apply process sends the changes to the non-Oracle database.

- When non-Oracle to Oracle replication is involved, the user application needs to read the transaction logs of the non-Oracle database and then format them as LCR events to enqueue into an Oracle database queue.

References

The following is the list of references consulted and used for the book.

Oracle Streams - Concepts and Administration 10g Release 1 (10.1); Oracle Corporation

Oracle Streams - Replication Administrator's Guide 10g Release 1 (10.1); Oracle Corporation

Oracle Streams - Advanced Queuing User's Guide and Reference Release 10.1 ; Oracle Corporation

Oracle Corporation. *Multiple Articles and Metalink Notes related to Oracle Streams*

PL/SQL Packages and Types Reference 10g Release 1 (10.1); Oracle Corporation

Oracle Database Utilities 10g Release 1 (10.1); Oracle Corporation

White Papers – GoldenGate Software;
http://www.goldengate.com/products/technology.html

White Papers - Quest Software; http://www.quest.com/documents/list.aspx

Index

W

About Madhu Tumma

Madhu Tumma is an expert and leading Information technologist specializing in Cluster Solutions, Server management, Database architecture and Performance management. He is a frequent speaker in many technical conferences such as IOUG Live, Oracle Open World, Veritas Vision and Sybase Techwave. He has co-authored three books on the subjects related to Oracle Database, Grid and Clusters.

Madhu held progressive technical and managerial roles mostly in financial services and managed services area in his 20 years of IT career. In recent times, he has provided consultancy to variety of clients on database clusters, business continuity and high availability solutions. His experience ranges across multiple relational database systems and varied operating platforms.

Madhu has Master Degree in science and attended Business Management graduate program. He lives in Princeton, New Jersey with his wife Hema and two children Sandi and Sudeep. At free time, he loves to read about people, cultures, origin, anthropology and history.

About Mike Reed

When he first started drawing, Mike Reed drew just to amuse himself. It wasn't long, though, before he knew he wanted to be an artist. Today he does illustrations for children's books, magazines, catalogs, and ads.

He also teaches illustration at the College of Visual Art in St. Paul, Minnesota. Mike Reed says, "Making pictures is like acting — you can paint yourself into the action." He often paints on the computer, but he also draws in pen and ink and paints in acrylics. He feels that learning to draw well is the key to being a successful artist.

Mike is regarded as one of the nation's premier illustrators and is the creator of the popular "Flame Warriors" illustrations at www.flamewarriors.com, a website devoted to Internet insults. "To enter his Flame Warriors site is sort of like entering a hellish Sesame Street populated by Oscar the Grouch and 83 of his relatives." – Los Angeles Times. (http://redwing.hutman.net/%7Emreed/warriorshtm/lat.htm)

Mike Reed has always enjoyed reading. As a young child, he liked the Dr. Seuss books. Later, he started reading biographies and war stories. One reason why he feels lucky to be an illustrator is because he can listen to books on tape while he works. Mike is available to provide custom illustrations for all manner of publications at reasonable prices. Mike can be reached at **www.mikereedillustration.com.**